PENGUIN BOOKS

AMAZING TALES FOR MAKING MEN OUT OF BOYS

Presenter of the hugely popular BBC series *Coast*, Neil Oliver is an archaeologist and author. His television credits also include *Two Men in a Trench* and *The One Show*. Neil lives in Glasgow with his wife and three children, Evie, Archie and Teddy.

Amazing Tales for Making Men out of Boys

NEIL OLIVER

PENGUIN BOOKS

PENGUIN BOOKS

Published by the Penguin Group
Penguin Books Ltd, 80 Strand, London WC2R ORL, England
Penguin Group (USA) Inc., 375 Hudson Street, New York, New York 10014, USA
Penguin Group (Canada), 90 Eglinton Avenue East, Suite 700, Toronto, Ontario, Canada M4P 2Y3
(a division of Pearson Penguin Canada Inc.)
Penguin Ireland, 25 St Stephen's Green, Dublin 2, Ireland (a division of Penguin Books Ltd)
Penguin Group (Australia), 250 Camberwell Road, Camberwell, Victoria 3124, Australia
(a division of Pearson Australia Group Pty Ltd)
Penguin Books India Pvt Ltd, 11 Community Centre, Panchsheel Park, New Delhi – 110 017, India
Penguin Group (NZ), 67 Apollo Drive, Rosedale, North Shore 0632, New Zealand
(a division of Pearson New Zealand Ltd)
Penguin Books (South Africa) (Pty) Ltd, 24 Sturdee Avenue,
Rosebank, Johannesburg 2196, South Africa

Penguin Books Ltd, Registered Offices: 80 Strand, London WC2R ORL, England

www.penguin.com

First published by Michael Joseph 2008
Published in Penguin Books 2009
6

Copyright © Neil Oliver, 2008
All rights reserved

The moral right of the author has been asserted

From 'The Call of the Wild' by Robert Service used by permission of the Estate of Robert Service.
From Under Milk Wood by Dylan Thomas, published by Orion.
Reproduced by permission of David Higham Associates

Picture permissions can be found on pages 343–4

Typeset by Palimpsest Book Production Limited, Grangemouth, Stirlingshire
Printed in England by Clays Ltd, St Ives plc

ISBN: 978–0–141–03559–8

www.greenpenguin.co.uk

Penguin Books is committed to a sustainable future
for our business, our readers and our planet.
The book in your hands is made from paper
certified by the Forest Stewardship Council.

For Archie

Have you suffered, starved and triumphed, grovelled down,
    yet grasped at glory,
Grown bigger in the bigness of the whole?
'Done things' just for the doing, letting babblers tell the
    story,
Seeing through the nice veneer the naked soul?
Have you seen God in his splendors, heard the text that
    nature renders?
(You'll never hear it in the family pew).
The simple things, the true things, the silent men who
    do things –
Then listen to the Wild – it's calling you.

They have cradled you in custom, they have primed you
    with their preaching,
They have soaked you in convention through and
    through,
They have put you in a showcase; you're a credit to their
    teaching,
But can't you hear the Wild? – It's calling you.
Let us probe the silent places, let us seek what luck betide
    us,
Let us journey to a lonely land I know,
There's a whisper on the night-wind, there's a star agleam
    to guide us,
And the Wild is calling, calling ... let us go.

From 'The Call of the Wild', by Robert Service

Contents

Introduction

There was a time not so very long ago when boys were taught to be men. Efforts were made in those just forgotten days to ensure that if you were born male you learned skills and acquired a clear understanding of what being a man was all about. It was straightforward, unquestioned and it worked.

Men used to live by the skill of their hands. They made new things and fixed old. They maintained their houses, cars and motorbikes. They knew how to grow food and how to hunt and fish. They dressed like men, talked like men, walked and worked and played like men.

Their jobs had names that are becoming as unfamiliar to us as calloused hands and ingrained dirt. They were fitters, turners and carpenters; blacksmiths and wheelwrights; ploughmen and woodsmen; wheel-tappers and shunters; masons and glaziers; tailors and cobblers; riveters and welders. They walked the line. Out of the ground beneath their feet they won coal and copper, tin and lead. They built bridges and railways, ships and trains and when they ran out of room here in Britain they did it all over again all over the world.

If you learned the lore of manhood and managed to pass your Manliness Finals there were all sorts of manly futures to be looked forward to:

Steam-engine driver
Engineer
Miner
Inventor
Cowboy (riding the range – not ripping off old ladies for

shoddy plumbing work and unfinished driveways)
Explorer (actually mapping new countries – not just being
   followed about by TV crews, up mountains and through
   forests we've all seen before anyway, from our couches)
Sheriff
Astronaut (with the hope of actually going somewhere, like
   the moon, or maybe even Mars, and not just endlessly
   orbiting the Earth in a shuttle, a spaceship that, let's face
   it, always looked a bit . . . well, clumpy)

All these proper, manly jobs and dozens more besides were
there for the taking, provided you'd done your manly home-
work.

Part of the education of boys came from reading tales of
brave and selfless deeds, or hearing from fathers and uncles and
grandfathers about how other men had lived their lives, met
their challenges, reached their goals and faced their deaths.

It was simple, honest stuff about standing up straight with
your shoulders back and eyes to the front like a soldier. It was
about making light of physical hardship and keeping going until
the job was done. Being a man was about comradeship and
standing by your friends whatever the circumstances. It meant
understanding that sometimes it was more important to die a
hero than live a coward's life. It was about always having at least
one more pair of clean underpants in your backpack when
lesser types were kicking up something fearful.

All of this became part not just of being men but, more
specifically, of being British men. And there was a time when
to be a British man was the greatest aspiration of them all.

It's rubbish being a British man at the moment – at least as
far as the rest of the world is concerned. Obviously it's still
good to *live* in Britain: we've got a national health service and
access to proper dentists. The telly's still satisfactory most of the
time and we make the only decent pop music in the world

apart from the US (but we invented the US anyway – that's really us as well). We don't yet live under the tyranny of a despot and we're still entitled to trial by jury, free speech, weekends off and several bank holidays every year. But those are just perks about being British, not being British *men*. Nowadays the rest of the world sees British men as the performing seals of George W. Bush's Wild West show. We're the sick men of Europe too, with our lazy great fat guts and our binge-drinking and the fecund under-age breeding of our young.

The rest of the world hates us so much now they won't even let us win the Eurovision Song Contest any more. Things have got that bad.

Being a proper British man used to be about things like 'Women and children first', 'Hold the line' and 'Play up, play up and play the game'. It was about keeping the garden tidy and the woodwork and railings freshly painted. It was about staying on top of the allotment. It was about firm handshakes, stiff upper lips and never, *ever* blubbing in public. It was Marquis of Queensberry Rules, rallying round and always having a clean hanky in case a lady needed to wipe her nose. It was about keeping a straight bat and cheering on the underdog. And when there was nothing else for it, it was about 'Fix bayonets, boys, and die like British soldiers do.' We invented all of that stuff from scratch.

It definitely wasn't about wanting to be noticed. It was about doing the right thing because manly behaviour was its own reward. *Middlemarch*, written by George Eliot in 1871, ends with these lines:

> . . . for the growing good of the world is partly dependent upon unhistoric acts; and that things are not so ill with you and me as they might have been is half owing to the number who lived faithfully a hidden life, and rest in unvisited tombs.

Hidden lives and unvisited tombs: that's a big lesson to learn as well. A manly man doesn't expect recognition – he does what he does because it's the right thing to do. And that's enough.

One of the many priceless moments in *Zulu*, the 1964 film about the Battle of Rorke's Drift, has a frightened private of the 2nd Battalion, 24th Regiment, a callow boy, look out at the approaching horde of enemy warriors and ask: 'Why us?'

In a matter-of-fact voice free of emotion, barrel-chested and richly moustachioed Colour-Sergeant Bourne replies: 'Because we're 'ere, lad ... an' no one else.'

That's what a manly man would say.

The Battle of Rorke's Drift was fought in the afternoon and evening of 22 January 1879 and on through the early hours of the following day. A hundred or so British soldiers defended their little supply post in Natal in southern Africa against an attack by 4,000 warriors of the Zulu nation, bent on slaughter and mayhem. When all was said and done, 11 of those men were awarded Victoria Crosses by a grateful Queen and Empress. It's still the most VCs ever awarded for a single battle.

On the morning of 22 January, just 12 miles away from Rorke's Drift, a British column of 1,700 men had been all but annihilated on the slopes of a mountain called Isandlwana by a Zulu army 25,000 strong. This was the greatest defeat ever inflicted on the British Army by an enemy armed with spears and shields. Rorke's Drift and Isandlwana: triumph and tragedy side by side.

A memorial on the site of Isandlwana bears these words:

> Not theirs to save the day
> But where they stood, falling to dye the earth
> With brave men's blood for England's sake and duty
> Be their names sacred among us

Neither praise nor blame add to their epitaph
But let it be simple like that which marks Thermopylae
Tell it in England, those who pass us by
Here, faithful to their charge, her soldiers lie.

Brave men's blood! Who can read those words without feeling the hairs rise at the nape of the neck?

Somewhere along the line we've forgotten – or discarded – the value and importance of being manly men. Somehow that whole way of being was ridiculed, then eroded and finally discouraged. Being an old-fashioned man in the time-honoured way became outdated, outmoded and forgotten.

Manly men were hunted to near-extinction in these British Isles, along with all the other wild animals that once roamed the quiet places of the land – the bear, the boar, the wolf. There's always talk these days of bringing back the Wild – reintroducing the beasts we've lost. Eccentric landowners stock their private forests with boar. Others lay plans for loosing packs of wolves in the high lonesome glens of the far north. No one mentions men. No one talks about bringing back the sort of men who once roamed the world, lived defiant lives and damn the consequences.

But the urge to be a man like men once were is a primal thing and lives still in the unformed hearts of boys.

Maybe it's just me and maybe I'm hopelessly wrong. Maybe the place for men like men used to be is somewhere in the past. Maybe it was all misguided and led to nothing but trouble. But it was *something* – something easily understood and worth getting out of bed in the morning for. It was as clear and clean and straight as a well-ironed shirt-collar and it gave boys something to live up to. It was a certain standard to be met in an uncertain world.

It's too late for me. I've been cosseted in this world of new men and stay-at-home dads for far too long. There's no hope of me making the grade. But at least I know what I've missed out on – what I haven't become.

It's not too late for our sons, though. It's not too late for *my* son. It's not about making soldiers of them all either, although soldiery is still an honourable and worthwhile pursuit, in spite of all the indignities foisted upon our armed forces by career politicians who aren't fit to polish our servicemen's boots (that's assuming they'd know how to properly polish a boot, which most of them wouldn't). It's about placing value on something else, something much bigger than the self. It's about being a manly man!

Some of what's required if our boys are to know once more what some of manhood is about is to let them hear the old tales and to learn what men are for and what men can do. Whenever I hear these stories I visualise a scene I've only ever witnessed in the movies: it's the one where a grand old duffer, white of hair and stout of girth, is holding court after an ample dinner. With fat cigar clamped between his teeth and the port ready to hand, he is using salt and pepper pots and assorted pieces of fruit to represent himself, his men and many foes on a hastily cleared tabletop that has become the field of some well-remembered battle.

If you read these stories without feeling the hackles rise and the chest swell, well ... well, then you're dead already. Boys will be boys, but boys want to be men. It's what I always wanted to be when I grew up.

It's hard knowing which stories to tell them. What's encouraging for the future of *man*kind is that there are so many to choose from. All of them demonstrate the qualities you'd want in your heroes – selflessness, devotion to the brotherhood, stubborn resourcefulness and refusal to quit regardless of the circumstances.

And behind them all is one story that has always stood out

for me. It's the beginning and the end of what I've tried to understand about the making of manly men. It's a story about one man, his team and their grand adventure and it depicts the ways of manly men more completely than any other. It forms the backbone – the ramrod-straight backbone – for all the rest.

It's a long story and takes a while to tell. I may be some time.

Holding out for a hero

Kathleen Bruce was 29 years old and had her heart set on a career as a sculptor when she attended a lunch party in a smart house in Westminster Palace Gardens, in London, in 1907. Given how keen she was to establish herself among the capital's creative and artistic types, she must have been pleased to note, as she walked into the dining room, that her fellow guests included the playwright J.M. Barrie, the novelist Henry James and the esteemed theatre critic Max Beerbohm.

The youngest of a family of 11, she had lost both her parents before her 16th birthday. She'd been taken in then by her grand-uncle, William Forbes Skene, historiographer of Scotland, and there in his Edinburgh home she had grown into a woman of the sort described, in those far-off days, as being 'of independent spirit'. Later she enrolled at London's Slade School of Art, and by the age of 21 she was in Paris, studying at the Académie Colarossi and every inch the art student. She knew Auguste Rodin, and it was while working for him in his studio that she met and made friends with the American dancer Isadora Duncan. She had lived and worked in Florence as well, and by the time of the lunch party in London she had been back in England for just a year.

It certainly was a glamorous gathering. She was introduced to the young would-be actor Ernest Thesiger, a grandson of the 1st Baron Chelmsford and a relative of the late Lieutenant General Frederic Thesiger, 2nd Baron Chelmsford and commander of the British forces during the Anglo-Zulu War of 1879. It was while making polite conversation with the younger Thesiger that she noticed, seated between Mr Barrie and Mr Beerbohm, 'a simple and austere naval officer'.

Ernest was being quite persistent, however, and after the briefest of glances at the other man, who seemed somehow out of place in such company, she resumed the business of being charmed. Ernest had been enrolled at the Slade and had had early ambitions of being a painter. He had quickly switched his attention to drama, though, and in 1907 was just two years away from the debut of a long and successful acting career.

Then, as Kathleen later noted in her diary, '. . . all of a sudden and I did not know how', she found herself face to face with the uniformed man. As he introduced himself she saw that he was of medium height, with broad shoulders, slim waist and thinning hair. 'He was not very young,' she wrote, 'perhaps 40, not very good-looking but healthy and alert.' More promisingly, he had 'a rare smile and . . . eyes of a quite unusually dark blue, almost purple. I had never seen their like.'

Kathleen Bruce's scrutiny of this middle-aged man was anything but casual. As well as making her name as a sculptor, she had another quite different creative ambition. Now, as she approached her 30th birthday, still without a husband, it was always at the back of her mind. While still in Paris she had told at least one girlfriend she was determined to have a son.

'A son,' she said, 'is the only thing I do quite surely and always want.'

Kathleen was not a beautiful woman – handsome would be nearer the mark. In photographs her features are certainly clearly defined and strong. There's a prominent nose and chin. Her dark hair is long and unstyled. How do women describe that Edwardian fashion of piling hair into a roll on the back of the head . . . a chignon, maybe? Her eyes were blue and set off by the only piece of jewellery she liked to wear – a pendant made from a single blue stone.

Anything she lacked in the looks department, though, she made up for in charm and presence. She certainly wasn't without male admirers. But when her girlfriends bothered to point out that she should have no difficulty in getting what she wanted, Kathleen replied that no one she had met so far was worthy of being the father of her son. The way she spoke about the business of breeding made the whole thing sound more like a mission – a destiny perhaps – than any mere fancy.

As Kathleen looked into the near-purple eyes of this naval officer, she began all at once to wonder if she was meeting the gaze of her Mr Right, 'the father of my son for whom I had been searching'. She wasn't certain – and seemed rather to be asking herself the question in an air of mild disbelief. 'Is this *really* him?'

What Kathleen either didn't know at that moment – or hadn't admitted to herself – was that she was looking for a hero, a manly man. Heroes are hard to find, and step out into the daylight when they are needed rather than when they are sought.

Heroes and manly men don't conform to a look or to a style and they have come from all classes and every race. They are a rare breed and, most inconvenient of all, they don't know they *are* heroes and so cannot identify, far less introduce themselves as such. Like beauty, heroism is in the eye of the beholder. It is up to us lesser mortals to spot our heroes and they are to be found in the strangest places, even lunch parties in south-west London.

The man Kathleen Bruce was talking to quite awkwardly in the dining room of the house at 32 Westminster Palace Gardens was Captain Robert Falcon Scott – Scott of the Antarctic. She had recognised him, of course – he had already made his name as an Antarctic explorer, and in an age when military men and explorers were among the A-list 'stars', this naval captain was shining brightly.

But was he a hero, or even a manly man? *He* didn't think so, not always at any rate. In fact from the age of 20 he had been confessing to his diary what he saw as his shortcomings as a man, far less a manly man.

He didn't even look the part. Average height, average build, no oil painting as far as his looks went – losing his hair by his middle years and definitely balding well before the end. When he was a young boy his family considered him to be on the soft side – frail and delicate, with a weak chest and a tendency to be knocked down by any passing chill or virus. Like Oscar Wilde, it seems, he was susceptible to draughts. He was also absent-minded, shy and apt to come over all peculiar at the sight of blood or the suffering of animals. He may have inherited his delicate constitution from his father, John. John Scott certainly never went to sea. When Grandfather Robert Scott retired, he went into the brewery business with his brother Edward. Young John was kept safe at home, to train as a brewer.

A Navy doctor who examined Scott before he joined the service reported that he didn't have a robust enough physique. A later biographer described him as 'shy and diffident, small and weakly for his age, lethargic, backward and above all, dreamy'.

Some of his early diary entries suggest he suffered from the great blight that is mild depression, or just good old-fashioned existential angst: '. . . this slow sickness which holds one for weeks,' he wrote, 'how can I bear it? I write of the future, of hopes of being more worthy, but shall I ever be? Can I alone, poor weak wretch that I am, bear up against it all? How can I fight against it all? No one will ever see these words, therefore I may freely write: What does it all mean?'

Poor weak wretch! This is marvellous stuff for us! These are the innermost thoughts and words of the young man destined to be Captain Scott of the Antarctic! This means you don't have to be born manly and heroic. You can start out weak and feeble and progress to manliness by sheer force of will! And all that introspection and self-doubt confessed to the pages of a diary: there's hope for us all.

He was born on 6 June 1868 in the family home, a place called Outlands, near Stoke Damerel just outside Devonport. In all, there would be six children for churchwarden John Scott and his wife, Hannah. Robert was the third child and the eldest boy – his siblings were Grace (known as Monsie), Rose, Kitty, Ettie and Archie. He was probably named Robert after his paternal grandfather, a Navy man who had reached the rank of purser by the time he retired. Family legend had it that they were all descended from one John Scott – a Jacobite sea captain who'd been captured and hanged for his part in the '45 Rebellion (another great story – another layer of glamour and intrigue). His middle name, Falcon, was the surname of his godparents, and his family and close friends always knew him, not as Robert, but as 'Con'.

In the quest for manliness, it doesn't hurt to have a cool name like Con, especially when it's short for Falcon. Names matter, and can set a chap off towards a manly destiny right from the word go. I was at school with a boy called – and I'm not making this up – Steel. Imagine growing up with a name like Steel. You couldn't help but be straight-backed with a firm handshake and confident gaze if your mum and dad had decided to name you after something hard, sharp and shiny! My niece went to infant school alongside a boy called Luke Walker. Nothing unusual or obviously cool in that, you might say. Little Luke's middle name, however, was Skye – spelt like the island off Scotland's north-west coast. So, Luke Skye Walker – a boy could go far with a name like that.

All three of grandfather Robert Scott's brothers went to sea as well, so it was an obvious career path for young Con, in spite of the reservations of the doctor. The historic port of Plymouth was just up the road from the family home – further inspiration for a life before the mast – and after a few years being coached for a Navy cadetship at Stubbington House, in Fareham, Hampshire, he boarded the training ship *Britannia* aged 13. He sat his exams in 1883, aged just 15, and was subsequently rated as a midshipman.

It's impossible to know what means Con Scott used to transform himself from a sickly little boy into a young man capable of putting up with, far less thriving within, the unremittingly harsh world of Her Majesty's Royal Navy. For boys like Scott the training was little changed from that dished out in the days of Nelson, with severe discipline enforced by beatings and extra drill. Regardless of the weather they would be sent up the rigging, to heights of 120 feet or more, to literally 'learn the ropes' while the deck rolled beneath them and their perches swung sickeningly. They slept in hammocks slung close together below decks and there was neither acknowledgement of, nor sympathy for, any of the natural feelings of homesickness, fear or lack of confidence. Where did Scott find the emotional and physical strength to cope with it all? Who did he model himself upon? Whose example did he try to follow?

Was he inspired by the thought of that shadowy Jacobite ancestor, perhaps? Or had he read and been told about the lives of other manly men?

Growing up close to Plymouth he would have known by heart the stories of the great seamen who'd sailed from there into their places in history. Sir Francis Drake set out to tackle and defeat the Spanish Armada; Sir Walter Raleigh departed for Guinea and, in 1576, Sir Martin Frobisher set sail with the *Gabriel* and the *Michael* in search of the fabled North West Passage to Cathay.

But in Robert Falcon Scott's day all young boys knew the lore of the heroes. In order to become manly men, they needed to know how manly men behaved – how they carried themselves, how they lived their lives and, when necessary, died their deaths.

The world he'd been born into in 1868 was one unrecognisable to us. It was a place so different from the one we know – in terms of our values and morals at least – that it's as distant as the imagined world of Homer.

The American Civil War had ended just three years before. The Crimean War of 1854–6 was only a dozen years distant. Legendary conflicts like the invasion of Afghanistan in 1838 (and the disastrous retreat from Kabul that ended it in 1842) and the Indian Mutiny of 1857–9 were still well within living memory when Con was a boy. Such stories! Such lessons to be learned!

Rudyard Kipling was born in 1865, in Bombay. At the age of five he was sent to live with a foster family in Southsea, back in wet and draughty England. He was desperately unhappy. But Kipling would of course grow up to deliver many of the lines that helped shape the attitudes and aspirations of generations of manly men:

> If you can make one heap of all your winnings
> And risk it on one turn of pitch-and-toss
> And lose, and start again at your beginnings
> And never breathe a word about your loss
> If you can force your heart and nerve and sinew
> To serve your turn long after they are gone
> And so hold on when there is nothing in you
> Except the Will which says to them: 'Hold on!'

So this is not about wanting to fight or to kill or to die, far from it – it's about wanting to value an upright and noble way of living. It's not about conquering or wanting to build empires, either. Men like Kipling, Raleigh and Frobisher and dramas like Afghanistan and the Crimean War and the rest have other things to say; they tell us that there are bigger stories to be told, and parts for us to play in them. One of the lessons to be learned from the old stories was that being a man meant there were more important things to think and care about than your own wellbeing.

When boys like Con Scott realised this – boys with weak chests and nervous hearts, who felt faint at the thought of suffering or at the sight of blood – it must have brought feelings of release and relief. It was possible to change, to become more than they had been before!

What is also true, of course, is that there are still brave men. It's not as though they've stopped turning up when need arises, far from it. It just feels sometimes that we've stopped paying them the attention they used to get – the attention they deserve.

In his own time and after, Scott would cast a long shadow against which young men would measure themselves. But examples are still being set, shadows cast, and the bravery of good men is as constant as the sea.

The Penlee lifeboatmen

Mousehole is a dream of a Cornish fishing village: white painted granite cottages, a single winding cobbled street with a few lanes running off it. Lying three miles to the west of Penzance, it probably takes its name – pronounced 'Mowzol' in the Cornish way – from the narrow entrance to its harbour. One of the breakwaters was built at the end of the 14th century, the other 1,000 years before that. The harbour mouth can be closed with wooden beams, to keep out tidal surges. Southerly gales have long been the bane of this part of Cornwall, and Mousehole is a place that has learned the ways of the sea.

Tradition has it that as the village prepared for Christmas one year long past, the sea was too rough for fishing boats to venture out. With the inhabitants facing starvation, one Tom Bawcock braved the gale and landed enough fish to feed every man, woman and child. The catch was turned into 'Stargazy Pie', in which the fish are cooked whole with their heads sticking up through the crust. This is the dish still eaten in the village every 23 December – Tom Bawcock's Eve – at least by those who know their history.

Dylan Thomas spent time hereabouts and may have immortalised the atmosphere in his imagined village of Llareggub in Under Milk Wood. *In recent years Mousehole has been taken over by 'second-homers' who've pushed house prices beyond the reach of locals. Now most of the cottages overlooking the harbour lie empty for 10 months of the year while their owners earn city salaries to pay for their part-time dreams. And while they sleep elsewhere, their empty houses in Mousehole are left, as the Welshman once said of other homes, blind as moles. Thomas told a friend he'd written his play after World War II to remind himself there was still beauty in the world. And yet, '. . . the shops in mourning, the Welfare Hall in widow's weeds. And all the people of the lulled and dumbfound town are sleeping now.'*

During the Middle Ages the harbour bade farewell to pilgrims making for Santiago de Compostela and the Holy Land. In 1595 it was raided and burned to the ground by Spanish soldiers. Dolly Pentreath, the last person to speak only Cornish, died here in 1777 aged 102, and there's a memorial to her in the local church.

In a place of honour nearby is a memorial to eight Mousehole men who knew the sea and so understood – in the way that only seafaring men do – the danger they faced as they answered a call for help on the night of 19 December 1981.

The Morton family was having an unusual start to the Christmas holidays that year. Henry Morton was the captain of a brand-new 1,400-ton coaster, the *Union Star*. She was on her maiden voyage from the Dutch port of Ijmuiden to Arklow in Ireland's County Wicklow, with a cargo of fertiliser. So they could all be together for the festivities, Morton had collected his wife Dawn, 32, and her two teenage daughters Sharon, 16 and Deanne, 14, en route. Counting the captain, there was a crew of five. The addition of Morton's family brought the head count to eight. In fact, Dawn was several weeks pregnant so perhaps nine was a more accurate total of the lives aboard.

By 19 December they were in trouble. The weather had deteriorated during the trip and by teatime that day they were in the grip of a full-blown hurricane, 60-foot waves and winds gusting to 100 miles an hour. Eight miles east of the Wolf's Rock lighthouse in south-west Cornwall the *Union Star*'s engine failed. Seawater got into the fuel line somehow and despite the efforts of Morton and the rest of the crew they couldn't get her started again. She was dead in the water.

A first offer of help came from a nearby Dutch tug, the *Noord Holland*, also making her way through the English Channel that night. Her captain wanted to put a line aboard the *Union Star* and take her in tow – but that would have made her 'salvage' and Morton baulked at the cost. Unaware of how much danger he was in, he told the *Noord Holland* thanks but no thanks and turned instead to the rescue services.

'*Union Star* calling Land's End Coastguard,' he said calmly into the radio. 'We are approximately eight miles east of Wolf's Rock. Engines have stopped and we are unable to get them started at the moment.'

A Sea King helicopter was scrambled from the Royal Naval Air Station at Culdrose and word was sent to alert the lifeboat crew at Mousehole.

Fifty-six-year-old Coxswain William Trevelyan Richards was at home watching television with his widowed mother Mary when he got the call. Some of his crewmen, he knew, would be in Mousehole's Ship Inn. It was the last Saturday night before Christmas and, bad weather or not, celebrations were already under way. The rest of the men were likely at home with wives and families, listening to the worst storm in living memory as it screamed its fury at the sea and sky.

Trevelyan Richards put on his coat, said goodnight to his mum and stepped out of the door into the howling dark. Down at the Ship Inn he asked for quiet and told them the score. He needed seven volunteers and a dozen men raised their hands, including the pub's landlord, Charlie Greenhaugh.

Down at the boathouse, fish salesman and lifeboatman Nigel Brockman, 43, turned up accompanied by his 17-year-old son, Neil. They'd been at home watching television with the rest of the family when word of the call-out reached them. Neil was a crewman too – a volunteer of just a few months' standing, but Trevelyan Richards wouldn't risk two members of the same family on such a night and refused to take him along.

'I was absolutely gutted,' Neil told a newspaper 25 years later. 'If you're on the crew, you always want to go.'

The lifeboat was the *Solomon Browne*, a 47-foot Watson Class vessel – shaped a bit like those little Royal National Lifeboat

Institution collection boxes seen on the bars of pubs throughout the land. 'Funded entirely by voluntary contributions', they say. She was built in 1960 at a cost of £35,000 – the money coming from the wills of three women, Miss Lydia Mary Dyer Browne, of Launceston, Miss Sara Wilhelmina Davies, of Timperley, and Miss Blanche Waterhouse, of Huddersfield. This is the way and the form of the RNLI – it's a gift we make to ourselves.

She bore the unmistakable livery of purple hull and orange cabin – colours which, at sea, mean so much more to stranded mariners than the reds and yellows of onshore rescue vehicles mean to drivers. Nothing compares to the sight of an orange and purple outline appearing over the horizon of waves, its crew made larger than life by their puffy waterproofs and crash helmets and bearing down upon you with the promise of continuing existence. 'Guardian Angel' is an expression that's bandied about quite a lot nowadays – but the men of the RNLI are the real deal.

Although the *Solomon Browne* was crewed by Mousehole men, she was stationed at Penlee Point and was generally known as the Penlee lifeboat. There had been a lifeboat there since 1913, and 91 people had owed their lives to the bravery of its crews down through the years. Many medals had been awarded to crewmen past and present before that night of all nights on 19 December 1981.

The men who climbed aboard along with Trevelyan Richards were second coxswain James Stephen Madron, 43, assistant mechanic, Nigel Brockman, 43, emergency mechanic, John Blewit, 43, Charlie Greenhaugh, 46, Barrie Torrie, 33, and 23-year-olds Kevin Smith and Gary Wallis.

It took masterful seamanship to get the *Solomon Browne* out on to the water that night. By the time those men arrived at their lifeboat station they were fighting to stand up in the face of a full-blown hurricane – the kind of weather event most of us will never even see. Yet they looked out into the dark of that winter's night, at 60-foot waves whipped up by 100-mile-an-hour winds, and decided to get aboard a 47-foot boat and head out into it. Remind yourself that they're volunteers, who do the job because they know what it's like to be on the sea when it all goes wrong. They understand what it means, and rather than stay safe on dry land while it all plays out, they find it easier to go out there and help. I find it almost impossible to imagine bravery like that.

The very existence of the RNLI is down to one Englishman, a Yorkshire-born Quaker called William Hillary, who never learned to swim. They say that in the old days, fishermen and sailors chose not to master the art – it gave them more respect for the sea.

In the days before he concerned himself with the plight of shipwrecked sailors, William was a soldier and adventurer who used his wealthy first wife's money to fund a private army to stand against any invasion by Napoleon. King George III eventually gave him a baronetcy for his trouble.

In 1808 Sir William moved to the Isle of Man, with a new wife, and there heard many tragic tales of local lives lost to the sea. The worst had been the loss of the Manx fishing fleet in 1787, when around 50 ships and more than 160 crewmen drowned in Douglas Bay. Caught out by a storm and running for safe haven, they foundered on rocks. There was no rescue service then, of course, and no one thought of making an attempt to pluck those souls from their watery graves.

And then in October 1822, Sir William watched with his own eyes as the Royal Navy cutter *Vigilant* made an attempt to sail out of Douglas Bay into a storm. She was caught by the wind and waves and driven on to rocks.

Sir William ran from his home overlooking the bay, down to the harbour wall, and there promised to pay any men who would help him crew a rowing boat and make some effort to help the sailors. Enough volunteers stepped forward to man two boats and they braved the storm to reach the stricken vessel. Fixing lines to the *Vigilant*, they managed to pull her back towards shore – close enough for rockets to be fired from the beach, carrying hawsers that could be used to draw her closer still. Despite ever-worsening conditions, Sir William and the rest of his volunteers then rowed back and forth between the *Vigilant* and the beach, eventually saving nearly 100 lives.

Sir William saw at once the need for an organised rescue service, teams of men all around the coast ready to brave the worst weathers for the sake of those in peril. He began a campaign and by 1824 the 'National Institution for the Preservation of Lives and Property from Shipwreck' was born. In time it would be renamed the Royal National Lifeboat Institution. Down through all the years from that day to this, the RNLI has remained independent and voluntary. Government doesn't pay for it, so the grey men in suits don't get to say how it's run, which is probably just as well.

For his bravery during the subsequent rescue of members of the crew of the *Fortrondet*, Sir William was awarded one of three gold medals he would collect during his time as a lifeboatman. Of more significance to him that day, though, was the fact that he was accompanied during the rescue by his son Augustus, who received a silver award. It would not be the last time that a son would follow a father into the role of lifesaver.

The steep slipway was being pounded by waves as big as houses, but perfect timing and judgement from Trevelyan Richards enabled them to break through into deep water and head off towards the last known position of the *Union Star*. It was 12 minutes past eight.

First to the scene, however, was the Sea King helicopter, flown by Lieutenant Commander Russell Smith, a United States Navy pilot on exchange with the Royal Navy.

Among other things, Morton told him: 'We have one woman and two children aboard.'

'Sorry,' came Smith's uncertain reply. 'Say again.'

Morton had to repeat that his wife and stepdaughters were aboard.

A winchman was lowered from the belly of the helicopter, down into the suffocating soup of gale and foam and spray. In a hurricane at sea, the air is made more of water than anything a person can breathe, but the winchman did his best to assess the situation on the deck of the *Union Star*. Below him he could see, rising and rolling, the fresh green paint of the brand-new deck. For a few seconds he glimpsed a pair of pink court shoes as one of the girls contemplated making a run towards the lights of the helicopter. It was not to be. The wind was threatening to snap the rotor-blades. Far from making a rescue, the pilot was fighting just to stay in the air. Defeated, he pulled back to a position from where he and the winchman could watch whatever the approaching lifeboatmen might try.

In the wheelhouse of the stricken coaster Morton listened as a new voice came over the radio. It was that of Trevelyan Richards, now within reach of them after an hour-long voyage through impossible waves and about to make his first move.

'Do you want us to come alongside and take the women and children?' he asked.

'Yes, please,' said Morton. 'The helicopter is having a bit of difficulty. So if you can pop out and get the women and two children off, I'd be very much obliged.'

Pop out and get the women and two children off. Very much obliged. It sounds so calm and reasonable and yet 36-year-old Morton's predicament was as bad as it could have been. Maybe his pregnant wife and two stepdaughters were within earshot – back from the deck and taking shelter while they could. No doubt he wouldn't have wanted to make matters worse for them by letting them hear how anxious he was and so he would have swallowed it down and tried to do what good husbands and fathers do: be brave.

What Trevelyan Richards and the rest of the crew of the *Solomon Browne* certainly knew, even if Morton didn't, was that the rocks of the Cornish coast were looming closer with every passing second. If something were not done immediately the coaster would be smashed to pieces.

Through that maelstrom of wind and water Trevelyan Richards ploughed his course. Once again Morton told his wife and daughters to make their way down on to the deck, there to ready themselves to leave the *Union Star*.

I don't suppose there's any way to teach coxswains like Trevelyan Richards how to do what they do in the teeth of hurricanes. It must come only from years spent learning the lessons of the sea. He charged at his target with all the power the *Solomon Browne* could give him, judging the waves, the rise and fall of the coaster rearing many feet above them like a cliff of steel. As the helicopter pilot and winchman looked on, the lifeboat made one run after another in an attempt to get into a position from which they could take the crew to safety. Time and again they were driven off.

At the subsequent inquiry, held at Penzance, a letter from pilot Lieutenant Commander Smith was read out: 'Throughout the entire rescue the Penlee crew never appeared to hesitate,' he wrote. 'After each time they were washed . . . or blown away from the *Union Star*, the Penlee crew immediately commenced another run-in. Their spirit and dedication was amazing. They were truly the greatest eight men I have ever seen.'

Trevelyan Richards's calm, matter-of-fact voice came over the radio again.

'We're going to make an attempt to come alongside,' he said.

'OK, skip,' said Morton. 'Yup.'

It's all so free of drama. The two men talked to one another without a hint of panic or of fear, their quiet words more humbling than any battlefield command.

A local news reporter was braving the hurricane up on the cliffs at Boscawen Cove. Through the blinding rain and wind he could just make out the outline of the coaster and, dwarfed beside her, the *Solomon Browne*. As the waves and gale pushed them towards the coastline, the two vessels were bow to bow: David and Goliath. A wave picked up the lifeboat and tossed it on to the *Union Star* like driftwood. She slithered and screamed across the green of the larger ship's deck, crumpling steel guard-rails like pipe cleaners, before rolling off, stern first, into the roiling sea once more. According to the reporter and the helicopter pilot, this happened not once but twice. The *Solomon Browne* weighed 22 tons, but to a sea driven by a hurricane she was as inconsequential as a cloud of foam. Thanks to watertight compartments fore and aft, she was self-righting and bobbed like a cork in most conditions – but pitted against Cornish rocks and mountainous seas, she was as fragile as an egg.

For a few moments the lifeboat stayed in place alongside the much larger vessel, held there as if by providence or collective will. As the reporter and the helicopter crew looked on, a handful of shadows leapt from the deck of the *Union Star*, out into the smothering, whirling blackness and down into the outflung arms of the lifeboatmen waiting so very far below.

'Penlee lifeboat calling Falmouth Coastguard,' said Trevelyan Richards, calm as ever. 'We've got four off, male and female.'

It was Dawn Morton, her two daughters and one of the coaster's crewmen. Of course that could never have been enough for the coxswain and the crew of the *Solomon Browne*. Now the lives aboard both vessels were mixing together and becoming one, all 16 of them woven together.

Trevelyan Richards took his boat back alongside the coaster once again. He was after every last man and his crew expected no less. The reporter watched, and the crew of the helicopter too. Falmouth Coastguard could only listen to their radio. What came next was everlasting silence.

'Penlee lifeboat,' called the coastguard. 'Penlee lifeboat. Falmouth Coastguard. Over.'

Nothing.

The coastguard repeated his call over and over, not believing.

No one knows for sure what had happened; the full facts of that night, the minute-by-minute details of 16 lives fought for, were lost along with so much else. What does seem certain is that the two vessels came together in the dark one last time. Falmouth went on calling out to them.

It's thought that perhaps they'd been driven too close to shore and that finally a trough between waves exposed the jagged and unforgiving rocks of the seabed. Both vessels then received damage too great to be survived.

William Trevelyan Richards, James Stephen Madron, Nigel Brockman, John Blewit, Charlie Greenhaugh, Barrie Torrie, Kevin Smith, Gary Wallis, Henry Morton, James Whittaker, mate of the *Union Star*, George Sedgwick, engineer, Anghostino Verressimo, crewman, Manuel Lopez, crewman, Dawn Morton, pregnant with her third child, Sharon Morton, Deanne Morton; all of them lost.

Brockman and Greenhaugh were married fathers of three children each. Madron was a father of two, as was Blewit. Smith was a merchant seaman, home on leave. He'd been too young when he first joined the crew, lying about his age in his eagerness to be among them all. The *Solomon Browne* was smashed to pieces, matchwood; the wreck of the *Union Star* was found next morning, upturned and washed against the base of the cliffs. Of the 16 who were lost, only eight bodies were recovered – four from each vessel.

Mousehole is a small village. The loss of eight fathers, brothers, uncles and sons was a dreadful wound. William Trevelyan Richards was buried on the morning of Christmas Eve, Nigel

Brockman in the afternoon. There were more funerals to come.

The loss of the *Solomon Browne* with all hands is still, more than 25 years on, the last time the RNLI lost an entire crew. May that sad record stand for evermore. Trevelyan Richards was posthumously awarded the Institution's gold medal for bravery. The rest received posthumous bronze medals. The Penlee lifeboat station was awarded a gold medal service plaque.

Communities that live by the sea and on the sea always say they understand the risks and expect loss of life from time to time. But how can anyone really understand or expect what happened to the men of the *Solomon Browne*?

On the morning after the tragedy volunteers stepped forward to fill the empty places. Just as strong as the sense of grief, perhaps even stronger, was pride in what the lost men stood for. Duty pulled the new crewmen forward as irresistibly as a tide. Neil Brockman was one of them and today he is the coxswain of the new lifeboat. His own son is keen to join him and even to replace his dad if the time comes. Brockman understands the need. He gives thanks that he had his own father until he was 17 – other children in the village lost theirs while still babies or too young to remember the lost men.

'I've got no doubt in my mind that when I'm on my lifeboat with my six crew these days, there's eight others there with me,' he said. 'No doubt in my mind at all.'

The new lifeboat is based a few miles from Penlee now, at nearby Newlyn. The old lifeboat house at Penlee Point stands empty as a memorial to the men of the *Solomon Browne*.

Nearly an hour after the last transmission from Trevelyan Richards that night, a lookout on the cliffs swore blind he saw the lights of the *Solomon Browne*, making her way home.

Dusk is drowned forever until tomorrow. It is all at once night now. The windy town is full of windows, and from the larruped waves, the lights of the lamps in the windows call back the day and the dead that have run away to sea.

Every year, at eight o'clock on 19 December, the Mousehole Christmas lights are turned off for an hour as a mark of remembrance.

William Trevelyan Richards's mother Mary spoke about the last time she saw him that night. He took the call, put on his coat and said goodbye to her. It might sound commonplace and routine: the coxswain of a lifeboat is called out countless times – and, every time he leaves, must say farewell. Mary saw her son off to the lifeboat again and again over the years, and welcomed him back after every call but one.

Although I have no real cause to, I think there was something different about that night – and that both of them knew it even as it began to happen.

Like Trevelyan Richards, it somehow seems to me, Mary knew their goodbye in the face of the hurricane was forever.

'With that he was gone,' she said. 'And the door slammed behind him in the wind.'

A few good men

Why is it harder to hear about acts of bravery carried out within our own lifetime than in distant moments from the past?

I was 14 at the time of the Penlee lifeboat disaster and I remember the reports in newspapers and on television – footage of the search for survivors, the wrecked hull of the *Union Star*. On the 25th anniversary, the BBC screened a documentary that looked back at the events of that night. It was called 'Cruel Sea' but Neil Brockman said in his interview for the piece that you couldn't blame the sea for anything – the sea just does what it does.

Hardest to listen to were the recordings of the voices of William Trevelyan Richards and Henry Morton as they talked politely to one another over their radios about what needed to be done.

Even 25 years later it struck me as a brave move by the programme makers, to go back to that village and interview those hurt by the tragedy. Wounds like those never go away. I don't think I could have steeled myself to make those first phone calls.

The bravery of the Penlee lifeboatmen and their successors has a *raw*ness to it – a rawness that it's harder to feel when reading about stories from more remote history. Men caught up in events of the 19th century or earlier can seem unreal – like comic book characters from *Boy's Own* adventure annuals. And so it matters to remember fresh bravery too – the better to reinvest the characters from long-ago dramas with all the flesh and blood of the living.

Robert Falcon Scott feels distant, long lost and almost unreal, like a fictional character or a figure from a legend. But it's possible to get closer to him by hearing about the years before he became fixed in history as Scott of the Antarctic. He becomes more real still when you know that exploring the southern continent – and finally struggling towards the South Pole itself – wasn't even his own idea. In *The Voyage of the 'Discovery'* he wrote: 'I may as well confess that I had no predilection for polar exploration.'

But before any excitement of that order – life-threatening, testing hardship on the great southern continent – he had to concentrate all his energies on succeeding as an officer of the Royal Navy.

After his time on *Britannia*, he saw service aboard Her Majesty's ships *Boadicea*, *Lion*, *Monarch* and *Rover*. He spent the winter of 1887–8 at the Royal Naval College at Greenwich, where he passed his lieutenant's exams. He was a good and diligent student, but never top of the class.

The inspiration for those voyages to the Antarctic came originally from Sir Clements Markham, secretary and later president of the Royal Geographical Society (RGS). Like Scott, Markham was a Navy man. In 1850–51 he was aboard the *Assistance* when it went in search of survivors of Sir John Franklin's ill-starred expedition of 1845 in search of the North West Passage. There wasn't a single member of the party to be found, of course, as all 129 lives had been lost.

Markham left the Navy in favour of a career in the Civil Service. By 1877 he had moved on again, this time to concentrate on his fascination with geography and, more particularly, the work of the RGS. He had developed a detailed knowledge of Antarctica at a time when no one else much cared for the place. For Markham, however, that great, uncharted wilderness of the south represented an opportunity to underline the pre-eminence of British exploring zeal. It lay unclaimed by human hand, or even foot, and Markham was determined that it should have the British flag unfurled upon it as soon as possible.

While Scott was still serving aboard the *Rover*, Markham had identified the young sub-lieutenant as a candidate for the job of leading an expedition to explore the southern continent. It was Markham's belief that youth was a vital qualification for exploration. It was all very well, he thought, to have wise old heads back at home making plans and offering up the fruits of their experience. But the job of going to new places was for young bloods alone: 'How can novel forms of effort be expected from stiff old organisms hampered by experience?' he asked.

He pointed out that no useful work in either the Arctic or the Antarctic had been undertaken by men over 40 years of age, and the best pioneers had been nearer 30. What he didn't know – or didn't say – was that the polar regions take a terrible physical toll on the human body. When conditions are right, or rather wrong, the places are just one big dead zone. The fact is that the bodies of younger men and boys – still blessed with the recuperative powers of youth – have the best chance of repairing themselves and staying alive in temperatures of 40 degrees below and worse.

Antarctica was certainly a new and unexplored territory. For millennia before anyone set foot on the place, its existence was just a myth. Greek philosophers had argued that a great body of land had to exist on the bottom of the world to counter the weight of all the continents at the top. Captain James Cook came within 75 miles of it in 1773, but never saw land. The great navigator was of the opinion that the place had to be so barren there was no point trying to land there anyway.

The Russian Thaddeus von Bellingshausen was first to lay eyes on the edge of the continent, in 1820, and the following year saw Captain John Biscoe sail right around it. In 1895 an eight-man team aboard the whaler *Antarctic* made the first confirmed landfall. But exploration of the place in any mean-ingful way would have to wait.

At 2,800 miles across and with an area of nearly 5½ million square miles, Antarctica is the fifth largest continent on Earth. That it had resisted investigation for so long was largely due to its extreme isolation – 600 miles from the tip of South America and 1,500 miles from Australia. It is surrounded by the Southern Ocean, the most challenging and unforgiving body of water on the face of the planet. Life must fight a constant battle to survive on the landmass at its centre, the vast majority of which is permanently covered in ice. For large parts of the year the continent is either in total darkness or bathed in constant sunlight.

A 25-year-old Norwegian by the name of Roald Amundsen was among an international expedition to Antarctica led by the Belgian Adrian de Gerlache in 1897. Their ship became trapped in the pack-ice and Amundsen and the rest became the first people to spend a winter enfolded in the continent's unremitting darkness. It was a grim foretaste of what awaited all the others who would venture there in the future.

Suffice it to say that by the turn of the 20th century, Antarctica was a forbidding place that called out only to the hardiest and most eccentric souls.

This is what manly men are all about. There are many fine qualities to be acquired in libraries and universities and other places of learning. Many men have lived noble lives without ever straying more than a few miles from home. They've raised families, held down jobs, paid the bills and done what's right. Those are good men too.

But there's a wide world out there beyond the horizon and the far-flung places of it demand a different sort of chap. I'm not saying he's better, or that he's the only sort worth being, but we need him as well. He walks a different path, and to the beat of a different drum.

The SAS and the Battle of Mirbat

For most men of my age, the Special Air Service appeared as if from nowhere, at about half past seven in the evening of 5 May 1980, on to the roof and balconies of the Iranian Embassy building in London's South Kensington. One minute we were watching the World Snooker Championships on the BBC – next thing, men dressed all in black, their faces concealed by balaclavas, were sliding down ropes and blasting their way through the windows of a white-fronted terraced building. From inside came the unmistakable and chilling sound of gunfire, and of men and women screaming.

For the past five days that address, on leafy Princes Gate, had been held by a gang of desperate Iranian terrorists, opponents of the Ayatollah Khomeini and his revolutionary regime. They'd taken 26 people hostage and were threatening to kill them all if their demands were not met. By 5 May they'd released five of their prisoners, but during that day their patience had begun to run out. About half an hour before the men in black appeared, the terrorists had thrown the body of murdered press attaché Abbas Lavasani into the street.

We didn't know the details right then, of course – all we could do was watch the events unfold while BBC journalist Kate Adie delivered an unscripted running commentary from behind the open door of a car parked at the scene. For a 13-year-old boy it was all too exciting for words. My abiding memory is of the way the black smoke and debris from the explosions billowed out of the windows a split second before you heard the sound of the blast. This was live – it was really happening. It was the most unbelievable telly-event of my life up until that time. But who were these guys?

Gradually the facts started to emerge. The men storming the embassy – that was always the word the journalists used to describe the raid, '*storming*' – were from an elite regiment within the British Army called the SAS, the Special Air Service. These were the best of the best, tougher than tough. They'd practised their storming of the embassy in a mock-up of the building at an army base elsewhere in the city before awaiting the order to carry out the real thing – and within a quarter of an hour it was all over. Five of the six terrorists were shot dead and all but one of the remaining hostages were rescued alive.

There were stories (perhaps apocryphal, but who knew?) of the hostages – grown men and women – being thrown bodily from soldier to soldier by those supermen in a bid to speed up the evacuation; of one terrorist's corpse having 30 bullets in it; of the sole surviving baddie avoiding death only because some of the hostages stepped in to stop him being executed. It was also said Prime Minister Margaret Thatcher, who had sanctioned the raid, spent the evening drinking whisky with the soldiers and hearing their version of events at first hand.

For weeks thereafter the subject of the SAS was constantly on the lips of every boy I knew. Sales of black balaclavas, the kind with just eyeholes, up until then the preserve of Irish terrorists, must have gone through the roof (my mum wouldn't let me have one – she said it would make me 'look tough'! – that's the whole point, mum!). By then, of course, the men in black had quietly disappeared back into the anonymous obscurity that was their natural environment.

But the SAS didn't spring from nowhere in 1980 (though it's said their success in ending the siege that evening secured the regiment's future at a time when it had been facing disbandment). In fact the idea for their creation had come from the mind of a Scottish soldier, while he was lying in a hospital bed in Cairo, in Egypt, in 1941, recovering from a leg injury sustained during a parachute jump.

Colonel Sir Archibald David Stirling was born on 15 November 1915, son of Brigadier-General Sir Archibald Stirling and the Honourable Margaret Fraser, daughter of Lord Lovat. His was a lineage with a long and proud history of defending the realm. He was educated first at Ampleforth College in Yorkshire and then at Cambridge University. He was an impressive figure – six foot five inches tall and supremely fit. Before the outbreak of World War II he'd been preparing to climb Mount Everest, but joined the Scots Guards as a subaltern – a junior officer – as soon as the fighting started. He volunteered for the newly formed No. 3 Commando Group under Lieutenant Colonel Robert Laycock and although 'Layforce', as it came to be called, was disbanded in 1941, Stirling remained convinced that small teams of soldiers could wreak havoc on enemy supply lines.

He took up parachute jumping – still an unusual practice at that time – and it was on his first attempt that he suffered the injury that put him in that hospital bed and gave him time to think. He was familiar enough with the channels of communication in the British Army to know that he stood little chance of getting his idea in front of the right people quickly enough. So according to legend he went straight to the top. Turning up at 8th Army's Middle East headquarters in Cairo, still on crutches, he sneaked past a sentry on the door in a bid to find Commander-in-Chief General Claude Auchinleck. As he hobbled along the corridors he heard footsteps coming his way and ducked into the first open office he could find. Inside, seated behind a desk, was General Sir Neil Ritchie, Deputy Commander of the Middle East.

Ritchie was apparently so impressed by Stirling's ideas, jotted down in pencil on scraps of paper, that he personally made sure they became a reality. The new fighting unit was called 'L-Detachment, Special Air Service Brigade' – a grand title designed to make the Germans think the new outfit was a whole lot bigger and more established than it really was.

Stirling's idea had come to fruition as a result of timing as much as anything else. While he'd been lying in his bed developing his notion of an 'army within the army', the Allied forces had been getting themselves hopelessly bogged down in the deserts of North Africa.

In September 1940 an enormous Italian force numbering more than 200,000 men had invaded Egypt. Desperate to prevent the Axis powers gaining control either of the Suez Canal or the vast oil reserves of the Middle East, an outnumbered Allied force set about the invaders with a vengeance. Led by General Archibald Wavell – and his field commander Lieutenant General Dick O'Connor – a combined force of British, Australian and Indian soldiers first stopped the Italians in their tracks and then chased them all the way to the sea.

In their haste to escape with their lives – and having convinced themselves it must be *they* who were outnumbered – the Italians left just about everything but their uniforms behind them in the sand. Over 130,000 men, together with hundreds of guns, tanks and other vehicles, were scooped up by the victorious Allies. British secretary for war Anthony Eden said afterwards: 'Never has so much been surrendered by so many to so few.'

But the success was short-lived. Hitler responded by sending in his newly created Afrikakorps, under the command of the charismatic and talented General Erwin Rommel – the 'Desert Fox'. What then ensued was a desperate struggle between well-matched forces, neither of whom seemed about to repeat the behaviour of the lately departed Italians. The Desert Fox would push the Allies all the way back to Egypt, leaving the city of Tobruk completely surrounded.

While all this was going on, what Ritchie wanted from Stirling's Special Air Service Brigade was some quick and spectacular results. He started with 65 men, mostly scavenged from the remains of Layforce, on a hastily prepared training ground at Kabrit, by the Suez Canal. But there in that first batch of volunteers were men whose names remain legends within the SAS: Australian John Steel 'Jock' Lewes (there's that name Steel again), formerly a soldier with the Welsh Regiment, an Oxford rowing Blue and inventor of the Lewes bomb that would, in time, be used to destroy or disable countless enemy aircraft; Irishman Robert Blair 'Paddy' Mayne, a former rugby player whose sheer physical strength, courage and eagerness for a fight created the blueprint of the ideal SAS man that stands to this day; and John Edward 'Gentleman Jim' Almonds, one of the toughest soldiers ever to fire a rifle, survivor of countless raids, keeper of the tidiest dugouts ever seen and never once known to lose his temper nor heard to utter a single profanity.

Training for the new unit was brief and ad hoc – relying on the natural resilience and toughness with which such men are born. The first raid by the Special Air Service Brigade, in November 1941, was, nevertheless, an unmitigated disaster. Fifty-five men parachuted down behind the German lines. They were supposed to gather intelligence about enemy positions and do whatever they could to cause disruption, but Stirling had green-lit the raid despite appalling weather conditions. The cloud-cover over the drop-zone was so low the pilots couldn't see the ground below them – with the result the raiders were dropped miles out of position. In the end, only 21 of the officers and men made it back alive – and only then because they were picked up by a Long-Range Desert Group patrol.

Gentleman Jim had missed out on the raid. His infant son had been taken desperately ill back home and Stirling had let him stay behind so he could write a letter home to his wife.

After his comrades had boarded their aircraft and disappeared out of sight he wrote in his diary:

> I am not there. I sit back here in the safety of the camp and wish I was with them. One more would make the load lighter. Reality beats fiction for sheer, cold, calculating courage. Some of these lads cannot be beaten. Films and books of daring and adventure fall short of this, the real thing.

When Lewes, his great friend, was killed during an attack on an enemy airfield at Nofilia, in Libya, on Christmas Eve 1941, Almonds was devastated. Although the mission had been reasonably successful – with two enemy aircraft destroyed on the ground – Lewes was cut down by large-calibre rounds fired from a Messerschmitt 110 that strafed the squad as they made their escape in Land Rovers. It took Almonds and the rest of the men a week to complete the 200-mile journey back to base, travelling by night and lying low by day. He was awarded the Military Medal for his part in the mission, but his thoughts were only for his lost comrade, dead at 28. He wrote:

> In many homes the Old Year is being watched die, and new hopes rise with the prospect of the New Year. I thought of Jock, one of the bravest men I ever met, an officer and a gentleman, lying out in the desert barely covered with sand. No one will ever stop by his grave or pay homage to a brave heart that ceased to beat. Not even a stone marks the spot.

Jock Lewes had been the organisational genius behind Stirling. While the public schoolboy had succeeded in getting the idea for a specialised force past the bureaucrats, it was the deep-thinking Australian, with his talent for planning and logistics, who had dotted the 'i's and crossed the 't's. His loss was the worst possible blow to morale for the new regiment.

But despite the shaky start, Stirling's force had learned from its mistakes and would mature into one of the most effective military tools imaginable. Stirling himself pushed his luck a bit too far in the end, and was captured in Tunisia in 1943. He spent the rest of the war incarcerated at Colditz Castle. His men carried on their work in his absence and by the end of the war had inflicted thousands of casualties on the enemy as well as destroying thousands of aircraft and vehicles. Hundreds of railway lines and trains were also put out of action.

Field Marshal Montgomery said: 'The boy Stirling is quite mad – quite, quite mad. However, in a war there is often a place for mad people.'

Often described as 'the most un-decorated soldier of the Second World War', Stirling was knighted in 1990. He died later the same year.

But while the SAS has enjoyed near-mythical status in the minds of the British general public, it hasn't always been so valued by the country's leaders. Old-school attitudes – and a belief in large-scale war by large-scale armies – have long survived in the minds of many of the Army top brass. The existence of small 'private armies' – as units like the SAS are described by sceptics – has been in jeopardy many times over the years. The Regiment was actually disbanded after the end of World War II and was only re-formed to help cope with the Emergency in Malaya in the 1950s. It took the Iranian Embassy siege to fend off a more recent attempt to consign them to history. During the 1960s and 70s, they existed only in the shadows, operating in parts of the world many people would struggle to point to on a map ...

Tourists visit the ports and harbours of Oman's Dhofar province nowadays to watch the dhows landing their catches of abalone, lobster, shark and tuna fish. As long ago as the 9th century traders from around the world were coming here in search of Arabian horses, human slaves and frankincense. The

Queen of Sheba had cargoes of the precious, fragrant resin put aboard ships at the port of Samhuram for transportation to Israel and the court of King Solomon himself. Trade routes carried more of it throughout Asia Minor and all around the shores of the Mediterranean Sea.

The city of Mirbat, east of Samharam, was another centre for the frankincense trade, but horses seem to have been the main interest here in ancient times – in fact the name 'Mirbat' means horse market. It was a prosperous place then, the wealth of its citizens displayed in the elaborate architecture of their homes and other buildings, some traces of which are still visible today.

More recently, of course, it's oil that has shaped the destinies of the countries of the Middle East. It's doubtful Britain would have cared much at all about Oman and the fate of its people in the 20th century had it not been for the black gold. But care we did, and during the middle years of the last century we got ourselves comprehensively mixed up in that nation's affairs.

Many of Oman's modern domestic troubles were the fault of her Sultan, Said bin Taimur, whose rule was reactionary and repressive. Slavery was still commonplace in the Dhofar province, along with other practices bordering on the medieval. Popular uprisings, eventually drawing much of their funding, training and armament from Iraq and Saudi Arabia, steadily took root.

Said was overthrown, and replaced on the throne, by his own 29-year-old son, Qaboos, after a bloodless palace coup in July 1970. With his father living in comfortable exile in London, the new Sultan tried various liberal policies in a bid to mollify the rebels, but with little success. Civil war still plagued the Dhofar region.

Oman had links to Britain stretching back into the last years of the 18th century, and it was to the British Government that Qaboos looked for help. He had been educated in Britain and received his officer training at Sandhurst before serving with the Cameronians, so it was hardly a surprising move on his part. British-trained soldiers had been operating unofficially in the country for years, on his father's behalf as well, and now in the 1970s fresh supplies of fighting men arrived to bolster the Government. But this was to be an undeclared war for Britain, kept secret from the public, and our men were there in the guise of advisers and trainers for the Omani forces.

There was talk of a 'hearts and minds' mission to draw popular support away from the rebels and direct it towards the new young Sultan and his Government, but there was bloody fighting to be done as well. By July 1972 the city of Mirbat, ancient capital of Dhofar, was the permanent base for a 10-man team of British soldiers, and their presence had attracted the attention of the rebels. They were out to spill British blood, and the unit stationed in the ancient castle seemed an ideal target.

Advisers and trainers those British soldiers may have been, but they were also part of 22 SAS. (In the 1950s the old Sultan of Oman had been helped by British forces as he tried to fight off a rebellion led by an Imam, Ghalib bin Ali. Explorer and writer Sir Ranulph Fiennes, himself an SAS man, spent time as an adviser at the palace in the years before he started circum-navigating the globe and climbing mountains.)

The country was under the protection of Great Britain and the fighting that followed drove the rebels underground. But in 1957 the Imam's brother Talib bin Ali entered Oman from exile in Saudi Arabia and established a stronghold high in the beautiful green mountains of Jebel Akhdar. At first the Sultan and his advisers believed only a full-scale assault by an entire brigade would dislodge the rebels from their remote position – a place believed by many to be impregnable. But in 1959 two squadrons of SAS men scaled cliffs to launch a surprise attack. The result was an outright victory, and those rebels that survived the encounter fled to Saudi Arabia. During the 1960s the rebellion resurfaced, now calling itself the Dhofar Liberation Front and with a Marxist-Nationalist agenda.

But when the new Sultan turned to Britain for help with the old problem in 1970, it was decided that our assistance would have to be covert. This time the SAS men entered the country as a British Army Training Team (BATT), ostensibly to prepare the Sultan's own troops for the job of domestic security. An offensive codenamed 'Operation Jaguar' – a joint effort between the British troops and the Omani Air Force – scored considerable success. There were casualties for the SAS but it was the rebels who were left licking the more serious wounds. With their support weakening in the face of one defeat after another the rebels – known as *adoo*, an Arabic word meaning 'enemy' – were on the lookout for a quick success. If they could score a victory over a British garrison, the people might be persuaded to rise one more time and overthrow the Government.

The SAS unit in Mirbat had reached the end of its three-month stint. As night gave way to dawn on 19 July 1972, the men's thoughts were given over to the prospect of moving on, perhaps even returning home for a while. Their tour had passed quietly enough. A few *adoo* mortar rounds had been lobbed towards the camp from time to time – more to demonstrate the rebel presence than anything else – and no real damage had been done: just another day at the office.

Captain Mike Kealy, the 28-year-old commanding officer, was awoken from his sleep in the BATT house, within the simple razor-wire compound that was the town's principal defence, by the sound of gunfire. It was just after 5 a.m. Jumping from his bed and slipping his feet into a pair of flip-flops, he ran upstairs on to the roof of the building to try to get a glimpse of whatever was going on. So early in the morning there was almost no light in the sky, just the first rumours of grey within the black, and all he could see was the flash of gunfire and the jagged comet tails of tracer rounds.

Several hundred yards away, at the top of a small hill called Jebel Ali, a picket of Dhofar Gendarmerie (DG) – locals trained by the British – were exchanging fire with the first of around 250 *adoo*. It was a huge force to have approached so close to the town undetected – and the SAS men would say later that these were some of the bravest and most able soldiers they would ever have to fight.

The rebel attack had begun with stealth – some of the DG had been dispatched in their bunks, their throats slit from ear to ear by the *adoo* while they slept. A handful of DG on routine patrol had then stumbled on to the enemy, still going about their gory work, and with the element of surprise gone the rebels had launched their full-scale attack. The DG fought bravely, but with four of their number shot dead the survivors decided to retreat back towards the compound and the fort.

It was this exchange of fire that had awoken Kealy. But with the blanket of night still covering the landscape, all the detail of the attack was still unknown to the SAS men now gathering themselves to face whatever the day had in store.

Kealy assessed his situation. As well as the 9-strong SAS team, he commanded some 30 Askaris – Omani soldiers fighting under British officers; 40 or so Firqat – Dhofari tribesmen loyal to the Sultan; and 25 DG, an unknown number of whom now lay dead on the slopes of Jebel Ali, or pale and bloodless in their bunks. Most of the Firqat, however, were on patrol, having been sent out by Kealy two days before to check out reports of a rebel force within reach of the town. It was only the SAS men, the Askaris and the remnants of the DG that stood now between Mirbat and whatever *adoo* force was massed against them.

Within the wire perimeter was an old mud fort built by local tribesmen – who knew how many years before – and beside it a gun-pit housing a World War II-vintage 25-pound artillery piece. Kealy immediately ordered a trooper to man the 81mm mortar positioned in front of the BATT house and to open fire towards the advancing *adoo* up on the hill of Jebel Ali. Seconds later the telltale whump ... whump ... whump ... of mortar rounds en route became the baseline accompaniment for the rest of the action. Without the need for any other commands, the rest of the SAS men took up firing positions around the encampment, or manned the two machine guns on the roof of the BATT house.

For the *adoo* it must have seemed victory would not be long in coming that morning. They had surprise on their side and were attacking in overwhelming numbers. They were well motivated, well trained and armed with Russian-made AK-47 assault rifles, heavy machine guns, recoilless rifles – even Carl Gustav 84mm rocket-launchers stolen from the British at Aden some years before. It was monsoon season and an early morning mist, coupled with low cloud, ought to deny the defenders any hope of air cover or airborne reinforcements. They had already driven the DG off the hill and were now raking the British position with rifle and machine-gun fire.

The situation facing Kealy and his men has been likened to that of the British soldiers at Rorke's Drift on 22 January 1879 during the Anglo-Zulu War. But what the *adoo* commander could not possibly have known was that the resolve of the British men he faced now was the same as that which had been demonstrated by those 100 of their fellows less than a century before. Worse still for the enemy, by sheer bad luck they had chosen a time in the calendar when the end-of-tour handover was about to take place. Yet more SAS men were just 30 miles away at the British base of Umm al Gwarif.

While heavy machine-gun rounds began to fizz and whine around the compound like angry bugs, a signaller got on the radio to make SAS headquarters there aware of their predicament. All he could report so far was the sound of gunfire and a few mortar shells – and at first it was assumed at the other end that this was just another stand-off battle that might well come to nothing. It was only as dawn began to make inroads on the night that Kealy and the rest began to see, through the drizzling rain, large numbers of the enemy moving about in the gloom. Was it possible they were facing a frontal attack?

The rest of the British soldiers, together with the local men they'd worked so hard to train, started the fight-back. It was around 5.30 a.m. and by now there was enough light in the sky to enable the defenders to make out worryingly large groups of *adoo* picking their way towards points all around the perimeter.

'We opened fire simultaneously, unleashing a hail of 0.50 calibre bullets and machine-gun fire at the assaulting *adoo* rebels,' said one trooper. 'The running figures became a focal point where the red tracer and exploding incendiary rounds converged.'

Outnumbered though they were, the defenders were managing to lay down a galling fire. The *adoo* advance, which had looked unstoppable in those first moments, began to waver for a while. The line began to falter and even collapse in places as man-shaped gaps were punched through it. But the *adoo* were well disciplined and there were plenty of reinforcements stepping up to fill the breaches left by the fallen.

Just at the moment when the courage of the enemy seemed as though it might break, a figure appeared among them with enough resolve to drive them forward once again. More than one of the defenders later reported seeing a tall man, resplendent in well-pressed khakis, who stood to the fore among the wavering *adoo* infantry. While bullets, shells and mortar rounds filled the air around him, he marched back and forth, urging his men to drive their attack home. Suddenly, but with his job done, he was dropped by a British rifle bullet to the head.

'Still they kept coming,' said the trooper. 'Wave upon wave over the plain.'

One of the SAS men was a Fijian corporal named Talaiasi Labalaba. As soon as the thunder of battle started he'd run and crawled over 500 yards under fire from the BATT house to reach the gun-pit in the shadow of the old fort, where an Omani gunner called Walid Khamis was manning the 25-pounder. Together they set to work slamming the heavy rounds into the breech and ducking down as each was launched on its murderous arc towards the enemy.

By getting the big gun into action, they had of course made themselves the principal target for the attackers. Mortar rounds and hot lead from heavy machine guns and automatic rifles peppered the air around the Fijian and the Omani as they manned the sharp end of Mirbat's defence. As the sand and gravel kicked up around them, stirred by an endless barrage of incoming rounds, they worked together like a frantic machine – until a lucky round from the attackers hit Khamis in the stomach. Without a sound he slumped to the floor of the gun-pit and curled into a ball around his torn middle.

Undaunted Labalaba took on the job of two men – loading and firing as the enemy growled and howled on the razor-wire of the perimeter just 40 yards away. Then all at once the world went black for the giant as a bullet smashed into his chin, tearing away bone and flesh. He regained consciousness a few moments later and raised a hand to his ruined jawline. He knew he was badly hurt but there was work to do and, shaking off the pain of the wound, he reached for his walkie-talkie.

Back at the BATT house, Labalaba's voice came through, broken and barely recognisable, saying he'd been shot in the chin and needed back-up. Lab had never been one to complain about injuries, and all who heard his call instantly understood he must be properly cut up.

(One of the legends of Mirbat – and there are several – tells of Labalaba's first sight of the town and its fort all those weeks before: as the team circle overhead in their helicopter prior to landing, Labalaba turns to a colleague and says quietly: 'This is the place where I'll die.')

Listening to the walkie-talkie was another Fijian, by the name of Takavesi, and at once he asked Kealy for permission to go to the aid of his countryman. Kealy agreed and within seconds 'Tak' tore out of the door of the BATT house, Armalite in hand and making for the gun-pit. Up on the roof of the building, the rest of the troopers could only watch as that graceful athlete, a rugby player in his former life, made the run of his life. Bullets flew around him like bees, or kicked up dust and stones around his feet as he weaved and ducked over the broken ground separating him from his goal. Miraculously, he dived unscathed into the gun-pit.

Labalaba had applied a makeshift field dressing to his ruined face but he was bleeding heavily (some accounts have it that his jaw was almost shot away and hanging from his face at a sickening angle). Without a word, and possibly unable to speak any more, he gestured towards a pile of unopened ammunition cases. Takavesi understood at once – the survival of the camp depended upon the 25-pounder gun continuing its job. The pair manned it together, crawling around the base of the gun-pit as enemy bullets threw up clouds of sand all around them.

By now the *adoo* soldiers had cut and blasted gaps in the razor-wire and were charging in small groups towards the gun-pit, bellowing as they came on. So close were they, Labalaba had to level the gun-barrel and blast shells into those enemy faces at point-blank range.

Back at the BATT house it was Tak's voice that was heard next on the walkie-talkie. 'I'm hit, I'm hit,' he shouted. And then silence.

An *adoo* round had smashed into his back, leaving him too

weakened to help operate the 25-pounder. Still able to use his automatic rifle, he laid down covering fire while Labalaba, understanding the desperate danger of their situation, made a lunge for a small 60mm mortar lying close by. While the giant Fijian was in mid-air, his arm outstretched towards the weapon, an *adoo* round passed cleanly through his neck. He fell lifeless to the ground, his prophecy fulfilled.

The intensity of the *adoo* fire dropped as they moved around the perimeter then, collecting and tending to their wounded. In the brief hiatus, a second radio message was sent by Kealy to HQ requesting airborne support. They were holding out for now – but they could not survive indefinitely without help.

Another legend has it that when an SAS man has reached that point in a battle where he and his comrades are about to be overwhelmed by the enemy – when hope is in exceedingly short supply – he uses one particular form of words on the radio when calling on back-up. It sends the instant message that every SAS man within reach must stop whatever he's doing, pick up a weapon and lend a hand. What Captain Kealy had done was to summon 'the beast', and now the beast was coming.

It was around 8 a.m. when the SAS men back at Umm al Gwarif got the call. Just arrived from Britain, they'd had their breakfast and were preparing to join their officers and NCOs out on the firing range. Instead they piled into waiting heli-copters, carrying enough firepower to start a war – or finish one.

All too soon the rebel firing in front of Mirbat recommenced, and it was obvious to the British soldiers that their survival depended on the heavy gun. Rockets were coming over the razor-wire defences as well, finding their mark on the old fort and reducing it to rubble. They had to get the 25-pounder back into action.

Kealy and another of the troopers, an SAS medic called

Tommy Tobin, fought their way over towards Labalaba and Takavesi. It was into a hail of lead and rocket bursts that they were advancing, but it was either die on the move or stand still and wait to be overrun. Having made it across the 500 murderous yards of terrain, using a shallow dry riverbed for cover, Tobin dived head-first into the pit. Kealy, right behind him and seeing there was no more room beside the gun itself, flung himself down behind the sandbags of the ammunition bay beside it.

Despite his injury Tak managed a defiant smile and kept firing bursts of rounds over the sandbag defences towards the *adoo* just yards away. Tobin set about administering a drip to the downed Omani gunner, but one look at the gaping wound on Labalaba's neck was enough to tell him nothing could be done for the hero of Mirbat. An *adoo* bullet smashed into the side of Tobin's face as he turned back towards Tak, causing terrible damage. He dropped to the floor of the gun-pit, mortally wounded.

Using the walkie-talkie, Kealy ordered the men back at the BATT house to use the 88mm mortar to try to weaken the *adoo* attack on the gun-pit. They did so, but the attackers were so close the troopers had to take turns bracing the mortar tube between their legs so they could aim horizontally. The rounds found their targets but the soldiers' thighbones were fractured in the process. Fractured or not, they kept on firing, dropping rounds frighteningly close to Kealy and the rest of the men cornered in the pit as they battled to hold back the *adoo*.

The situation for the defenders was reaching breaking point. Kealy and Takavesi were running out of ammunition for their rifles and *adoo* grenades were landing right beside the sandbags now as well. Suddenly an *adoo* soldier appeared above Kealy but he managed to cut his would-be attacker down with a burst of fire from his SLR.

Just when it seemed the tide was about to break over them, the air was filled with the scream of jet planes. Despite the low cloud, RAF pilots had flown their Omani Air Force Strikemaster jets out over the sea to get a glimpse of ground level. Then, hugging the contours of the land, they flew dangerously low over the terrain until they could bring their cannons to bear on the *adoo*. Time and again they dived down out of the cloud, scudding just tens of feet above the ground as they pounded the increasingly demoralised rebels. The pilots would report seeing hundreds of attackers advancing upon Mirbat, but cannon fire and a well-placed 500-pound bomb scattered them like sheep.

Helicopters too faced the hellishly difficult flying conditions, not to mention *adoo* rocket fire, to bring help where it was so urgently needed. Covering the 30 miles from Umm al Gwarif in less than 10 minutes, they unloaded the 23 fresh SAS men armed to the teeth with, among other things, 25,000 rounds of ammunition. The beast had arrived and its work was quick and bloody. Sweeping through the town from the south, they drove all before them. The *adoo* lost a total of 38 men dead before finally withdrawing altogether and disappearing back into the surrounding countryside. Their rebellion would never recover.

Given that no British soldiers were officially fighting in Oman, nothing of the defence of Mirbat was reported at the time. The bravery and sacrifices of that battle – like so many actions involving the SAS – are remembered best by their comrades. Two of the surviving troopers were eventually awarded the Military Medal, while a third received a posthumous Distinguished Conduct Medal. Sergeant Labalaba was given a posthumous Mention in Dispatches, although many of his colleagues thought he deserved more, even the VC. 'Tak' Takavesi had taken wounds that would have dropped a horse. Nonetheless he insisted on walking unaided to the helicopter that would ferry him to hospital for urgent treatment. In 1980, still fighting the good fight, he would be part of the storming of the Iranian

Embassy in Princes Gate, a leader of one of the teams tasked with abseiling down from the roof and blasting their way in through the windows. At the time of writing, he is apparently busy in Iraq as a mercenary.

Captain Kealy received the Distinguished Service Order. In 1979, after a three-year break from the Regiment, he decided to return to active duty. Determined to prove he could still cut it with the best of them, he volunteered to take part in the traditional endurance march for would-be recruits, in the Brecon Beacons.

The weather conditions when he set out were atrocious – and steadily deteriorated. Having filled his Bergen rucksack with bricks rather than kit, he was without the recommended waterproof clothing when the snow really set in. While other students came off the mountains, Kealy pressed on. By the time some younger men were passing him on the way down and suggesting he should quit too – but being assured by him that he was all right and happy to continue – he may well have been suffering the first stages of hypothermia. Two trainees found him, unconscious and covered with snow, at 10 a.m. They tried to revive him but he died before he could be got off the mountain.

This is the way of such men. Driven by restless hearts, they are sometimes incapable of choosing the safe way home.

It is the legend of the SAS that survives most determinedly of all – and stories like the Battle of Mirbat will always be remembered best by boys.

In 'The Golden Journey to Samarkand', by the English poet James Elroy Flecker (1884–1915), as they prepare to depart the Master of the Caravan turns to a band of ragtag travellers on the road and asks:

> But who are ye in rags and rotten shoes
> You dirty-bearded, blocking up the way?

Their reply is engraved on the wall of the clock tower at the home of the Regiment in Hereford, and is their best monument and memorial:

> We are the Pilgrims, master; we shall go
> Always a little further: it may be
> Beyond that last blue mountain barred with snow
> Across that angry or that glimmering sea.

How curiously the course of one's life may be turned

Show me a man who says he never once dreamed of being an SAS man like Jock Lewes and I'll show you ... a man who's not being entirely honest, not least with himself. In fact any boy who didn't spend at least part of a school summer holiday running down grassy slopes and sand dunes while firing an imaginary machine gun and hurling imaginary Lewes bombs must have had a deprived childhood. The acid test is to look at the logo on a D.C. Thomson *Commando* comic – in which the 'C' of 'Commando' is wrapped around a Fairbairn-Sykes fighting knife. If you don't instantly remember wanting to *own* a Fairbairn-Sykes fighting knife when you were about nine, then it's quite possible that you are, in fact, a girl.

Manly men carry within them, unmarked by the years and with the dreams still burning brightly, the boys they once were (and to some extent still are). And of course, they are not supermen. I remember thinking they were when I was 13, but I'm much older now. What the intervening years have taught me is that they were and are ... men, plain and simple. They are men who seek an adventurous life and whose abilities lead them somehow into war. They are also the sort who want to be the best in the world at their jobs. It is their calling and their profession, and that such men exist at all should attract only gratitude from the rest of us.

Although Lieutenant Scott had impressed Markham, he was not the number one choice for a pilgrim to cast light into that southern darkness, to cross its mountains barred with snow. Our Con was placed only at number six on the list.

A year after being commissioned as a sub-lieutenant he was

posted to the Pacific, and then to the Mediterranean. By 1891 he was back in England, often visiting the family home at Outlands. He completed a two-year course aboard the torpedo-training ship *Vernon* and the first-class certificates he received in his final exams showed he was emerging as a talented officer.

In spite of his successful career there was a large black cloud on Scott's horizon during those years. In October 1897 his father died of heart disease at the age of 66. The family had no money to speak of – far from it. Three years before John Scott's death they had had to give up their home at Outlands in favour of more humble digs nearby. John's death only made matters worse. He left neither savings nor life insurance and his widow and daughters had to move house again. Two of the girls rented rooms above a shop in Chelsea and their mother moved in with them. It fell upon the two sons – Robert and Archie – to try to support their mother.

For a young officer like Scott, this was a severe financial handicap. The means to entertain, to furnish oneself with the best of clothes, were important considerations if the right impression was to be made and social advancement achieved. Scott was living only on his modest officer's salary and though he never begrudged his mother a penny of the support he was able to provide for her, he felt the best things in life were passing him by.

He had no way of affording the social life enjoyed by many of his fellow officers, and the expense of taking a young woman out on a date was completely out of his reach. During this time Scott withdrew into himself, retreating into the reticence and shyness that were always part of his nature.

Another man in such circumstances might not have been overly bothered, might have been content with his lot – but it burned Scott. He had within him the desire to be someone, to matter in a bigger story. Lacking either the money or the social status to rise to prominence, he would need to find another way.

A further spur came in the form of his younger brother Archie's sudden and unexpected death from typhoid fever in 1897. In a letter to his sister Ettie he wrote:

> ... it is easy to understand that he died like a man ... It is a strange chance that has taken him who perhaps of all of us found the keenest pleasure in life ... I saw that despite his health he was not strong and I meant to have a long talk with you about it. Too late – doesn't it always seem the ending of our wretched little mortal plans?

When he wrote to his mother about Archie, he praised her for the job she had done of raising good men:

> Don't blame yourself for what happened, dear. Whatever we have cause to bless ourselves for, comes from you. He died like the true-hearted gentleman he was, but to you we owe the first lessons and examples that made us gentlemen.

Scott correctly identifies another of the ingredients important in the making of manly men – good mothers. While it's true that brave and manly men have come from backgrounds lacking in family love of any kind, there is no doubting the value of a loving mum in the shaping of a hero.

Scott's tendency towards depression, or at the very least a kind of lethargy, seems close at hand in his words to his sister. But there's also an awareness that life is short and might be snatched away at any time. For Scott, the time for action to shake himself out of his doldrums was at hand.

In the summer of 1899 his path crossed that of Markham, who told him in person about the plans for an Antarctic expedition. After years of research, preparation and salesmanship, the wily campaigner had got the go-ahead from both the Royal

Society and the RGS. All at once there was a need to appoint an expedition leader.

With the urge to seize the day burning strongly inside him, Scott applied at once. In June 1900 he was appointed to the job – despite protests from members of the Royal Society who'd wanted a civilian scientist for the role. Markham had argued that only a services man like Scott could provide the kind of backbone required for such an expedition.

Always honest about the way in which he had been drawn into the adventure that would shape and define his life, Scott freely acknowledged the role of fate and serendipity. As he wrote in *The Voyage of the 'Discovery'*, '... how curiously the course of one's life may be turned'.

The random hand of kismet presents the situations to be faced in life, but men are judged by the way they respond when the moment comes. Some of that response is determined by the expectations of others, and Scott lived in a world that demanded a certain kind of behaviour from its boys and men.

Those expectations were clearly outlined in, among other places, the tales of other men's lives. As well as hearing about how British men had behaved when faced with life's challenges, Scott would have grown up knowing about the wars and exploits of those of other nations too.

By 1868 the French were still licking their wounds after an ill-fated attempt to establish an empire in Mexico. It had been an exploit the French Government probably wanted to forget. But for one group of men, none of them French, it would never, ever be forgotten.

The Demons of Camerone

Les Invalides in Paris was once a hospital for the care of France's wounded soldiers. For most of its existence it has been a resting place for her honoured dead. The body of Napoleon Bonaparte was interred there in 1841, having been repatriated from its first grave, in exile on the island of St Helena in the South Atlantic. Les Invalides is a place of memory and remembrance. High on one wall is a word inscribed in letters of gold. It reads: 'Camerone'. In the town of Aubagne is the Legion Hall of Honour, dearest of all places to the men of the 'La Légion des Etrangers' – the French Foreign Legion. Inside, in a place of the highest honour, rests a carved wooden hand.

On the morning of 30 April 1863, just 62 non-commissioned officers and men of the 3rd Company of the 1st Battalion of the French Foreign Legion were fit for duty. Their normal complement was three officers, 112 NCOs and other ranks, but illness had taken its toll. They had been in Mexico just a few weeks, supporting efforts to establish a French colony under the puppet-rule of one Archduke Ferdinand Maximilian Joseph von Habsburg, an Austrian aristocrat hand-picked for the job by Napoleon III, Emperor of France. Maximilian would be accompanied by his new Belgian wife, Marie Charlotte Amélie Léopoldine, taking on the Mexican form of her name to make her the Empress Carlota.

The Americas offered the hope of wealth beyond the dreams of avarice, and with a civil war occupying the attentions of the inhabitants of the north of the continent, opportunist European nations were making inroads on the disputed and turbulent lands of the south. Mexico had also run up debts with several foreign powers and by 1861 a coalition of British, Spanish and French troops were in occupation in the country in hope of getting their money back. The three proved incapable of agreeing on a strategy and within months both Britain and Spain had abandoned the operation, leaving the French in sole occupation.

Although a French Expeditionary Force had been in action in Mexico from the start, the Legion had had to petition Napoleon himself for permission to join them on the campaign. Two battalions under the command of Colonel Jeanningros had landed in Vera Cruz on 28 March 1863, but their arrival had not been a happy one. Having expected to march towards the city of Puebla, the main seat of local opposition to the French invasion, instead they suffered the indignity of being placed on escort duty, babysitting supply convoys in the east of the country. The low-lying marshlands sweated and stank and the Legionnaires were succumbing in the main not to bullets and bayonets but to cholera, typhus and yellow fever. It was a miserable posting enlivened only by the constant threat from snipers.

Puebla had been besieged by the French since the middle of March, but there was no sign yet of victory. On 29 April, a month or so after the Legion's arrival, word reached Jeanningros that a hugely valuable convoy was to be sent by road from Vera Cruz to the besieged city. Along with vital equipment and rations the wagons would be carrying 3 million francs' worth of gold bullion for the soldiers' pay. It would be the job of the Legion to ensure its safe passage.

Sorely depleted by illness though it was, Jeanningros selected 3rd Company for the job. It was anyway the only body of men available and they would have to make the best of it. Three other officers volunteered to go along: Second Lieutenant Maudet, company pay officer Lieutenant Vilain and Captain Jean Danjou.

Vilain and Maudet had risen through the Legion's ranks.

Almost certainly French by birth, they had enlisted as other nationalities – Frenchmen being forbidden by law to join the Legion (the men they commanded were a mix of Italian, German, Polish and Spanish). Vilain and Maudet were good soldiers, winning their promotions at the Battle of Magenta in 1859 during the Austro-Sardinian War. While the enlisted men had a grudging respect for Maudet, they held a seething loathing for Vilain, who, they believed, had used his position as pay officer to keep them short of money. He had a long way to go if he was to win their loyalty.

Captain Danjou was from a proud French military family. He had graduated second lieutenant from the best military academy in France, the Ecole Spéciale Militaire de Saint-Cyr, and was sent straight to French Algeria. During fighting there in May 1853 his left hand was so badly wounded it had to be amputated below the elbow. He had a fully articulated wooden replacement made and fitted, and carried on his soldiering undaunted, winning promotion to full lieutenant later the same year. He fought next in the Crimean War, seeing action at the siege of Sebastopol. His captaincy came in June 1855. Captain Danjou must have cut quite a dash – even by the standards of the day when battle scars were commonplace among career soldiers. As was the custom of men of his rank, he wore a carefully maintained moustache and a thick goatee beard. By all accounts he was a handsome man.

Like Vilain and Maudet, Danjou fought in the Austro-Sardinian War at Magenta and at Solferino. He served then in Morocco before being sent along with the French Expeditionary Force in 1862 into Mexico, where he was made Quartermaster to Colonel Jeanningros.

It was still fully dark when the little company of soldiers of 3rd Company set out from their base in the village of Chiquihuite. Despite the stifling heat promised by the day ahead, they were dressed in their standard uniforms of knee-high black boots, baggy red woollen pantaloons and blue woollen tunics. On their heads they wore kepis, to cover and protect their necks from the heat of the sun. Each man carried a 70-calibre smooth-bore musket.

These were men of a sort seldom seen in our world now. They were foreign to the land through which they marched, foreign to the land that sent them and foreign to one another. This was a legion of strangers, after all, and each was far from home. They had left forgotten lives many years and many miles behind them and when asked what country was home to them would reply only, 'La Légion est ma Patrie' – the Legion is my country. They were hard men, hardened by drill and by battle and toughened by years of self-reliance and discipline. But what they had and held most dear was brotherhood. They depended on each other as they depended upon themselves.

As they'd prepared to leave Chiquihuite that morning, Colonel Jeanningros had wondered aloud if they were enough to protect such a valuable convoy and see it safely to Puebla.

'They are Legionnaires,' said Captain Danjou.

Out on the road he assembled his company into a defensive formation. He was at the centre with a small group of men and some of the mules loaded with the ammunition and rations necessary for the journey. Two equal-sized columns of Legionnaires marched in parallel either side of – and 100 yards away from – the road. He deployed no scouts, reasoning that since his men were infantry and not cavalry, soldiers on foot would provide little in the way of early warning of attack. Better if they all stuck together. The bullion and siege equipment would depart Chiquihuite two hours later and follow the scouting company at a safe distance.

Trepidation marched along the road as well. The Legionnaires were long enough in the tooth to know that word of what the convoy contained would be travelling ahead of them into the ear of the enemy. There was little doubt that a Mexican Army force would be sent to intercept them en route. It was only a question of how strong and how determined that force might be.

As Danjou and his men passed through the Legion post of Paso del Macho in the early hours of the morning, the company commander there offered to supplement the company with a platoon of his own. Danjou refused and 3rd Company carried on its way.

The Mexican force out hunting the convoy was 2,000 strong – 1,200 foot soldiers and 800 horsemen. The cavalry were armed with US-made Remington and Winchester repeating rifles – far superior weapons to the muskets carried by the Legionnaires. The commander was General Francisco de Paula-Milan, and his spies had provided him with accurate information about the Legionnaires he sought – and the cargo they were tasked with protecting. As he rode in pursuit he was confident his men would quickly destroy the defenders and relieve them of their riches.

Some time around dawn Danjou and his men marched through the ruinous remains of a hamlet the locals called Hacienda Camarón. In time the men of the Legion would come to know the place as Camerone but for now it registered as no more than a cluster of dilapidated buildings and huts enclosed by a high, stone wall. 3rd Company did not stop, marching for another mile before Danjou called a halt and told the men to prepare their breakfasts. A handful of sentries were posted on the perimeter of the makeshift camp. Now at least there was daylight, and while they waited on water to boil for coffee the Legionnaires could look around at the unfamiliar vegetation smothering the landscape. Maybe a few of them noticed that the waist-high profusion might at least prove a hindrance for any enemy cavalry coming their way.

There would be no time for coffee this morning. Most of these Legionnaires would never taste it again. With the water still cold in the billycans the sentries sounded the alarm. Cavalry! It was the outriders of Milan's force and hundreds of mounted men were bearing down on the tiny company. Buglers licked dry lips and sounded the call to arms as best they could.

Legionnaires were men for whom drill was second nature and they formed their defensive square without having to think about it. Disciplined volley fire from their muskets was keeping the Mexicans at bay for now – but there was no hope of survival out here in the open. Danjou ordered a fighting retreat towards the only hope of salvation – the buildings and walls of Hacienda Camarón. Still in their square the Legionnaires began a steady withdrawal, keeping to the thickest of the vegetation to deter any solid charge by the mounted men.

Confident of victory, Colonel Milan held his horsemen back and had them simply circle the Legionnaires, harrying them and picking them off one by one.

It was now that Danjou suffered his first setback – when the mules carrying the company rations and ammunition bolted out of the square and into the clutches of the enemy. Now the defenders had only the musket balls and powder they carried in their pouches and webbing. Danjou remained in control. Twice on the way back towards the hacienda he brought the square to a halt and ordered volley fire. Mexican cavalry fell from their saddles, but there were too many.

Then came the second blow – 16 of Danjou's Legionnaires had been cut out of the square by the encircling horsemen. By the time the survivors reached the relative safety of the hamlet, their captain was in command of just 46 men. Several of those were wounded. Suddenly rifle fire poured into the company from within Camarón itself – some of Milan's men had made it there first and were in sniping positions in the upper floors of the ruined farm building.

Even by the standards of men accustomed to making the best of awkward situations, this was dire. The men of 3rd

Company were surrounded by unknown and potentially over-whelming numbers and already their only sanctuary was compromised by an enemy within.

Danjou had no room for thoughts about their chances as he gave orders to barricade all entrances to Camarón and to throw up a makeshift perimeter between the scattered walls and sheds. The courtyard remained vulnerable to the snipers in the main building but Danjou did not have enough men to risk trying to winkle them out. Again and again enemy horsemen rushed at the barricades and each time the Legionnaires drove them back.

Now a Mexican officer, Lieutenant Ramón Laine, approached the walls under the flag of truce. The Legionnaires held their fire and Laine was permitted to offer terms for the defenders' honourable surrender. The encircling force numbered 2,000 – what hope did the Legionnaires have in the face of such odds? Danjou went to each of his men in turn and told them he would accept the terms if just one Legionnaire thought it the right thing to do. Each man told Danjou what the captain already knew, that they would rather fight. Laine was informed of the decision and sent on his way.

The sun was hot now as the morning advanced. The Mexicans came on. Milan was enraged by the refusal of his terms and the force of these fresh attacks was greater than before. Again the enemy was driven back but this time at a terrible cost. Captain Danjou had fallen – shot and mortally wounded. The bullet probably came from a sniper, seizing his moment while Danjou rallied his men in the face of the latest attack. He died there in the courtyard, but not before winning from his men their vow to fight on. And so it was and so they did.

Lieutenant Vilain, the hated pay officer, now stepped up into command. 'Mes enfants!' he cried. 'I command you now. We may die, but never will surrender!'

By now Camarón was besieged not just by cavalry but by

infantry soldiers, 1,200 of them and crack shots all. The firing was as hot as the day. The sun rose ever higher in the sky and so the suffering of the defenders increased. Within the walls musket smoke coiled and hung like a shroud. Muskets grew so hot with incessant firing it was almost impossible to hold them. There was no water in any of the buildings and a run to the well in the courtyard, into the sights of the snipers, was to invite certain death. It was said later that the men of 3rd Company were reduced to drinking their own blood and urine before it was over. Again Milan offered terms of surrender. This time it was Vilain who went from man to man, asking what was in their hearts. They had fought for Danjou, they said, and now they fought for Vilain. There would be no surrender.

Some time in the middle of the afternoon a bullet took Vilain. History does not record whether he was loved or loathed at the end. In any case the Legionnaires fought for him and died beside him. What is true is that Lieutenant Maudet stepped up now and asked the survivors if they would surrender or fight on. They chose to fight, of course.

Now came a desperate attack by the Mexican infantry to test the defenders' mettle once more. Steady and disciplined fire from the remaining 70-calibre muskets drove the Mexicans back.

Unable to clear the defenders from the hacienda, the besieging soldiers set fire to the place instead. Now the smoke and flames of burning straw and timber were added to the heat of the sun. By late afternoon Maudet commanded no more than a dozen Legionnaires and they stood or lay in a manmade hell of thirst and fire and dying.

Beyond the walls they could hear the fury of Colonel Milan as he demanded of his officers how it could be that 2,000 men and cavalry had not yet accounted for the defenders of Camarón? There was no answer to be had.

Finally, with bugles sounding, rifles blazing fire and men

howling, the Mexicans began a final desperate push. Maudet and his survivors made it into an outhouse. The officer looked around at his fellows. There were five men still alive beside him – Corporals Berg and Maine and Legionnaires Constantin, Leonard and Wensel. Between them they had a handful of ammunition. Still the attackers came on, frenzied now as the defenders pulled back from one ruined outbuilding to another.

At bay, in a lull in the firing, Maudet looked into the faces of his comrades for the last time, taking in every detail. Their future was simple. They'd already been through the ammunition pouches of the fallen and had just one round apiece.

'Load your weapons,' ordered Maudet.

He looked towards the shattered doorway through which they had come and through which he planned to leave, for good or ill.

'On my command, fire,' he said. 'Then follow me and we'll finish this with our bayonets.'

With Maudet leading the way, the survivors plunged headlong into legend. Their lieutenant fell mortally wounded.

The firing stopped. The Mexicans pressed forward and, as the smoke of gunfire cleared, in one corner of the courtyard stood the last three defenders of Hacienda Camarón. Their ammunition was spent and they were standing shoulder-to-shoulder, muskets raised and bayonets fixed. The attackers were moving forward as one, ready to finish the job, when an officer's voice ordered them to halt. It was a Mexican colonel named Combas, and with sabre in hand he shouldered his way through the encircling soldiers until he could see with his own eyes who it was that had defied them for so long.

When he saw the trio standing firm – Corporal Berg, Corporal Maine and Legionnaire Wensel – he asked of them, 'Surely you must surrender now?'

It was Corporal Maine who replied, having first glanced left and right to check he was the senior of the surviving men.

'If we may keep our arms and tend our wounded, then we will surrender,' he said.

'To men such as you,' said Combas, 'one may refuse nothing.'

And so it was that the three were brought before the Mexican commander, Colonel Milan. On hearing what had happened in those last hours and minutes and moments he said, 'Pero, non son hombres – son demonios!' Truly, these are not men, these are demons!

Picking their way back through the buildings of Camarón, the Mexicans found a few more men of 3rd Company still alive and, true to their word, saw to it that those wounded defenders were well treated.

All were imprisoned, but eventually returned to the Legion in exchange for Mexican prisoners taken elsewhere. While still incarcerated, Corporal Berg managed to get a message back to Jeanningros. Among other things he informed his commander, '3rd Company is no more, but I must tell you it contained nothing but good soldiers.'

On release from his Mexican prison cell, Berg was commissioned and fought in other wars in other places – before dying in Algeria in a duel with a fellow officer. Corporal Maine rose up through the ranks too, finishing his army career as a captain.

In their defence at the Hacienda Camarón the men of 3rd Company lost three officers and 23 Legionnaires. The Mexican Army lost 300 men and saw a further 500 or more wounded. They never did capture the convoy – by leaving it to follow two hours behind him Danjou had ensured it was in a place of safety when the fighting started. The wagons carrying the gold simply waited on the road until they could be collected by a relief force sent out by Jeanningros.

The city of Puebla fell to the French on 17 May, followed

by Mexico City itself on 7 June. A year later, on 12 June, Emperor Maximilian and Empress Carlota entered Mexico City in triumph.

Thereafter the story was a less than happy one for the French occupation. Distracted by its own civil war, the United States of America had had no option but to turn a reluctantly blind eye to events unfolding in the lands of its southern neighbour. President Abraham Lincoln had made it known he supported the Mexican Republicans opposed to France, but was unable to send any help.

Following his assassination on 14 April 1865, Lincoln was succeeded by his Vice President, Andrew Johnson. Immediately after the end of the war, Johnson sent General Ulysses S. Grant to the Mexican border at the head of an army 50,000 strong. The message was clear and unequivocal – France was to withdraw its forces from the country or face the consequences of riling an overwhelming enemy. On 31 May 1866, Napoleon III announced he was pulling his men out of Mexico and by November of that year, the French soldiers were on their way home.

Denied the support of his erstwhile masters, Emperor Maximilian was on borrowed time, and he knew it. A reinvigorated Republican President Benito Juarez gained the upper hand in the fighting and Maximilian was captured on 15 May 1867. He was tried and sentenced to death, and despite pleas for clemency from no lesser figures than Victor Hugo and Giuseppe Garibaldi, was duly executed the following month. His widow, the Empress Carlota, went into exile, living first in Italy and finally in Belgium. Her estate was surrounded by the German Army during the Great War of 1914–18 – but since she was the widowed sister-in-law of the Austrian President, none was allowed to set foot upon her demesne. She never stopped loving her husband and believed always that he was not dead, that he would one day return to her. It was said she slept every night beside a doll she named Max. She died in 1927.

For the duration of the French occupation of Mexico all units of the Legion were under orders to halt whenever they had occasion to pass the site of the place they now called Camerone. To this day the men of the 1st Regiment wear the Mexican Eagle as their cap badge. The ashes of the dead of that battle are held in an urn carved in the shape of an eagle and it is passed from regimental chapel to regimental chapel in an endless rotation down through the years.

Some time not long after the Battle of Camerone, a farmer working the land near the former hamlet found the wooden hand of Captain Jean Danjou. By a circuitous path it was eventually returned to the Legion and is now their most honoured relic. Every year on 30 April the Legion celebrates Camerone Day and the hand of Jean Danjou is paraded before the men of the assembled regiments. All new recruits are told the story of the Demons of Camerone and left in no doubt that those are the standards expected of every Legionnaire.

On many battlefields since, when the last bullet has been fired and nothing remains but men and valour, a cry goes up from the Legionnaires, 'Faire Camerone' – do as they would have done! And they fight to the last man, and beyond.

At Camerone itself there is little to see. In the aftermath of the fighting the Mexicans went to some lengths to forget the place where so many of their men had died trying to oust so few. A railway line was deliberately routed through the site of the former farmyard where so many men fell.

In 1892 the French were permitted to place a commemorative plaque on the low ruins of one partially surviving wall. It has these words on it:

Here there were fewer than 60 opposed to a whole army. Its mass crushed them. Life abandoned these French soldiers before courage.

The trouble with the truth

Whenever I try to tell someone the story of the Demons of Camerone – and I'm the sort of person who does that kind of thing – I find it hard to speak before the end. When I get to the bit where Maudet and his men are trapped in that outbuilding, like Butch Cassidy and the Sundance Kid, my throat thickens and my voice starts to break. It's ridiculous and I know it. But that tale will never lose the power it has over me – and its power comes from the way it has become more than just another story from history, it has become a legend (when I first told my partner Trudi the story of the Demons she said, 'Stupid idiots', but she's a girl and girls don't understand).

Maybe events at the Hacienda Camarón didn't unfold *exactly* as described here. But there are more important things to ask of great stories than the truth. Historians spend a lot of time on the details, winnowing the seed from the chaff, trying to pin down *precisely* who did what, and when, and why. That's all very well, but sometimes it takes the thrill out of things. That's the trouble with the truth. The message to be learned from the Demons of Camerone is about the power of the brotherhood. It has been passed down through the years because the people who bothered to remember it and retell it cared deeply about what those men represented. The story is bigger than the sum of its facts. The important thing is to believe such behaviour is possible.

There's no way of knowing if Scott ever heard about the Demons of Camerone – but he came from a world and a time when knowledge of such stories was commonplace among boys and men. Somewhere along the line he certainly learned about sticking together with his men to the bitter end – but he was a military man and military men are trained to be like that.

Men are always impressed by military types (whether they admit it or not and even if they're not especially manly). Markham was right – in certain situations, like trying to keep people organised and motivated when the temperature's 50 degrees below zero, the huskies' paws are stuck to the ice and it's seal stew for lunch for the 100th day in a row, you want leadership from someone who reverts to training without a second thought.

No one in their right mind thinks war is a good idea but, as Plato said, only the dead have seen the end of it. It's no use pretending the real wide world will ever be any different and so it's a good idea to have people trained to cope with the worst of times.

There's also no denying that many of the great stories of manly men come out of war. By far the majority of British men alive today have never been to war and that's the way any reasonable person would want things to stay. But there are lessons for us civilians to learn from hearing about the kind of men who've been forged in that furnace.

(The older I get, the more I realise how easy I've had it all my life. Having been born white and male, into a loving family, living in Great Britain in the last third of the 20th century, I've been dealt what amounts to a winning hand from the cosmic deck of cards. All of the opportunities of life have been available to me since day one. I've never had to live with poverty, or endemic disease. I've never experienced any kind of prejudice or disadvantage born out of race, religion or creed. I've been kept safe all of my life by nameless strangers, from dangers both foreign and domestic. Our politicians are as keen to send our soldiers into wars in foreign parts as they ever were, but having been born beyond the grasp of conscription or National Service, as I have, such dangers have always been the other chap's problem. At 40, I've lived long enough to be too old for conscription even if they reintroduced it tomorrow. My safety has been provided for me by people I don't know and whom I haven't bothered to thank. I have effectively enjoyed an endless childhood. I've acquired certain responsibilities along the way – jobs, mortgages, partner, children – but nothing on a par with the responsibilities borne by men of all the generations before me. To paraphrase Jack Nicholson's deluded colonel in *A Few Good Men*, I've slept under the blanket of security provided for me by other people.)

Most of the 30 to 40-something men alive in Britain today started paying attention to war when they saw it in the form of action movies on screens both big and small. This is what it's like when you live in perpetual childhood – the only deadly dangers you ever see are the fictional ones faced by fictional characters. And so you start to see everything as a made-up story. Danger is just a thrill. Who nowadays gets the chance to sit at a dinner table listening to a genuine old duffer recounting a tale of battle? It's movies that have to get that job done now.

Who could resist the impact of watching *The Wild Geese* for the first time? A team of mercenaries hand-picked by Richard Burton sets out to rescue an imprisoned African leader – only to find themselves betrayed by their employer, Stewart Granger, and left to fight for their lives against a bloodthirsty army of Simbas somewhere in the African bush.

At the climax, Burton's best friend, Richard Harris, is running alongside a beat-up old DC-3 'Dakota' the team have managed to get hold of as their getaway vehicle. Roger Moore is at the controls (they're all in this one), and Burton and the rest of the survivors are already aboard ready to take off and make their escape to victory. Only Harris is still on the runway, fighting a desperate rearguard action to keep the Simbas at bay. They've been sharpening their machetes and you just know they're going to show Harris a pretty thin time if they can get their hands on him.

He's at the door of the plane, just about to be hauled in by Burton, when a lucky bullet gets him in the leg. He falls away from the plane and as both he and Burton realise he's a goner now for sure, soon to be taken and horribly murdered by the Simbas, he knows it's his time to die.

Having already thrown away his own rifle, he begs Burton to do the necessary.

'For God's sake, shoot me!' he cries.

Burton is horrified – unable at first to contemplate killing his friend.

'No, no – I can't,' he says.

Finally, through tear-filled eyes, Burton turns his rifle on Harris and cuts him down with a burst of machine-gun fire.

Harris's body falls lifeless to the runway and the plane lifts into the sky. Look out Stewart Granger, you evil swine!

On every occasion when *The Wild Geese* is repeated on TV, everyone watching for the second time or more prays things will work out differently – that Harris will somehow get on the plane. (Hollywood missed a trick by not filming alternative endings. Imagine the impact on Boxing Day if Steve McQueen managed to leap his Triumph Bonneville over the last line of barbed wire and escape the Nazis! There'd be dancing in the streets.)

But of course it never happens. Richard Harris dies on the runway, Steve gets sent back to solitary confinement and Frank Sinatra's Von Ryan never catches that blasted Express.

The point of this is that most boys nowadays begin learning

about manly men by watching the way they're portrayed in the movies. Eventually, though, boys grow old enough to understand that some of the movies are not fiction, but based on real-life events.

It's quite a revelation – that some of those brave men had once been real, heroes made of blood and bone. And out of countless viewings of films about the truth, can come an obsession with wondering how it would really feel to know that *this time* your luck has run out.

The Battle of Isandlwana

In the Zulu language 'Isandlwana' is a word with more than one meaning. The most literal translation is something about 'that hill looks like a little house' – and from some angles the steep-sided, 300-foot-high bluff of rock that bears the name does suggest the outline of a Zulu hut. Sometimes it looks more like a weathered and rounded sphinx. Light and shade dress it in different colours as the sun passes across the sky. Little house, lion – in sunshine or in shadow – the hill is the central character in a story that hangs around it like smoke. Isandlwana dominates the landscape, catching the eye from miles off and holding the gaze on the long approach down a deeply rutted dirt road. As visitors draw close, passing through the gates of the reserve, they emerge on to a stage always set for drama. The battle seems very close.

It's easy to overlook the memorial lying off to the left, just beyond the gates. Low to the ground, it's the most discreet of the many erected around the site in the years since 22 January 1879. It was unveiled in 1999, 120 years to the day after the fighting stopped, and takes the form of a necklace called an iziqu. Pronounced in the Zulu way, with a click forming part of the last syllable, 'iziqu' sounds like the letters 'e' and 'c' followed by an exasperated 'tut' – 'e-c-tut!'

This decoration is the Zulu equivalent of the Victoria Cross – the highest honour given by the king to the bravest of the brave. The iziqu monument at Isandlwana is modelled in bronze, 10 feet or so across and made up of thorn-shaped beads interspersed with lions' claws. Lying on its foot-high circular plinth it has the look of something cast aside – an afterthought – yet it's the most poignant memorial of all on this battlefield, placed by a nation whose light burned brightest in its final moments.

Towards the end of 1878 the British High Commissioner in South Africa, Sir Henry Bartle Frere, set about provoking a war. His aim was to create a confederation of states in southern Africa, bringing the whole place under British influence without the trouble and expense of imposing direct rule. It was a land of opportunity and as far as Frere was concerned those opportunities ought to be at Britain's disposal. As he and others saw it, the only obstacle was the independent kingdom of Zululand.

Zululand was and still is an astonishingly lovely place, ranging from the heights of the Drakensberg – the Dragon Mountains – in the west, through the gently rolling grasslands of the interior, down to the subtropical coast of the Indian Ocean. Legend has it that when the Bantu-speaking peoples first ventured into the area from further north, they were so struck by its beauty they called it *kwaZulu*, 'the place where heaven is' – and themselves *amaZulu*, 'the people of heaven'.

The Zulu king Cetshwayo kaMpande wanted to be left alone to rule this land and its people as he saw fit. The nation was young – created just 60 years before under the martial brilliance of Shaka – and had no need of trouble from a force as powerful as the British Empire. Cetshwayo had no clearly defined interest in any territory outside his own borders and just wanted to keep hold of what he had. But the boundary between Zululand and Natal had often been a blurred one, and towards the end of the 1870s the British authorities encouraged whites living in the northern fringes of their colony to fear imminent invasion by their black neighbours.

This anxiety on the part of the whites was based largely upon a British misunderstanding of the nature of the Zulu 'army'. Men like Frere believed Cetshwayo held a force of as many as 40,000 warriors in constant readiness, eager to do his bidding – a weapon of mass destruction, if you will. More unsettling still was the knowledge that Zulu warriors were forbidden to marry without the express permission of the king. It was widely believed this permission was only granted once braves had 'washed their spears' in enemy blood. Not only was this army huge, then, it consisted of sexually frustrated young men whose only hope of relief lay in the murder of white men, women and children! The continued existence of such a volatile force could hardly be tolerated. The sooner those restless warriors were stood down from their perpetual state of military readiness, and returned to the life of peaceful farmers, the better. And as peaceful farmers they could of course be put busily to work for the good of Britain, the Empire and the confederation.

The truth of the matter was rather different. Cetshwayo's authority did depend upon his control of the young men of his kingdom, but it was hardly a standing army. From about the age of 18 every Zulu boy was placed in an *ibutho*, or regiment, made up of other boys the same age. He would owe allegiance to this same regiment for the rest of his life. Throughout the year the king might call upon one or more of the regiments – collectively the *amabutho* – to come to his capital at Ulundi and provide some or other service for him. It might occasionally be military service but was just as likely to be labouring in the king's fields, repairing his huts or hunting for his food. For the rest of the time the men were returned to their homes and families to tend their own animals and crops. It was true that Zulu men could not marry without the king's permission – and this permission was unlikely to be granted before the age of 30 – but Zulu society allowed a fair degree of sexual activity outside marriage, provided no pregnancy resulted. In effect, the Zulu army was not the permanent fighting force the British imagined, but something more like a version of our own Territorial Army.

Nonetheless British minds were made up and Cetshwayo

was handed an ultimatum. By 11 January 1879 he was to do away with all the regiments. Zulu men were to be freed from any obligation to the king and allowed to marry whenever they pleased. There were other similarly humiliating conditions and the king had also to accept a representative who would live in the royal homestead at Ulundi, enforcing the British will. Failure to submit to all of this would be interpreted as an act of war and would swiftly be followed by invasion.

As Frere well knew, all of this trapped Cetshwayo between a rock and a hard place. If he met the demands he would make himself powerless within his own kingdom. If he refused he would be invaded by a vastly superior military force and have his power taken forcibly from him. Left with no room for manoeuvre, he summoned the *amabutho* to his kraal. He told them to bring only their weapons and to be ready for war. The deadline for the ultimatum came and went without word from Cetshwayo − as Frere had always known it would − and a British force promptly crossed from Natal into Zululand.

Lieutenant General Frederic Thesiger, 2nd Baron Chelmsford, the senior British commander in southern Africa, was the man in charge of the invasion. He was a 51-year-old career soldier, tall and statesmanlike with a carefully trimmed goatee beard. Well liked by his men, he had a reputation for being cool under fire. He had fought in India and Abyssinia and, more importantly, had already drawn blood on African soil − fighting the warriors of the Xhosa tribe on the Cape Frontier of southern Africa.

For the invasion of Zululand Chelmsford had split his force into three columns. The right crossed the Thukela River and headed towards the country's east coast, while the left was directed towards the west. Chelmsford himself rode at the head of the centre column as it splashed through the Mzinyathi River into Zululand at a crossing called Rorke's Drift. As the General watched his 4,000-strong force step out on to the Zulu bank, he was planning to deal with the new foe like he'd dealt with the Xhosa. In that earlier, ultimately successful campaign, he'd had to cope with the guerrilla tactics of a people who avoided pitched battle at all costs. Chelmsford put this down to cowardice as much as anything and firmly believed the Zulus would behave the same way. As the men and wagons progressed slowly into Zululand, he was convinced its inhabitants would flee before him, forcing him to hunt them down.

As it turned out, the Zulus had different tactics in mind. These were not soldiers who ran from a fight. Rather they ran towards it, barefoot over thorn and rock, thinking nothing of covering tens of miles before engaging the enemy. This was no standing army, but each man within it understood and venerated personal bravery above all things. Not for him the relative security of standing back from an enemy and firing bullets at him either. Instead the Zulu brave did his killing face-to-face. To do anything less was to show a lack of respect for self and foe. He was armed with shield, spear and club. Training had taught him to use the outside edge of his six-foot-tall hide-covered war-shield to drag down the weapon of his foe, while with the other hand he plunged his short, broad-bladed stabbing spear into the exposed upper body. We give those spears the name '*assegai*', but to the Zulu they were '*iklwa*' – the sucking sound made by the blade as it was tugged back out of the flesh. If the spear was dropped or knocked aside he could use the '*knobkerrie*', a ball-ended club shaped from a single piece of wood and more than enough to crack a man's head open like an egg.

The Zulu religion taught that killing a man was an unclean act. Each brave had to go through complex rituals before a battle to ensure he was protected from the taint of causing the deaths of other men. Regimental chaplains – *izinyanga* – conducted the necessary ceremonies beforehand and would be ready again after the fighting to help each man cleanse his body and soul. Living close to death as they did – the death of animals and humans alike – Zulus were familiar with what happened to corpses left lying around in a hot climate. They believed the bloating of the dead body was caused by the struggling of the soul trapped inside the stomach. After killing a man a brave would therefore split open the belly with his *iklwa* to ensure the soul could fly free. Failure to do this, the Zulus believed, would lead to their own, unclean but still living bodies swelling up the same way. It was also important to wear a piece of the dead man's clothing until such times as the *izinyanga* could perform the cleansing rituals – and for this reason they were also in the habit of stripping the bodies of their slain.

On 17 January, outside his kraal at Ulundi, Cetshwayo addressed the largest army ever to gather before a Zulu king. He was a handsome man: over six feet tall, broad-chested and heavily set. In his full ceremonial regalia he was a towering sight. Those who knew him well understood that while he could be easy-going and warm, he was shot through with a ruthless streak. He was understood to be at his most dangerous when backed into a corner.

Perhaps as many as 24,000 men, purified by their *izinyangas* and existing now in a place set apart from the world of everyday life, a place of war, listened as their great king asked them a question: 'I have not gone over the seas to look for the white man yet they have come into my country ... I have nothing against the white man and I cannot tell why they came to me. They want to take me. What shall I do?'

His braves bellowed back that they would not allow their king to be taken while even one of them remained alive.

Cetshwayo said they must kill the red soldiers (the British infantrymen wore red tunics) who had come into Zululand to take away the king and the womenfolk and the cattle. Most prophetically of all, he urged them to stay clear of those red soldiers wherever they had dug trenches or forts to protect themselves.

Find them out in the open, he said, where they have failed to build up their defences, and: '... you will be able to eat him up.'

He sent them away from him then, with instructions to the commanders – the *indunas* – to set a relaxed pace. They would need all possible energy for the fight ahead.

Battle-ready too were the men now marching into Zululand. Many of the British soldiers had been fighting for years in the service of the Empire. They'd grown accustomed to the conditions in the hot places of the world, their faces, necks and hands tanned by the sun, their once-white pith helmets darkened by dust and sweat to a more practical light brown. The infantry soldiers were armed with the state-of-the-art firearm of the day, the Martini-Henry rifle. It was loaded with a 0.45-calibre cartridge and delivered a lead bullet not much smaller than the last joint of a man's little finger. One round could stop a buffalo and a hit anywhere on a man's body above the knees was likely to cause enough damage to kill or at least permanently disable him.

The force under Chelmsford's command was by no means all-British. Along for the fight as well were men of the Natal Native Horse (NNH), the Natal Mounted Police (NMP) and the Natal Carbineers (NC) – locals with lifelong experience of the terrain and of fighting their black neighbours. It wasn't an all-white army either. Disaffected Zulus, together with men of other neighbouring tribes, formed companies of the Natal Native Contingent (NNC) under the command of white officers. These were dressed and armed like the enemy, with spears and shields, and wore coloured headbands to enable the whites to tell them apart from other Zulus in the heat of fighting.

By 20 January Chelmsford was watching his men make camp on the level ground in the shadow of the east face of Isandlwana mountain. A few days before he'd notched up a minor victory against the braves of a local Zulu chief called Sihayo – and the way the enemy had broken and run before his men deepened his conviction that no Zulu army would willingly stand before him. He didn't order his men to dig trenches around the camp – or even to arrange the wagons in a protective ring or *laager* around it. He would say later that he saw no need for such defences – demanded by the textbook in the case of fighting in enemy territory – because it was always his intention to move the camp forward within days. The ground was anyway, he said, too hard for digging.

The Zulus, looking for an enemy out in the open, would be well pleased.

As he looked out at the terrain surrounding Isandlwana, Chelmsford felt uneasy and impatient for the fight. Reports had informed him that a Zulu force had left Ulundi three days before, and the mountains between him and the Zulu capital could easily conceal a huge force. On 21 January he dispatched Major John Dartnell in command of a detachment tasked with conducting a thorough reconnaissance of the broken, mountainous terrain off to the south-east. At 1.30 the following morning, word came back from Dartnell that a large Zulu force had been detected and he was keeping his detachment out overnight in order to maintain surveillance.

This was exactly what Chelmsford had expected – the Zulus were staying out of sight in broken ground suited to guerrilla tactics. Well before dawn on 22 January Chelmsford rode out of the camp at Isandlwana accompanied by four of the six heavy guns he had brought with him and around half the available fighting men. The camp was put under the command of Lieutenant Colonel Henry Pulleine, and Chelmsford also sent orders to an officer presently waiting at Rorke's Drift with a force of 250 mounted men. He was Brevet Colonel Anthony Durnford, of the Royal Engineers, and his orders were to move up at once to the camp at Isandlwana.

Durnford was a maverick. He was a heavy gambler and usually a heavy loser. He'd been married in haste, during a posting to Ceylon in the 1850s, to Frances Tranchell, youngest daughter of a retired lieutenant colonel of the Ceylon Rifles. The marriage had gone bad – the couple had lost two of their three children in infancy – and Frances had left her husband for another man. By the time Durnford reached southern Africa, he was a lonely man with a lot to prove, to himself and to others. He'd recently met and fallen in love with Nell Colenso, the beautiful 24-year-old second daughter of the Reverend John Colenso, the Anglican Bishop of Natal. He was 19 years older than her – but it wasn't the age gap that made their relationship one that could never be seen in public. Even though Durnford had been wronged by his wife, divorce would have ruined his military career. Whatever love he and Nell managed to share, was shared in private.

He had lived and fought in southern Africa long enough to learn to love and respect many of the black tribespeople. The mounted column he commanded at Isandlwana was composed almost entirely of black troops and they were fiercely loyal to him. Durnford, however, was a soldier fighting his way back from a disastrous military past. In 1873 he had been in command of an operation to capture a chieftain called Langalibalele, who had fallen out with the Natal authorities over the matter of some rifles obtained by his young braves. Langalibalele and his men made a run for it into the mountains, making for neighbouring BaSotholand. Durnford and his party of local colonial volunteers, including men of the Natal Carbineers, caught up with the fugitives at a place called Bushman's River Pass. The encounter was a dangerous fiasco – Langalibalele escaped and many of Durnford's men were killed or injured. Durnford himself suffered a spear thrust through his right elbow that would leave the arm useless for the rest of his life. Back in Natal, the blame was levelled squarely on his shoulders alone.

By the time he arrived at Isandlwana on the morning of 22 January there had already been some slight excitement. Some time after dawn a large body of Zulu warriors had appeared on a ridge beyond the left of the camp and Pulleine had ordered his men to form up on the makeshift parade ground in front of the tents. Pulleine was no warrior – he was an experienced administrator and better suited to paperwork and logistics than fighting. Chelmsford knew and understood this – and the fact that he had left such a man in command shows he never suspected any threat.

For Chelmsford, the morning was already looking like a frustrating waste of time. He had joined up with Dartnell and though there had been some lightweight skirmishes with small pockets of Zulus, any large enemy force had vanished – if it had ever existed. He would also receive sketchy reports of activity back at the camp throughout the day, but nothing that would persuade him to return there with any urgency.

As soon as Durnford arrived at Isandlwana, he met up with Pulleine to discuss how best to shape the day. In terms of rank Durnford was senior to the other man and might have been expected to take overall command. His personal orders from Chelmsford were vague, however, and he took the opportunity to retain both his own independence and that of the 250-strong force he commanded.

The Zulus who had appeared earlier had disappeared out of sight but he hadn't liked the sound of what Pulleine had to tell him. As far as Durnford was concerned, that same large body of the enemy might now be working its way around towards Chelmsford, in his exposed position several miles out in the bush. He told Pulleine he was taking his men out into the broken terrain well beyond the front of the camp – to be in a position to drive the enemy back in the direction it had come from. He split his command in two – sending some men up on to the ridge to the left, directly towards the area where the enemy had been seen earlier. The rest he led himself, due east into territory right in front of the camp. It was just before midday.

Two Lieutenants, Raw and Roberts of the NNH, led the party sent up on to the ridge. The men were in good spirits as they trotted across the high ground. It was another beautiful day beneath blue skies and light cloud. The enemy was behaving as it should, and would doubtless continue to keep well out of their way if they knew what was good for them. Even the grass around their horses' hooves was saying 'shush, shush'.

Up ahead, a mile or so distant, they spotted some Zulu herdboys trying to drive a few head of cattle out of sight of the approaching horsemen. Rustling those animals would provide some little diversion for the men, so Raw and a handful of troopers split from the main body and trotted towards the point where they'd somehow disappeared into dead ground.

Raw reported later how the ground suddenly dropped away in front of them, so steeply and so suddenly they had to rein in their horses and bring them to a halt. This was the lip of the wide and lovely valley of the Ngwebeni Stream, and spread as far as the eye could see across the bottom of it, hunkered down beside their great war-shields, were the 24,000 braves of the Zulu army.

Here within five miles of the British camp was the greatest force ever assembled by the Zulu nation. They'd travelled the 60-odd miles from Ulundi without being detected and had spent the previous night without campfires lest the smoke give away their position at the last minute. Later the British would come across great, flattened swaths of grass scything across Zululand, wider than modern motorways, revealing the path taken by that host.

The invaders had been so completely duped it was embarrassing. Those Zulus who had led Dartnell and Chelmsford on their wild- goose chase had been followers of a local chief who had been slow in gathering his men. The fact they were off to the south-east and still making for the rendezvous at the valley of the Ngwebeni when Dartnell ran across them was the kind of good fortune that favours the brave. Because it was where Chelmsford expected his enemy to be, it confirmed his belief in the nature of the war he faced. He had been led by hubris into the lethal mistake of dividing his force in enemy territory – behaviour contrary to every military textbook of the day.

There was a final moment of silence as Lieutenant Charlie Raw and his men became the first of the invaders to fully understand the situation in which the British now found themselves. Then with admirable presence of mind they bothered to fire a volley into the massed force below them before turning tail and galloping for home. First to rise were the teenaged boys of the uKhandempemvu regiment. Enraged by the gunfire and without waiting for the commands of their elders, they jumped up with their shields and spears and ran up the slope towards the departing horsemen. The Battle of Isandlwana had begun.

Historians have argued endlessly about the significance of the date of 22 January. According to some, the Zulus would have had no intention of fighting that day because it coincided with the arrival in the night sky of the new moon. For the Zulus this was the Day of the Dead Moon – a spiritually unclean time and therefore the wrong time for fighting a battle. Those writers say the Zulus would have been intending to wait until 23 January and only attacked when they did because they'd been discovered.

Others say that having got themselves so perfectly into position to strike at the camp – while half its defenders were chasing shadows through thorn trees and dry riverbeds a dozen miles away – the Zulu generals would not have overlooked their opportunity for any reason, spiritual or otherwise.

Greatest of those generals – and now a strong, clear voice

of calm within that turbulent sea of warriors – was Ntshingwayo kaMahole. He commanded the left flank while his opposite number Mavumengwana kaNdlela had the right. Having seen the young bloods of the uKhandempemvu bolt from the starting-gate without instructions, Ntshingwayo brought the rest of the left to heel. Working with Mavumengwana he fought for order, and won. Now the regiments received their final blessings from the *izinyangas* before being dispatched from the valley in the formation that was to become legend – '*izimpondo zankomo*' – the horns of the buffalo. Zulu tactics dictated that the 'horns' would run out and around both flanks of the enemy force while the 'chest' engaged the front. Once the 'horns' were around the flanks, they would encircle the rear and begin cutting their way back through the massed foe towards the 'chest'. The reserve regiments would form the 'loins', waiting quietly behind the 'chest' until required.

These then were the well-practised and proven tactics, but never before Isandlwana had they been attempted on such a scale. It was the job of Ntshingwayo and Mavumengwana to choreograph this majestic deployment without any of the modern means of communication we would take for granted. Discipline and training were the only tools – and they worked.

Raw sent word to Pulleine and Durnford telling them what he'd seen. It seems Pulleine couldn't believe what he was reading on the hastily scribbled note handed to him, back at the camp, by a breathless horseman. Still convinced Chelmsford was dealing with the main Zulu army – somewhere off out of sight towards the south-east – he decided to send a single company of men in the direction Raw had reported. Pulleine already had a company up there under a Lieutenant Charles Cavaye (he'd dispatched them soon after Durnford rode out of the camp at 11.30 a.m.) and felt sure that by doubling its strength he was doing enough to contain whatever any approaching Zulus might have planned.

As the new men, under Captain William Mostyn, arrived out on the ridge they saw Cavaye's troopers strung out in a line and firing into a large body of Zulus that was moving across their front from right to left. For some reason those Zulus were not even bothering to acknowledge the red men picking away at their numbers. What neither Cavaye's nor Mostyn's men could possibly have understood at that moment was that they were watching the right horn of the buffalo moving to outflank not just them but the entire British camp.

Durnford's experience was to be slightly different. No sooner had Raw's messenger reached him than a large force of Zulus appeared in front of him, travelling fast. This was the left horn of the buffalo – the whole beast deploying on such a scale that soon the points of the horns would be five miles apart, moving around the British position with perfect symmetry. Durnford's men dismounted and fired into the mass, some hundreds of yards distant, then got back on their horses to begin a fighting retreat.

Just before leaving the camp Durnford had ordered a rocket battery and a company of NNC, under the command of Major Francis Russell, Royal Artillery, to follow him out on to the escarpment in front of the camp. Finding the journey over broken, rocky ground more difficult than Durnford's mounted men – and hampered by the apparatus of their primitive rocket launcher – they arrived on the scene just in time to encounter the full force of the Zulu advance.

Hastily they set up the trough for their rocket and managed to launch the missile in the general direction of the advancing left horn. It burst harmlessly overhead and, though briefly alarmed by the bang and flash of the thing, the Zulus quickly overtook the battery, stabbing at the men with their *iklwas*. Russell himself was killed in the mêlée and just a handful of British and NNC survived the clash, falling in with Durnford's men as they continued their retreat back towards the camp.

The sounds of rifle fire could be clearly heard by the men still back among the wagons and tents of the camp – but there was no panic yet. This was the British Army! There were hundreds of thousands of rounds of ammunition close at hand. There were 1,300 highly trained officers and other ranks ready to face down any attack launched by men armed with spears and clubs. There should have been nothing to fear.

Pulleine ordered his two heavy guns out on to a plateau that offered a field of fire towards the ridge where the trouble had apparently started. He also sent two more companies of riflemen to support those already up on the ridge with Cavaye and Mostyn. Just on the tail of the mountain of Isandlwana itself was a company under the command of Captain Reginald Younghusband, there to cover any retreat by the soldiers further out to the north and east.

To the right of the guns, and in position out on the escarpment in front of the camp, were soldiers led by Lieutenant Charles Pope. Seeing that a firing line was now developing on terrain facing the ridge, Pope wheeled his men to the left to try to make them the right-hand anchor of the British position.

It was now that the battle began to enter its critical phase, when decisions taken in the heat of the moment – and mistakes made – would determine the final outcome. And it's always tempting to see this only as a British battle. It's easy to overlook the fact that those events were being watched by other than British eyes, movements shaped by other than British commands.

Up on the high ground, clear of the fighting, Ntshingwayo watched and waited. He was almost 70 years old and yet had jogged easily alongside the army as it made its way from Ulundi to the valley of the Ngwebeni Stream. Now, while Pope did his best to read events down on the firing line . . . while Pulleine played his cards one at a time . . . while Durn-

ford fought to win recognition as a brave and intelligent officer
. . . and while Cavaye, Mostyn and Younghusband spoke calming
and confident words to their men . . . Ntshingwayo made his
move.

As one, the regiments making up the chest of the buffalo
stepped out into view on the top of the ridge, in plain view
of the camp and the firing line for the first time. They poured
down the slope like spilled oil, their numbers transfixing the
riflemen who had until now only a hint of the scale of the
force massed against them. Cavaye and Mostyn were already
pulling away from it, back towards Younghusband and the hope
of finding salvation among the tents and wagons of the camp.
Roberts's men were there too, still retreating after the initial
encounter alongside Raw.

Both of the seven-pounder guns roared into action, trying
to cover the partial retreat. Some say a stray shot killed Roberts
himself. In any case, the red men were starting to realise how
great was their peril. Perhaps the taste of fear rose into mouths
here and there for the first time as they turned their backs on
the enemy and began to flee.

Durnford's fighting retreat, courageous and disciplined though
it was, had left Pope's men dangerously exposed to outflanking
by the Zulu left horn. Realising there was a gap of many
hundreds of yards between him and the mounted men, Pope
wheeled to his right and began to try to close it. Durnford
meanwhile had reached a deep, dry riverbed – called a *donga*
– and ordered his men to get down into it with their horses.
Once dismounted, they lined the lip of the *donga* and began
to put steady fire into the advancing Zulus.

For the first time, the attack began to stall. Though they
outnumbered the British many times over, disciplined volley
fire from Martini-Henrys in professional, steady hands presented
a wall of death for men protected only by hide-covered shields.
They were youngsters too – the untested teenagers of the

uKhandempemvu and the 20-year-olds of the iNgobamakhosi – and they flung themselves down in the long grass.

Seeing this, Ntshingwayo dispatched Mkhosana kaMvundlana of the Biyela clan – a man destined to emerge as the greatest Zulu hero of Isandlwana – to knock some heads together. Sprinting down to the front line, Mkhosana marched back and forth among the prostrate warriors, heedless of the bullets flying around him and kicking up clouds of dust by his feet. As the braves watched, awestruck by his valour, he reminded them of the greatness of their king, who had himself won many battles and crushed his foes and was therefore deserving only of their praise and courage.

'The Little Branch of Leaves that extinguished the Great Fire … gave no such order as this!' he cried, his head thrown back, his face towards the sky.

Shamed by their elder's words, the boys leapt to their feet and plunged forward once more, towards the rifles spitting fire and smoke into their shining faces. Still unbowed, still urging them onwards, Mkhosana was suddenly silenced, felled at last by a Martini-Henry round.

Durnford meanwhile was in his element – survivors would recall how he walked calmly back and forth among them as they fired their volleys. From time to time a rifle would jam in the hands of a less experienced soldier. The cartridges were not solid brass cylinders but made of thin foil. Often, and especially once the barrel of the rifle was hot, they would jam in the firing mechanism. Durnford had his ruined right arm in a sling, bound close to his chest. But taking the offending weapon from shaking hands, he would jam it between his knees and use his good hand to free the cartridge with one practised movement.

The greater problem was a rapidly diminishing supply of ammunition. Much has been made by historians of the role of the quartermasters in charge of supplies back at the camp. Some have claimed that a great deal of trouble was caused by jobs-worths who were reluctant to hand out the boxes of bullets. In any case, out in the *donga* Durnford decided it was time to move and he ordered his men to mount up and withdraw.

With thousands of Zulus bearing down on him he led his men back to a ridge of high ground near the camp, called the Nek, close to where the army's wagons were parked. He had picked up stragglers of other units along the way and by now he was accompanied too by men of the Natal Carbineers – colleagues of those he'd been with so unhappily at Bushman's River Pass. It says a great deal for Durnford's actions and charisma that day that those men chose to stand with him now, rather than take their chances elsewhere.

From here on the Nek the surviving British could see there was no hope of survival where they stood and nowhere to run. Beyond the mountain was the road that led back towards Natal, the way they'd come just two days before. But the right horn of the Zulus had long since completed its manoeuvre and was blocking all hope of retreat in that direction. Some refugees of the British force would head that way nonetheless, down a route remembered to this day as the Fugitives' Trail.

From a column of 1,700 men – both black and white – who'd awoken at Isandlwana that morning, no more than 300 would make it to safety. Of them fewer than 60 were European.

The firing line had been overrun all along its length. The Zulus had broken through en masse and now their sheer weight of numbers was a flood that would not be checked. British order began to fall apart as men, singly or in groups, turned away from the foe and fled in hope of safety back among the tents and wagons – anywhere.

It's always meaningless to attribute bravery or cowardice in broad brushstrokes. Here at Isandlwana every shade of human behaviour, from cowardice to heroism and all points in between, was displayed by men on both sides. There were boys there too

– drummer boys of 12 years of age or thereabouts – taking shelter where they could among the men. It was to be the last time the British Army would take children into battle. None of those at Isandlwana would survive the day.

One of the most famous stories of 22 January 1879 details the attempt by two lieutenants to try to save the Queen's Colour. This flag was the rallying point for soldiers in battle – and its loss to the enemy an unbearable shame. Nevill Coghill and Teignmouth Melvill, both on horseback, were said to have tried to see the flag safely off the field, with the blessing of Pulleine. They died in the attempt, overcome by Zulus, and the Colour itself was lost for many months. For years their flight was recounted as a tale of great heroism – but it seems that even at the time doubts were cast on their motives. Of the few who survived the battlefield, all but a handful were men on horseback who fled the field early enough to avoid the crush of the rout. It begs the question why two officers saw fit to leave their footsoldiers to their fate, while they themselves headed for safety with a flag. Heroes or cowards ... who can easily say?

Killing and dying were everywhere, and white man and black man either rose up to meet them, or cowered before them.

A Zulu who fought and survived would say later, 'The tumult and the firing was wonderful ... those red soldiers! They fought like lions and they fell like stones, each man in his place.'

Cetshwayo had ordered the killing of the *red* soldiers, after all – and only those on the battlefield in the tunics of other regiments, other colours, would live to tell the tale.

If men on both sides learned anything that day, it was mutual respect. The Zulus would say afterwards that they never fought anyone braver than British soldiers. Whites who made it out would recall the selfless courage of near-naked Zulus, driving themselves on to the bullets and bayonets of the British in the hope their own deaths might bring victory one step closer for their fellows. Before the end they would be throwing the bodies of their dead up on to the stubborn British bayonets so as to drag them down and create an opening for attack.

Up on the slopes directly beneath the sheer walls of the mountain, another knot of British soldiers was looking out over this greatest battlescape of the Victorian era. And right at the height of it all the greater forces of nature played their hand as well. The moon – the 'dead moon' that had concerned the Zulus – now passed in front of the sun. For the next half hour the horror would be played out in the twilight of a near-total eclipse.

There in the gloom was Captain Younghusband. He and his men had been fighting their way back towards the camp, using the cliffs to cover their rear. They too had run out of ammunition, and hundreds of Zulus were rushing up the slope towards them. Moved by the spectacle of so few against so many, a Zulu commander raised his voice above the tumult.

'Wait!' he ordered.

The braves did as they were told and looked on in silence as Younghusband went to each of his men in turn, shook his hand and said a few words. Then, according to the watchers, he took 'a long knife' from his belt. So it was with sabre in hand that Younghusband let out a defiant roar and led his men in a final charge down towards the waiting host.

'We fell upon them and we killed them all,' said the Zulu.

Perhaps before they died Younghusband and his men glimpsed the last of Durnford. He had earlier sent away two of his sergeants, along with his beloved horse Chieftain, and at the end he was shoulder to shoulder with his men, an ever-tightening knot of red, surrounded by black. Above all else it was his wish to lead his men bravely and to do his duty.

'Fix bayonets, boys,' he said as the wave broke over them, 'and die like British soldiers do.'

Zulus were pouring into the camp, driving before them the

cooks and bottle-washers along with the fighting men. Some time now Pulleine himself was killed, perhaps issuing final desperate orders to those who'd remained close to him in those moments.

The last act of the Battle of Isandlwana was performed amid scenes of savagery, where men used empty rifles as clubs, slashed and stabbed with bayonet and spear and finally fell upon the last man they could reach with fists and fingernails and bared teeth.

When there were no more men left to kill, the Zulus turned their attentions to everything from the oxen, to the horses, even to the pet dogs. The camp was torn apart – canvas cut into strips for blankets, all metals scavenged for re-use, all foodstuffs consumed, taken away or destroyed.

A Zulu boy who visited the battlefield some days later described the aftermath:

> Dead was the horse, dead too the mule, dead was the dog, dead was the monkey, dead were the wagons, dead were the tents, dead were the boxes, dead was everything, even to the very metals.

When Chelmsford returned to the camp that evening it was to a scene of horror. Every corpse had been stripped and disembowelled, the grass in every direction slick with gore. Never before had such a defeat been inflicted upon a British army by a native force armed only with spears.

The General allowed his men only the briefest stop – for fear they would be overcome by the full impact of the slaughter if they saw it in daylight – and marched them on towards Rorke's Drift before dawn on the 23rd. He feared the worst, but in fact the 150 or so British defenders there had survived with just a handful of casualties.

A force of 4,000 Zulus under the command of Cetshwayo's half-brother Dabulamanzi had grown bored sitting back in the reserves at Isandlwana with no hope of 'washing their spears'. During the afternoon of the 22nd they'd crossed into Natal, against their king's express instructions, and picked a fight with the first British soldiers they could find. In spite of their vastly superior numbers they were fought off by disciplined Martini-Henry rifle fire. They returned to their kraals to face the ridicule of their families and the wrath of Cetshwayo, who had been at pains to use his army only to defend his borders.

The British high command, keen to salvage some form of triumph from within disaster, used Rorke's Drift as a public relations opportunity. A total of 11 Victoria Crosses were awarded to the defenders, and this lesser battle rose to overshadow the disaster of Isandlwana for more than a century.

Victory for the Zulus on 22 January 1879 succeeded only in bloodying the nose of the British Empire. The red soldiers withdrew to lick their wounds and then returned all the stronger. Later the same year they reinvaded, finally wiping out the Zulu army at the Battle of Ulundi in July. Cavalrymen with lances were unleashed before the end, to spear the fleeing Zulus like animals as they ran. Their king was made a prisoner and his kingdom wrested from him.

But Cetshwayo had seen the future months before, while the fires still smouldered on the fields below the mountain of Isandlwana. In fact if he had spent his boyhood learning the lore of the heroes, he would have had an inkling of the nation's destiny for almost all of his days. The Zulus had been united under Shaka just over 60 years before – and he had ruled them with a cruel hand until his death by assassination in September 1828. As his killers, including members of his own family, plunged their *iklwas* into his body he cried out:

> Sons of my father, you will not rule this land when I am dead, for it will be ruled by the white people who come from the sea.

And so in the moment of his greatest victory, Cetshwayo kaMpande wept. As his army lined up before him at Ulundi, in the aftermath of their triumph, he could not help but notice a great many were missing.

'When will the rest come before me?' he asked.

His *indunas* told him there would be no return for 3,000 or more left on the bloodied soil, before the mountain that looked like a little hut. Many more, who had made it home, were so terribly wounded by bullet and bayonet they would never fully recover. Knowing all too well that the war had only begun and already his losses were unbearable, Cetshwayo said:

A spear has been thrust into the belly of the nation ...
If you think you have finished with all the white men
you are wrong, because they are still coming.

Like flowers upon the African veldt after rain, victory had sprung from a nation watered by its own blood. The blossoms would not come again.

The heroic age

The battlefield of Isandlwana is a haunting, haunted place. A strange trick of the geology or the topography seems to make the lion-backed mountain the receiver at the centre of a huge dish. You can be standing alone, out in the long grass in front of where the camp would have stood, and suddenly hear voices at your shoulder. You look around, startled, and see no one. Then, once you've calmed down, you spot a couple of people standing several hundred yards away. It's their voices you've heard, the sound conducted somehow over the distance by the shape of the landscape itself.

If you stand out there and imagine the impact of the sound of 24,000 Zulus, stamping their feet on the dry, rock-hard ground as they draw closer, beating their spears against their shields and shouting their war cries, it's enough to make the hairs rise on the nape of the neck on the hottest day. That men stood in the face of it, whether or not they were armed with rifles, and coolly obeyed the orders of their officers, makes a person wonder just what such men were all about. What did they know, or understand, or believe that enabled them to stand and fight to the death, 'each man in his place' like the Zulu said?

For a start, the world they lived in was much harder than our own. Life was tougher for every soul alive, made of hard graft, long hours, physical suffering and no expectation that things were about to change or improve any time soon. Although the boys who survived and made it to manhood might have looked the same as us, they were not the same. How could they be?

With Scott in place as leader and funds of £90,000, the best part of £5 million in today's money, Britain's first expedition to explore the interior of Antarctica was finally under way. A brand-new ship, the *Discovery*, had been specially designed and built in Dundee and on 31 July 1901 she set sail from London, bound for the Isle of Wight. With her steel-plated bow and 26-inch-thick sides crafted of English oak, she was no thing of beauty. She was also tiny by our standards: 172 feet long, 34 feet wide and displacing just over 1,600 tons, but incredibly strong. Some of the bolts holding her together were over eight feet long. To untrained eyes, though, she was just ungainly and slow among the shapely yachts gathered for Cowes Week. She had been designed for a different job, however, and on 6 August she left the lightweights behind and set a course for the end of the world.

This was the time recorded by history as the 'heroic age of polar exploration', and British men were queuing up to try to ensure their place within it. There were still undiscovered countries to be claimed, and those who set out in search of them were reaching as far into the unknown as any astronaut would in the Gemini and Apollo missions of the 1960s and 70s.

The food loaded aboard the *Discovery* for her 47-strong crew gives a perfect insight into the *style* of these voyages, the spirit with which they were undertaken. Stored by the ton were whole roasted pheasants, turkeys and partridges, along with rump steak, duck and jugged hare. There were green peas, pemmican (the staple fare of polar explorers, 'pemmican' is a Cree Indian word describing a 'cake' of dried meat mixed with animal fat), raisins, onion powder, chocolate, celery seed, blackcurrant vinegar, wild cherry sauce, candied orange peel, Double Gloucester and Stilton cheeses. To wash it all down there were gallons of brandy, whisky, port, sherry and champagne. And in an age when nearly every manly man smoked like a factory chimney, there were thousands of pounds of pipe and chewing tobacco as well.

There were early problems with the *Discovery* herself. For one thing she leaked and for another she seemed sluggish and graceless at sea, so heavy indeed that she never made more than about seven knots. She showed her mettle in the open oceans though, and bobbed like a cork in the teeth of howling gales in the Roaring Forties. They encountered their first ice on 16 November, around the time they crossed the 60th parallel, and it was here in this environment that she finally looked and felt the part of a ship made for dangerous endeavours. By the time they reached their final staging post of New Zealand, on the 29th of the month, Scott and his crew had developed a love-hate relationship with the old girl.

So the *Discovery* never did – nor ever would – win any beauty contests or talent shows. She was built to get a job done, nothing more nor less. What would make the difference was the quality of the men she carried inside her.

The Cockleshell Heroes

William Edward Sparks was born on 5 September 1922 in London's East End. He left school aged 14 and trained as a cobbler. His father had been a ship's stoker and so when World War II broke out Bill took himself along to a Royal Navy recruitment office with every intention of carrying on the family tradition. The recruiting sergeant had other ideas, however, and persuaded Bill to join the Royal Marines.

He completed his training at Deal in Kent before joining the battlecruiser HMS Renown, as a gunner, in August 1940. It was convoy duties at first, in the Mediterranean. Then on 24 May 1941 the Bismarck sent HMS Hood, pride of the Royal Navy, to the bottom of the Atlantic along with all but three of her crew of 1,418 men. Renown took part in the legendary and ultimately successful hunt for the German battleship before eventually being recalled to Britain for a refit.

Bill was home on leave in London when the news came through that his brother Benny had been one of 77 crewmen lost when his ship HMS Naiad was sunk by a German U-boat off the coast of Crete. It hit Bill hard and he spent the rest of his leave drinking heavily. He was in such a bad way he was two days late returning to Plymouth – and wouldn't have gone even then if his dad hadn't told him to. But had it not been for that sorry misdemeanour – and the resultant punishment of one week confined to barracks – he would never have seen the notice calling for volunteers for 'hazardous service'.

Seeing a chance to get back at the enemy for his brother's death, Bill put his name down on the list. He was summoned to an interview with one Major Herbert 'Blondie' Hasler and immediately selected for special training. When he reported to Eastney Barracks in July 1942, *one of 40 willing volunteers, he had no way of knowing Hasler was putting together a 12-man team for a top secret mission that would become a legend.*

Training for the Royal Marines is hard enough. What Sparks and the rest had to endure for the next three months was something out of a whole different league. They were put through their paces handling canoes, diving, learning escape and evasion techniques, hand-to-hand combat, explosives training and advanced navigation. The days were endless, taking a toll not just on the physical body but on the mind and even the soul as well. The exercises and drills were designed to break all but the toughest hearts.

As the weeks ran into months, many of the volunteers fell by the wayside – either dropped by Hasler and the rest of the instructors or admitting defeat by themselves. Sparks more than lasted the course – indeed he seemed to thrive in the unusual, less formal atmosphere of the new training regime. In particular, he excelled at the business of blowing things up. At the end of the 12 weeks he was named by Hasler as one of the dozen who would embark upon the mission itself.

So far they'd been told not a single word about where they would be going or what they'd be expected to do when they got there. All they knew at the end of their three months of hell was that they now formed the rather banal-sounding Number 1 Section of Royal Marine Boom Patrol Detachment (RMBPD). As far as outsiders were concerned, the group's responsibility started and finished with patrolling the defensive boom sitting off Portsmouth harbour.

Hasler, of course, knew the focus of their attentions would shortly lie elsewhere. By the time he came to putting together his unique team, he was already a soldier and sailor of proven talents. He'd fought in Norway in 1940, winning mentions in dispatches and the French Croix de Guerre along the way. He'd been a sailor from an early age and believed there was a crucial wartime use for small boats – in fact the smaller the better.

By 1941 he was trying to persuade the powers that be – and in particular the Combined Operations Head Quarters (COHQ) – that canoes could be used to get small teams into enemy harbours. Once in position, well-trained men could operate like foxes in a chicken-coop – almost impossible to detect and free to do untold damage with explosives before making good their escape. COHQ had been sceptical at first, but in the last weeks of that year Italian 'human torpedoes' wreaked havoc in the British port of Alexandria. Two British warships, HMS *Elizabeth* and HMS *Valiant*, were severely damaged by explosives placed against their hulls by frogmen of the Decima Flottiglia Mezzi d'Assalto special unit. They had penetrated the harbour's defences using small motorboats – and all of a sudden British high command were all ears to men like Blondie Hasler.

Following the attack on Alexandria, Churchill himself wanted a seaborne assault force with the same capability as that of the Italians, and Hasler was asked to join COHQ and develop his ideas. He proposed bringing together motorboats and canoes for use in highly specialised raids – and the result was the RMBPD. Sparks and the rest had become members of a new, elite force.

After the evacuation of the British Army from Dunkirk in 1940, Churchill had ordered the creation of 'butcher and bolt' raiding forces that could continue to do harm to the enemy war effort. The specially trained men who made up these new companies were sometimes described as 'special service'. But the name that was to fix itself most firmly in the British imagination was the one first heard during the Boer War of 1899–1902, in South Africa. The British Army had been pain-fully harried there by small teams of specialist fighting men the Boers called 'commandos'.

By the end of World War II there would be more than 30

commando units within the Army, Royal Navy, Royal Air Force and the Royal Marines – as well as others operating as independent units.

From the start it was the most dangerous profession imaginable – and not just because it involved fighting without support behind enemy lines. In October 1942, during a commando raid on the German-occupied Channel Island of Sark, five German soldiers were shot and killed. When Hitler was told the dead men had been found with their hands tied behind their backs – that they had been shot *after* being taken prisoner – he issued an order that was to become infamous. Any and all commandos who fell into German hands were to be executed – armed or unarmed, whether in uniform or not – no exceptions.

When the RMBPD finally set out on its mission, in December 1942, there was no room for failure and no hope of mercy from the enemy if anything were to go wrong. Hasler had deliberately kept his men in the dark about what lay ahead – reasoning that their curiosity would keep them sharp. Within the team all manner of rumours were circulating. Sparks himself subscribed to the belief they were shortly to be used in an attack against the giant battleship *Tirpitz*, sistership of the *Bismarck*, which had been sunk three days after sinking the *Hood*.

Still giving nothing away, Hasler moved the team up to the River Clyde to complete their training aboard the submarine HMS *Tuna*. When the sub slipped her anchor on 1 December, the commandos were led to believe it was simply the start of another day's training. In fact, they were finally on their way. They headed south for five days, evading a German U-boat attack en route, before arriving in the Bay of Biscay approximately 10 miles from the mouth of the River Gironde, in France.

The weather was bad – hardly surprising for December – and they had to spend the first 24 hours on the seabed waiting for things to ease off a little. As night fell on 7 December Hasler decided the moment had come and gathered his men around him. There would be no attack on the *Tirpitz* – languishing in the Norwegian fjords, where she would spend most of the war. Instead Hasler unrolled a map of France and outlined a plan overseen by the head of Combined Operations himself, Lord Louis Mountbatten. It was codenamed 'Operation Frankton' and they were going to paddle their six two-man canoes 80-odd miles up the Gironde to the port of Bordeaux. There they would use limpet mines to attack as many as possible of a fleet of German merchant ships. After that, it would be a long walk home through occupied territory.

Hasler got his men moving at once. The time for preparation was past and there was no point in delaying a moment longer. The canoes – they called them 'cockles' though the world would remember them as 'cockleshells' – were quickly prepared and loaded with the necessary explosives and other equipment. They had been designed with the dimensions of the submarine hatch in mind – but as one of them, called *Cachalot*, was being pushed through, it was damaged beyond repair. Hasler had no option but to tell Marines Ellery and Fisher, its intended crew, they would be staying behind. It's said the two men were so distraught that both were reduced to bitter tears. Before the commandos were even in the water, their team had been reduced to 10 men.

With no time for any more words – or any further consolation for Ellery and Fisher – the rest climbed into their cockles. It was a desperately cold night. The Bay of Biscay is notorious for its cruelty to seamen and on that moonless December night it was no different. A stiff wind was blowing and the waves were as much as five feet high – grim conditions indeed for men in canoes, paddling in the dark in strange waters.

When you picture that scene – those five little boats moving silently away from the hulking shadow of the submarine – you have to bear in mind the ages of the men. If like me you grew up reading D.C. Thomson's *Commando* comics, it's all too easy to visualise the characters that filled those pages, and to place those imaginary figures in the starring roles in a story like this one. The drawings were invariably of tall, broad-shouldered men with strong jaws and piercing, confident eyes. There was something ageless about them but they looked so tough it always seemed reasonable to assume they'd been around the block a few times. They certainly seemed like grown men – at least as old as your dad.

But Bill Sparks was just 20 years old when he paddled away from HMS *Tuna* that night. Even Hasler, the commander of the whole operation and sharing Sparks's cockle the *Catfish*, was only 28. Corporal Albert Frederick Laver and Marine William Henry Mills, in the *Crayfish*, were 23 and 21 respectively; Lieutenant John Withers Mackinnon and Marine James Conway, in the *Cuttlefish*, were 22 and 20; Sergeant Samuel Wallace and Marine Robert Ewart, in the *Coalfish*, were 29 and 20; Corporal George Jellicoe Sheard, in the *Conger*, was 27. There seems to be no available record of the age of his partner, Marine David Moffat, but it's fair to guess he was no older than the rest.

Far from improving, the weather and the conditions worsened around them all the time. As the team began to approach the mouth of the Gironde, a strong rip-tide caught hold of them and the *Conger* was almost immediately overturned, pitching Sheard and Moffat into the perishing cold water. Their cockle was lost almost at once, but the two men were grabbed by their comrades and towed through the waves. After a short while, both realising they were only slowing down the mission, Sheard and Moffat let go of the cockles and struck out for shore. Still far from land, the tidal race also claimed the *Coalfish* and now Wallace and Ewart were in the sea as well. At great risk to themselves, Hasler and Sparks broke away from the little flotilla and tried to recover the missing foursome.

Sheard and Moffat were never seen again and presumed drowned – and while the other two made it to dry land, a darker fate awaited them. Captured by the Germans, Wallace and Ewart were identified as British commandos and handed over to the Gestapo. They would be interrogated and shot. Sparks and Hasler rejoined the surviving members of the team and pressed on. The mission had hardly begun and yet now they were only six.

By now the tide had turned towards land, making the paddling easier and faster. But they were six men alone in occupied France and danger was everywhere – sometimes from civilians as well as German soldiers. The cold was also severe, sapping the men's strength and forming ice on the tops of the canoes. Too visible and vulnerable in daylight, as dawn broke that first morning the crews made for the riverbank and holed up among the reeds. Good sailor that he was, Hasler had brought an illicit bottle of rum along for the ride. Years later Sparks would recall how much relief and pleasure could be snatched from a tot of that blessed, warming alcohol. They had tea with them as well – and used it to wash down tablets of Benzedrine to fend off exhaustion.

On the third day they spotted a small island – Ile de Cazeau – and decided to lie up for a few hours while they waited for darkness. Unbeknown to them, the island had also been chosen as a base for a German anti-aircraft battery – and the six commandos might have stumbled right in among their enemy. Their field-craft was so finely honed, however – after all those painful weeks back at Eastney Barracks – that they were able to avoid detection.

Mackinnon and Conway were first to paddle away from the island that night . . . and were never seen again by their comrades. It seems most likely that their canoe was damaged somehow – perhaps on an obstacle submerged in the water. In any case they were forced ashore and had to try to escape overland.

Having made it over the border into neutral Spain, they apparently ran across some unfriendly civilians who betrayed them to the Germans. Like Wallace and Ewart they were handed over to the Gestapo, returned to France and later executed.

And now there were four.

The two surviving crews had set out once more, under cover of darkness. At some stage they were spotted by some French villagers – but the commandos apparently persuaded the women to say nothing of what they had seen. By the early hours of the morning of 11 December they had arrived at the mouth of Bordeaux harbour. Sparks would later recall how relatively secure their final hiding place had felt: deep within the reed beds they could eat, rest and prepare their limpet mines while just yards away the enemy base was busy with life.

As darkness fell that night the two crews paddled away from their sanctuary in the reeds and into the harbour itself. Laver and Mills in the *Crayfish* would attack the ships on the east side, while Sparks and Hasler in the *Catfish* set about tackling those on the west. While they were paddling between two ships, looking for suitable locations for their mines, the hulls towering above them began to drift together, almost crushing the two men and their canoe in the process. Somehow they managed to paddle free and successfully placed all their pre-timed explosives. Then, as they turned to leave the harbour, the lancing beam of a sentry's torch found their canoe. Sparks and Hasler laid their bodies flat along their deck and froze, awaiting the inevitable sounding of the alarm, or even gunfire. And nothing happened. Perhaps it was just good luck; maybe it was down to camouflage and training. Whatever – the sentry seemingly thought he'd spotted nothing more dangerous than driftwood and his beam passed on by.

Sparks and Hasler paddled out of the harbour and headed downstream, meeting up with Laver and Mills, who'd also succeeded in planting their mines, along the way. Some time around dawn they scuttled their canoes in the river and prepared to head for home. Reasoning that four was too big a group to move together, they agreed to travel in their pairs. The four commandos shook hands then and Hasler wished them all the very best of good luck. They would not meet again.

On 10 December a message had circulated from German High Command that a squad of British saboteurs had been picked up near the Gironde – and that its members had been interrogated and executed before they could cause any damage. At precisely 9 p.m. on the evening of 12 December the limpet mines planted on vessels in Bordeaux harbour exploded. Four vessels were severely damaged and a fifth was sunk completely. Churchill would later say the mission had been so effective – not least in terms of the enormous boost it gave to morale during an otherwise low ebb for the Allies – that it shortened the war by six months. The legend of the Cockleshell Heroes was born.

For the next three months the commandos were pursued through France and Spain by every means available to the enraged Nazis. Sparks and Hasler had the best of the available luck – successfully covering nearly 100 miles on foot to reach the town of Ruffec. There in the Hôtel Restaurant de la Toque Blanche they made contact with agents of the French Resistance and were passed from safe house to safe house in a desperate game of cat and mouse. They finally made it across the Pyrenees into Spain and, four months after their raid, embarked on the final leg of their journey home.

Things did not go so well for Laver and Mills. Betrayed by locals at Montlieu, they fell into the hands of the Gestapo and suffered the same fate as those of their comrades taken earlier in the mission. Some believe that none of the captured Cockleshell Heroes were executed until some time in March 1943.

There was even an element of farce for Sparks towards the end. While Hasler made it home to Britain unmolested, courtesy of his rank, Sparks was arrested by the British at Gibraltar. He and Hasler had been separated before the end of their journey and no one – not even the agents of MI5 – could corroborate his story. In fact so much time had elapsed since the explosions in Bordeaux, the whole lot of them had long since been written off as dead. Mountbatten certainly believed they'd all perished and so anyone turning up in Gibraltar claiming membership of the team was certain to be treated with suspicion.

And so, much to his annoyance, Sparks was kept under close arrest and placed on a troopship home. On arrival back in Blighty he was placed on a train bound for London Euston – but his guards failed to check the lock on his carriage and he made good his escape. Suspecting quite rightly that he would have been reported 'missing presumed dead' months before, he headed straight home to his dad. After two days back in the East End, he reported to his rightful base where he received a gentle reprimand for his lateness. He was subsequently awarded the Distinguished Service Medal by a grateful King George VI. Major Hasler, who'd had a rather more sedate return to COHQ after a flight home aboard a military aircraft, received the Distinguished Service Order. Laver and Mills were posthumously mentioned in Dispatches.

Lord Mountbatten said: 'Of the many brave and dashing raids carried out by the men of Combined Operations Command, none was more courageous or imaginative than Operation Frankton.'

Major Hasler continued with a distinguished military career, later contributing to the creation of the Special Boat Service (great minds do indeed think alike – Blondie's development of the SBS was happening at around the same time Sir David Stirling was shaping his SAS; cometh the hour, cometh the *men*). On return to civilian life he took up competitive sailing – even inventing the gear that enables yachtsmen to steer their

craft single-handedly. For the rest of his life, he always bridled
at the description of his team as the Cockleshell Heroes. They
were Royal Marine Commandos. He died in 1987.

And then there was one.

Bill Sparks survived the war, serving in Burma, Africa and
Italy. In 1946 he became a bus driver for London Transport,
subsequently qualifying as an inspector. He took time out from
that career to serve in Malaya as a police lieutenant during the
Emergency, in 1952. When he was 61 he took part in a re-
enactment of the Cockleshell raid by paddling up the Gironde
to Bordeaux for a second time. The effort raised a great deal
of money for Cancer Research.

For the rest of his life he remained grateful to those French
civilians who had been kind to his colleagues and who had
helped him and Hasler to escape. He often returned to Bordeaux,
meeting people who had helped shelter them after the raid.
On one occasion he visited the chateau where it's believed
Wallace and Ewart were imprisoned before being shot. He was
always disappointed that the sacrifice of his colleagues and other
men received scant recognition, or even remembrance from the
country they'd fought and died for.

He fought long and hard for a memorial to his comrades
– and when the call was taken up by his local MP and a national
newspaper, the money was raised in weeks.

Aged 65 he suffered the indignity of having his pension cut,
and in order to keep hold of his Sussex home he had to sell
his DSM.

He told a newspaper at the time: 'I have tried not to feel
bitter about this. But when I went to the DHSS and explained
my case, I was told absolutely nothing could be done. How
can I feel anything else but bitter and disappointed?'

His DSM, together with some others of his medals, was
bought at auction at Sotheby's in 1988 by an anonymous bidder

who placed them in a bank vault and told Sparks he could wear them whenever he wanted.

Bill Sparks died on 30 November 2002, aged 80.

And then there were none.

When Britannia ruled the waves

It had been a natural decision to have the *Discovery* designed and built in a Scottish shipyard. Scott came into *his* prime when Scottish shipbuilding was the greatest on the planet, a phenomenon. By the end of the 19th century, something like 80 per cent of Britain's ships were built in Scotland.

But this great industry was not based on the River Tay at Dundee. The true masters of the art, the giants, were to be found on the River Clyde between Glasgow, Govan and Greenock. As well as heroes and manly men, we used to celebrate our industries – not least because those industries built our men as well as our status and wealth. There was a time when 'Clyde-built' meant 'the best', and people the world over assumed that all the great ships on the seas had come out of Glasgow's mighty river, accompanied by the obligatory Scottish engineer in the engine room. 'Clyde-built' referred to a certain type of manly man as well – tough, loyal and uncompromising.

(My mum worked in the offices of a Glasgow shipyard in the years before she met and married my dad – and it's part of our family history that in childhood they both attended the launch of one of the greatest ships ever to come out of that city. They were both just a year old when they were taken to witness the event, from opposite banks of the river, by their respective families.)

It was a day and a ship that went down not just in our family history, but also in that of the whole world. She became an emblem of a time when the world was a different place – and Britain and her men held a different place within it . . .

While the bottle shards fell and bubbles ran, she remained

still, frozen by her own inertia for one last moment. She'd been painted white for the occasion – the better to be seen and immortalised by waiting photographers – and she dominated the skyline like a manmade glacier. Then, anointed with champagne and coaxed into life by that great city's cheers, all 1,000 feet and 81,000 tons of her began to move. Huge chains danced, thunder rolled and the river's waters parted to receive her.

For the three years of her construction she'd been known only by her yard number: 534. Now it was different. Moments before, Mary of Teck – Queen Mary, Consort of King George V – had given the leviathan her own name. It was as RMS *Queen Mary* that she thundered down the slipway and entered the Clyde for the first time.

All the schools had closed in honour of the great occasion – 26 September 1934 – and it seemed the entire population had turned out.

The new ship, a wonder of the age, pushed ahead of her a great wave as she came. It was only the presence of the River Cart directly opposite the yard, a wide-mouthed tributary that opened on to the Clyde, that had enabled the ship, bigger than RMS *Titanic*, to be launched at all. As her great length crossed the Clyde and nudged into the Cart, a wall of water rose and ran, surging towards and past the hordes of spectators gathered to see this latest of the Cunard Ship Company line take her place where she belonged. Scores who'd stood too close were caught out and drenched by the passing torrent.

Ten million rivets, 257,000 turbine blades; 200,000 horsepower from her steam engines; 2,500 square feet of glass; space for 2,139 paying passengers and 1,101 crew; 2,000 portholes and windows for them to look through; 700 clocks to measure the journeys and 600 telephones. Everything about her sounded like an exaggeration. She carried three steam whistles, each weighing a ton, that could be heard ten miles away.

Britannia still ruled the waves and the world knew it.

The Yangtze Incident

By the time the Queen Mary's hull was laid down in 1931 there were already legends aplenty in the Clyde's past. Great passenger liners for Cunard like RMS Aquitania, or her sister ship RMS Lusitania, torpedoed and sunk by a German U-boat in 1915; capital warships like HMS Australia, HMS Barham, HMS Inflexible, HMS Tiger and HMS Hood, greatest of all the pre-war battlecruisers and brightest symbol of Great Britain's invincibility. RMS Elizabeth, sister ship of the Queen Mary, would come next, and HMS Indefatigable, an early aircraft carrier, and HMS Vanguard, the last battleship built anywhere in the world. When the end of World War II silenced the call for warships, life was sustained by a balancing rise in merchant shipping.

All of these leviathans came out of just one yard – John Brown's – and yet there were dozens more working round the clock just to meet demand. In 1967 RMS Queen Elizabeth II (QE2) was the last hurrah for passenger-liner building on Clydebank before John Brown's became part of the Government-sponsored Upper Clyde Shipbuilders. UCS went into liquidation in 1971 and the following year RMS Alisa became the last ship ever to be built on those historic slipways. It brought to an end 101 years of shipbuilding on the site.

All of this – from the Queen Mary to the Alisa – happened well within a lifetime. Generations of Scots grew up hearing about the Clyde shipyards. They always sounded like a constant, something proud and permanent and vital to the body of the nation – like an arm or a leg.

But of course they were anything but permanent. The Clyde is a dead river now and the only ship plying up and down with any regularity is an ocean-going paddle steamer called the Waverley. She *takes tourists on day trips to Largs and Rothsay, past the skeletons of derelict shipyards that once employed tens of thousands of men.*

More than places of work, the Clyde shipyards were part of the identity of Scotland and of Great Britain. We would never have survived World Wars I and II without the warships and merchant ships that we built to keep ourselves alive.

Out of another Clyde shipyard came a ship that became an unforgettable legend of heroism and manliness. She was a Black Swan class sloop, built by Alexander Stephens and Sons yard at Govan and launched on 7 May 1943. When World War II was over she was reclassified as a frigate.

By April 1949 she was on China's Yangtze River near Shanghai. Her name was HMS Amethyst.

There had been civil war in China since the 1920s. But by 1949 Mao Tse-tung's communists had the upper hand and Chiang Kai-shek's nationalists were bowing to the inevitable. At the British Embassy in the city of Nanking, as elsewhere, staff and other British and Commonwealth nationals were on standby to evacuate the territory. Standing guard nearby was the destroyer HMS *Consort*, a reassuring presence. By the middle of April she was running low on fuel and orders had been sent to HMS *Amethyst*, anchored downstream at Shanghai, to steam up to Nanking and relieve her.

Since the 1858 Treaty of Tiensin the British Royal Navy had enjoyed the freedom to navigate any and all Chinese waters. British warships had been a familiar sight for nearly a century, but Mao Tse-tung's communists saw things differently. While the nationalists had quietly honoured the treaty, Mao was of the opinion that since he hadn't signed it, he was absolved of any need to respect its terms. More to the point, he was hostile to the possibility of British imperialist warships being at liberty, in his hard-won territory, to prop up the ailing nationalist forces.

The timing for the *Amethyst* could not have been worse. The communists were already in control of the river's north bank and were now looking hungrily towards the south. A temporary truce between the two sides had maintained a peace of sorts but it was due to expire on 20 April. Although the communists expected to cross the river unopposed, they were prepared to do it the hard way on 21 April if the nationalists got in their way.

And so the *Amethyst* was entering treacherous waters when she slipped her moorings at Shanghai early on the morning of 19 April and headed upriver at a sedate 11 knots. To this day it's unclear whether the British Navy were still within their rights – but Lieutenant Commander Bernard Skinner could have been forgiven for thinking his ship was unlikely to face any real threat.

After a first day's journey of around 100 miles they dropped anchor at Kiang Yin. The Yangtze River was notoriously difficult and dangerous to navigate in darkness, and the rest of the trip would be tackled the following day. There was no real sense of urgency, far less of danger.

By just after five o'clock on the morning of 20 April the *Amethyst* was under way once more. For around three and a half hours she steamed peacefully towards her destination – when all at once a burst of heavy machine-gun fire from somewhere on the north bank reminded Skinner and his crew they had entered a war zone. The rattling burst was followed in short order by 10 or a dozen artillery shells from a shore battery, all of which flew well wide of the ship. The sailors were not alarmed. They assumed the firing – surely too wayward to be aimed at them – must have been part of routine bombardment of the nationalist positions on the south bank by the communists in the north.

Skinner had earlier had his men paint two large canvases with Union Jack flags, and just to be on the safe side he now ordered both to be slung over the side of the ship. Around an hour later, just about 9.30 a.m., the situation changed dramatically and permanently. The *Amethyst* was approaching the village of San Chiang-ying when a communist shell passed over her bow, much too close for comfort. This wasn't communist against nationalist – this was communist against the Royal Navy.

Skinner ordered action stations, and in a bid to distance themselves from this much more accurate shore battery, the ship's engineers battled to wring full power out of the turbines. It was not to be. Before they could clear the field of fire a shell tore into the *Amethyst*'s wheelhouse and exploded. Leading Seaman Leslie Francis was at the wheel and somehow managed to stay on his feet, trying to stay on course. A second shell hit the bridge, killing or injuring every man. Skinner had suffered multiple wounds and was barely conscious, but managed to give the order to return fire. First Lieutenant Geoffrey Weston, bleeding heavily from a chest wound, tried to relay the order but found the explosions had cut communications between the bridge and the rest of the ship. As more shells found their target the *Amethyst* ran aground on a mud bank off Rose Island. It was just 9.35 a.m. – barely five minutes after the first explosion. Further hits took out the generator, the port engine room and the sick bay. Desperately, Weston made it to the ship's radio and sent a terse message to anyone listening:

> Under heavy fire. Am aground in approx position 31.10 degrees North 119.50 degrees East. Large number of casualties.

Dead and dying seamen lay all around, and now the *Amethyst* was a near-helpless sitting duck, within point-blank range of her undeclared enemy. To make matters worse, the position in which she'd run aground meant she couldn't retaliate with the two great guns on her foredeck. Only the stern turret remained in operation, and the gunners managed to get 30 shells away towards uncertain targets before a direct hit by the enemy destroyed one of the two remaining guns. Hoping that by holding fire he could persuade the communists to do likewise, Weston ordered the stern turret to fall silent. Unimpressed and unmoved, the enemy kept pounding shells through the *Amethyst's* armour-plating.

Fearing the worst, Weston ordered some of the uninjured men to crawl into sniping positions, armed with rifles and Bren guns, ready to repel boarders. Seeing men on the move on deck, the communists turned to heavy machine guns to rake the *Amethyst* from stern to bow. There was carnage aboard now. What had been a peaceful river-trip just minutes before was now a hell of dead and injured men strewn throughout the ship. The decks were awash with blood.

With Skinner mortally wounded and drifting in and out of consciousness, Weston had to assume command. Like the rest of the crew he knew the best chance of survival lay elsewhere – as far from the ship as possible in fact. He ordered most of the able men over the side into the water. The south bank and the nationalist forces offered the only hope of salvation, and it was either swim for it or die here aboard the stricken ship. Non-swimmers and wounded men scrambled into the only lifeboat still serviceable and began rowing south.

There was yet more hell to be got through – machine-gun fire and heavy artillery were turned on to the men in the water and more were cut down before they could make much headway. In all, 59 sailors and four Chinese kitchen boys made it on to the south bank, where they were given medical treatment in a nationalist army hospital before being transported in trucks back to Shanghai.

It was an isolated and desperate band of brothers left aboard the *Amethyst*. Weston had slivers of shrapnel in his liver and lungs and was later dosed up on a combination of morphine and Benzedrine to simultaneously dull his pain and keep him awake. The communist shore batteries had fallen silent but any movement aboard ship still attracted the attention of the machine-gunners.

So far there were 17 dead and 25 seriously wounded and the situation was hardly expected to improve any time soon. Only around 80 men were still fit for active duty but they were trapped like fish in a barrel. The *Amethyst* herself was holed above and below the waterline, more like a Swiss cheese than a ship of war. Men scrambled to plug holes with hammocks and mattresses and anything else that came to hand, but she was in a pitiful condition.

Hopes were pinned on the arrival of the *Consort*, now well aware of their plight and steaming towards them. Out of sight of the enemy machine guns, men prepared a tow-line at the stern of the ship so the destroyer would have at least some slim chance of coming in close and pulling them clear of the mud bank that held them. It was the roar of communist guns that told them she was making her approach. Up on deck they caught their first glimpse of their would-be saviour. Flying three Union Jacks and seven white ensigns, she was steaming towards them at a mighty 29 knots – the fastest speed that had ever been achieved on the Yangtze River. Her funnel was belching plumes of black smoke and all her guns were blazing fire towards the communist shore batteries.

Aboard the *Amethyst* men cheered as their ally knocked out one shore battery after another, but she was also coming under terrible fire herself. Her Commander, Robertson, wanted to make a rescue attempt – and sent an urgent transmission to that effect. Weston feared such an action would only cause the loss of a second ship and replied she was putting herself in too much danger. Initially undeterred, *Consort* made a first pass of the *Amethyst* and then wheeled around hard, still punching shell after shell towards the communist positions.

She was taking too many hits, though – that much was now

clear even to the stubborn Robertson – and with 10 of his men dead and three seriously wounded he wheeled around once more and headed downstream out of range. The trapped men could only watch as she steamed out of sight.

Desperate attempts to free the *Amethyst* from the mud banks of Rose Island were finally successful and she was able to limp a couple of miles upstream, out of range of the communist batteries that had so tormented them, where she dropped anchor at a place called Fu Te Wei.

All the while Weston and his men had fought to free their ship, a further rescue attempt had got under way. The transmissions from the *Amethyst* had been picked up in Shanghai and Vice-Admiral Madden was quickly on the move. Shortly after daybreak on 21 April two Royal Navy ships set a course for *Amethyst*'s last known position. They were the cruiser the *London* and the *Amethyst*'s sister-ship the *Black Swan*.

The news was transmitted to Weston along with the instruction, 'Be ready to move.'

With hope rekindled, the men watched the ships steam into view – but the communist guns found their range almost at once, severely punishing both almost from the start. Neither the *London* nor the *Black Swan* had any success returning fire and, having taken many serious hits and with dead and wounded on both ships, they were forced to withdraw. Madden sent a typically straightforward signal: 'Am sorry we cannot help you today. We shall keep on trying.'

It must have come as cold comfort to the men left aboard. How much longer could they hold out? What to do now for the best?

As it was, a new commander was already making his way towards them along 70-odd miles of rough road from Nanking in a borrowed jeep. He was Lieutenant Commander John Simon Kerans, the British Embassy's Naval Attaché, and he was determined to get things moving again come hell or high water. By the time he made it out to the *Amethyst* aboard a Chinese landing craft, some time in the afternoon of 22 April, Lieutenant Commander Skinner had died of his wounds. In fact Kerans climbed aboard a ship that was as much a home to the dead as to the living. Corpses wrapped in hammocks lay in neat rows upon the stern gun-deck, and elsewhere wounded men suffered in steadily worsening conditions without proper medicines or painkillers.

Taking command, Kerans ordered Weston to go ashore with those others of the wounded who could still be moved.

(When I told my dad I was writing about the *Amethyst*, he told me he'd known a man who served aboard her during the Yangtze Incident. He said it was someone he'd met at his golf club years before and he'd never thought to mention it. I asked him to tell me what he knew and the first thing he said was that he didn't want me to give the man's name. In fact he wouldn't even say it to me. 'He wasn't the type who would want that,' my dad said. 'He only mentioned it in passing once or twice. It wouldn't be right, he wouldn't have liked it.')

And so it goes with the men caught up in stories like these. You come close to them at times only to have them slip away once more, elusive to the last.

On 23 April Mao's communist forces finally crossed the river. Their nationalist enemies had melted away before them and now they controlled both banks. The *Amethyst* was completely surrounded.

Three days later Major Kung, the local communist commander, opened formal negotiations by inviting Kerans to go ashore for talks. In no mood to trust the man who'd provoked the fight in the first place, Kerans chose to stay aboard. Instead he sent one of his officers, Petty Officer William Freeman, dressed in the uniform of a lieutenant commander. Kung boasted to Freeman that it was his own shore battery that had caused so much death and destruction aboard the *Amethyst* during those first minutes. He even demanded the British admit to having opened fire first. With considerable presence of mind under the circumstances, Freeman refused point blank to make any such admission – and even managed to persuade Kung to send fresh supplies of food to the ship.

A stalemate then ensued – with neither side ready to back down and no end to the crisis in sight. By 18 May Kung's demands had become even shriller – with him insisting that Kerans accept the *Amethyst* had 'invaded' Chinese waters. The British ship had done no such thing, of course, and Kerans quietly told him so again and again.

And all the while, the tense stand-off had to be endured by the crew. They'd been trapped for weeks in hostile waters, enduring stifling heat and humidity as well as round-the-clock uncertainty. To make matters worse, the supplies from the Chinese were always inadequate and by the middle of May the men were existing on what amounted to half rations. Work provided the only relief from the boredom and tension. Kerans ensured the men were kept occupied repairing the worst of the shell damage and making every effort to keep the ship as clean as possible. The British Navy, like the rest of the armed forces, has always understood the value of discipline and routine – the last redoubt for men under pressure.

While Kerans played the game of diplomatic cat and mouse with the communists surrounding him, he had another option in mind. The *Amethyst*'s position looked bad, there was no denying it. But in spite of all the circumstances she was still a fighting ship of the British Royal Navy. They were not officially prisoners of war – since no war had been declared – but to all intents and purposes they were being held against their will.

'Move your ship and we will destroy it,' Kung had told them.

But the principal duty of all POWs is ... escape.

Kerans sought continual updates from his officers regarding

the state of the ship. Most frustrating of all was the news that the Chinese embargo on fuel was depriving them of the potential to make a dash for Shanghai. Kung was so confident the ship was hopelessly disabled, however, he authorised a delivery of oil to the *Amethyst* during the second week in July. Now Kerans faced a dilemma. For the next three weeks they would have enough fuel in their tanks to make an escape attempt; wait any longer than the end of the month and they would have used too much oil just idling at anchor. The question was: should he risk the lives of the starving and weakened men who depended on him for the right decision? He kept the answer to himself at first, but he was never in any doubt.

Without telling anyone the reasons why, he issued some unusual orders. First the anchor chain was to be covered in blankets smothered in oil. Second, the outline of the ship's superstructure was to be obscured by great sheets of canvas draped over her most distinctive parts. Kerans told the men it was to solve the problem of incomplete blackout at night, but at least some of them must have suspected the truth. With just days to go before the deadline, Kerans told his officers what he had in mind – as if they didn't know – and on 30 July the rest of the men were told it was time to leave.

Once it was fully dark, the muffled anchor chain was pulled up and the *Amethyst* floated free from her moorings for the first time in months. A Chinese vessel was spotted and it was taking the line they needed, downstream towards the open sea. As stealthily as was possible for a ship weighing more than 1,350 tons, she slipped in behind the merchant vessel and began her flight to freedom. Each man aboard knew what was expected of him – and all understood that detection now would bring about their doom.

Their secret remained intact for less than an hour before the communists realised their prisoners had made a break for it. The lancing beams of searchlights cut up the sky and flares exploded overhead as they sought their prey. With the night illuminated now, the *Amethyst*'s temporary invisibility was torn away. Having found her once more, the shore batteries opened up, filling the air with shells as they battled to find their range. It seems that in the confusion, it was the merchant vessel that initially drew the worst of the fire. Kerans ordered his own gunners to return the fire – the better to maintain the general air of chaos that arched across the Yangtze that night – and for some little while it seemed to work. It couldn't last of course, not with so far left to run, and soon the communist shells began to find their mark. Now the telegrapher sent a familiar message: 'I am under fire and have been hit.'

But there was nothing for it now but to keep on running as long as her men, hull and turbines held out. There could be no second imprisonment and no real hope of surrender. This time they were running for their lives.

And this time, the fates ran with them. After three hours of bombardment they saw they were approaching Kiang Yin, the last safe anchorage they had enjoyed before their ordeal had begun. Kerans chose his line past the guns and with the darkness aiding their flight they made it out of range. By three in the morning they were within 50 miles of the sea.

Suddenly out of the blackness appeared the unmistakable outline of a Chinese junk. With no other option available to him, Kerans ordered full steam ahead. The timber sides of the local vessel were no match for the armoured steel plate of the *Amethyst* and at a full speed of 19 knots she cut through the obstacle as though there was nothing before her bow but driftwood.

All that remained to obstruct them now was the mighty communist-held fort at Woosung, within sight of the sea. Searchlights played across the dark water and found the *Amethyst*, in all her battered, bloodied and magnificent defiance. She would not be stopping now, or even slowing down. This was the course she had chosen and she would not be thwarted by any foe.

And then the strangest thing happened. She was within easy reach of the communist guns. The searchlights had her lit up like a fair and every pair of lungs aboard had drawn in a breath and held it. But no gun fired. The moment dragged on and the peace remained unbroken. Perhaps right there at the end the communists were simply glad to be seeing her leave their company once and for all.

A boom lay stretched across the mouth of the river and without a thought the *Amethyst* burst through the final obstruction and plunged into the open sea. Directly ahead was a second ship of war, thundering towards them. It was the *Consort*, the destroyer that had tried so valiantly to help them months before, with the loss of many lives.

As the *Consort*'s crew cheered the return to the fold of that wounded frigate, a message was received over the telegraph: 'Have rejoined the Fleet south of Woosung,' it read. 'No damage or casualties. God Save the King.'

The *Amethyst* returned to Britain for a refit in November 1950. Thereafter she saw active service in the Korean War before starring as herself in the 1956 film of the Yangtze Incident entitled *Their Greatest Glory*. Richard Todd played the part of Kerans. According to legend, a special effects explosion caused more damage aboard than anything the communists had manage to inflict in 1949.

A year later she returned to Plymouth, where she was sold and broken up for scrap.

In the National Memorial Arboretum in Staffordshire, a grove of ginkgo trees commemorates her dead.

The loneliness of command

Great ships and manly men – these were the kinds of things we used to produce in this country. And the rest of the world accepted the truth of it like an immutable law of the universe. As a nation we used to have the best dreams and the grandest ambitions, and we fashioned from ourselves a breed of men that believed those dreams could be made reality with just a strong jaw, a firm handshake and a bit of backbone. We don't make anything now. We've given away or destroyed all our industries and thousands of our men spend the best years of their lives answering phones in call centres or doing something or other in IT. A lot of the rest are at home minding the kids. How did we let all this happen? Men can be tamed and domesticated – that much is obviously true – but most would be better off out in the woods and hills, like the lions and tigers and bears.

At the very least, surely there are better and more productive things we could all be doing with our time? You've only got to look back to the fringes of living memory to find the sort of spirit that believed all things were possible.

On arrival in the port of Lyttelton, New Zealand, Scott and his crew were welcomed ashore by the locals as if they were long-lost sons. The men, many of whom were bachelors, were soon invited to live in the homes of local families, and more than one took rather too much advantage of the generous hospitality extended to them. The Wild is often just below the surface.

It wasn't all good news. When you round up the sort of men ready and willing to leave the world behind and march off into the unknown wearing just scratchy woollen jumpers, scratchier tweed trousers and stout brogues, you have to be ready to deal with some rough and tumble. Scott wrote that the drunkenness of some of his crew disgusted him and vowed to 'have it out with them somehow'. He added: 'There are only a few black sheep but they lend colour to the flock.'

First Lieutenant Charles Royds, RN, one of the young naval officers assigned to Scott for the expedition, took a similar view of the men he commanded:

> Better men never stepped a plank whilst they are at sea, but in harbour they are nothing but brute beasts, and I am ashamed of them, and told them so, and penitent indeed they are, but only until they are drunk again.

This is one of the perennial problems of leaders, heroes and manly men – the nature of us lesser mortals. The mass of humanity is barely up to the job, any job, and this inertia must be overcome by those few who are born knowing what all of us could be doing. Great leaders have all the chutzpah required to turn a shapeless rabble into an engine fit for travel to the ends of the earth.

Manly men aren't just born – they are also made by other manly men who've been well schooled in the arts of discipline, routine and washing outdoors in cold water. But part of the loneliness of command, and therefore of commanders, is the acceptance of the fact that nothing very much is going to be achieved – ever – unless they drive it forward by the sheer force of their own will.

Scott went so far as to dismiss several of the worst offenders and replace them with others he was able to recruit in New Zealand. Finally on 21 December the *Discovery* was ready to continue her journey and steamed away from the earthly temptations of Lyttelton towards the *terra incognita* of Antarctica.

Did the burden of command weigh heavily on Scott's

shoulders at this time? If that were so, he went out of his way to conceal any trace of self-doubt or weakness from his officers and men. Much of this outward display of self-confidence was about the details. His officers noticed for example that he never once appeared in the wardroom unshaven. Though his efforts made it apparent he wasn't particularly skilful about the chore of laundry, he always did his own clothes washing and made self-reliance and independence a visible part of his character. Whether in fair weather or foul, he expected his brother officers to conduct themselves like gentlemen. At mealtimes there was always Grace and the offering up of the Loyal Toast. There were fines for swearing. As far as possible, too, he remained in good humour in front of all of the men, sending the signal that all was well.

It was the right way to be, for as they continued south the reality of the challenge ahead was being made clear to all of them. Their destination would be no place for weaklings, or those unable to take care of themselves and of their comrades. Soon after departing from New Zealand, they encountered the pack-ice for the first time. When they stopped in Lady Newnes Bay to kill seals for fresh meat, they saw ice 150 feet thick. As if this wasn't enough to demonstrate that here was a place owned and controlled not by man but by Mother Nature, the awesome Aurora Australis – the Southern Lights – put on regular performances.

Young Dr Edward 'Bill' Wilson, the expedition's assistant surgeon and a devoutly religious man, wrote to his wife to tell her of the otherworldly scenes he was daily witnessing. And there's another thing – letters. Not for these men the 25-word text or the hurried mobile phone call. Instead they devoted countless hours to writing pages and pages of letters to wives, parents, children, friends and acquaintances. They somehow managed to make more of their time than we ever do today:

'I long to do as much as I can that others may share the joy

I find in feasting my eyes on the colours of this wonderful place, and the vastness of it all,' wrote Wilson. '"The works of the Lord are great and very worthy to be praised and had in honour," but I do wish you could see them here.'

But no one new would be joining them for the foreseeable future, not their wives or anyone else. As far as the men aboard the *Discovery* were concerned, they were alone in the world. Alone at the top of the pyramid of command – with the lives of 47 men depending upon his abilities and judgement – Scott had to look inwards for inspiration. He would have to find the strength to match that of other great men – those who had faced the obstacle of sometimes unsatisfactory raw material and yet found ways to shape it in their own image.

Sir John Moore, the Iron Duke and the retreat to Corunna

Wellington's defeat of Napoleon at Waterloo, on 18 June 1815, towers above all other British victories of the 19th century. In terms of its place in the imagination of the British people, it may well be the greatest victory of all. Everything about it was monumental and grand. Hundreds of thousands of men took part and tens of thousands lay dead or wounded by the end.

There was a time when every schoolboy knew the story by heart, and the key, final moments from the traditional accounts of the battle are still familiar:

Napoleon, witnessing the 11th-hour arrival of Blücher's Prussians, tells his men the incoming troops are French reinforcements . . . and hears them reply, with misguided joy, 'Vive l'Empéreur!' . . .

. . . General Ney himself, bravest of the brave and convinced that help is at hand for the final push, is swept along on the wave, shouting, 'Courage! France is victorious!' . . .

Seizing the moment, as always, Napoleon takes personal command of his 'Immortals' – the Imperial Guard – and leads them in one last charge . . .

Wellington on horseback, in an exposed position high on a ridge and seeing the French advance, orders General Maitland to step out and meet them with his infantry, 'Now, Maitland, now is your turn,' he yells. 'Up guards, make ready, fire!' . . .

The French resist the pressure, briefly stopping the British troops in their tracks . . .

Wellington sees Lord Uxbridge take a round in the knee. 'By God, Sir, I've lost my leg,' says his wounded second-in-command. 'By God, Sir, you have,' he replies (the amputated limb will later be buried with full honours in the garden of a chateau) . . .

Undaunted, Wellington rises up in his stirrups and, by waving his hat in the air, unleashes the crucial advance of his reserves . . .

The French soldiers realise it is not their own reinforcements on their right, but the Prussians. Their emperor has lied to them! 'Sauve qui peut!' they cry − save yourselves those who can − 'We are betrayed!'

The news ripples like a cold wind through the ranks of La Grande Armée − the greatest force ever to march across Europe − and they break and run . . .

It's all so well known to us, and so well told in the classic accounts. Wellington comes home our greatest battlefield hero − the Iron Duke − and his legend is assured.

But while Waterloo was undoubtedly his most famous victory, it was not his best. He said himself it was a close-run thing. Even the weather had been on his side when it mattered: a downpour the night before had made the ground too soft for Napoleon's cavalry, forcing the emperor to delay his attack until noon and giving Wellington's allies precious time to get into position. What it came down to in the end was luck.

Napoleon himself, when asked whether he preferred brave generals, or brilliant generals, replied: 'Give me lucky men for my generals − I can teach them everything else.'

Luck, then. Even the greatest military commanders in history admit that it's luck that makes all the difference. Arthur Wellesley, Duke of Wellington, was a lucky man, a lucky soldier and a lucky general.

But there was a greater general, and he had been well known to Arthur Wellesley. If luck had been on that other man's side then he − and not Wellington − might well have gone down in history as our greatest soldier.

Sir John Moore was born in Glasgow, on 13 November 1761, the son of a doctor. In an age when advancement in the British Army was achieved by using family influence to secure favour, and family money to buy promotion, this was a modest background indeed. He was educated at Glasgow High School and joined the Army in 1776, as an ensign in the 51st Foot Regiment – later to be renamed the King's Own Yorkshire Light Infantry.

Although he had started life many rungs down the ladder from the stratum of society that ran the British Army, he had other qualifications by the sackload. Moore's superiors soon noticed that he was intelligent, skilful and brave and he rose quickly through the ranks on merit alone. He served always with distinction, seeing his first actions during the American War of Independence. Following his return to Britain he was elected as a Member of Parliament, before going back into active service, where he truly belonged. He fought well in the Mediterranean and was wounded on the island of Corsica, at the town of Calvi – where Nelson, his contemporary, would lose his eye in 1794.

Also in 1794, and still on Corsica, Moore commanded the land forces that finally succeeded in taking a tower at Mortella Point, which had held out against constant bombardment by two Royal Navy gunships for two days. Moore and the rest of the British commanders were so impressed by the effectiveness of the tower's design that it became the basis for the chain of 'Martello Towers' built around Britain's southern and eastern coastlines in preparation for any invasion by Napoleon ('Martello' being a plain misspelling of 'Mortella').

By 1798 Moore had attained the rank of major general and the following year, while commanding a brigade fighting in Holland, he was injured again – this time seriously. Here then was a soldier who, despite his seniority, always impressed his men with his own personal bravery and his willingness to put himself in harm's way. Having fully recovered from the wounds he received in Holland, he would display yet more heroism while leading the 52nd Regiment in Egypt.

In many ways, it seems, he was cut from the same bolt as

Lord Nelson. Like the Admiral – the son of a humble country parson – Moore had had to rely on his qualities as a man to ensure his advancement in his service of choice. He also looked the part of the hero – tall, handsome and dashing – which never hurts and is hardly likely to hold an ambitious young man back in his chosen profession. But above all other attributes it was his disregard for his own safety – coupled with conspicuous concern for the welfare of his men – that would win for Moore the admiration and love of those he sought to command. These are gifts that cannot be bought.

The Duke of Wellington was of a different sort entirely. Born in 1769, Arthur Wellesley was eight years younger than Moore. More significantly, he was born into privilege, the son of Irish gentlefolk of English descent. For the first years of his adulthood he rode along on the coat-tails of his smarter, better-looking, more successful elder brother, Richard.

Richard Wellesley, Lord Mornington, used his influence to have 17-year-old Arthur taken up as an ensign of the 73rd Regiment, in March 1787. The boy was an owlish late developer – slow of speech and with nothing of his brother's charisma or intelligence. He was of medium height and had a fair measure of good looks – high forehead, prominent chin and a beaky nose most flatteringly described as aquiline. In 1793 he approached his big brother again – this time to borrow money so he could buy the rank of lieutenant colonel. This he used to get himself into the war against France. He served in Flanders, with little distinction, before finding his way to service in India, where he spent as much time in the fleshpots of Calcutta and Madras as he did trying to acquire any skill or reputation as a soldier.

Travelling always by his side, though, tucked unnoticed in a pocket like a wind-blown seed, was luck. Lord Mornington was made governor-general of India, by his friend William Pitt (talk about luck), and at once promoted his doltish brother to the rank of full colonel. While this obviously advanced Arthur's career, it also drew down upon him the envy and bitterness of the fellow officers he had leapfrogged. Colonel Wellesley, however, was unabashed. Always sure of himself and with the inbred sense of superiority that came with his class, he seemed to care not a jot that his charmed life was upsetting others.

During the subsequent fight to take control of Mysore and defeat its ruler, Tippoo Sultan, Arthur regularly found himself in the right place at the right time. He arrived at the fortress of Seringapatam once the fighting was over and just in time to discover the body of Tippoo, who had been slain alongside hundreds of his men.

General Bernard had led the final, victorious assault – but as soon as the dust settled he was replaced, on the orders of the governor-general, by . . . Arthur Wellesley. Ensconced in the late Tippoo's own palace, and now senior military commander for the whole area, Wellesley had somehow changed from slow-witted teenager to a young man with a small part of the world at his feet.

But it was from this point on that he began to grow to fit the rank he had so effortlessly attained. In 1803 he was part of General Stuart's campaign to extend British rule in Central India by dispossessing the Hindu Maratha princes. At the climactic battle for control of the area close by the heavily defended fort of Ahmednuggar, Colonel Wellesley at last emerged from the shadow of his brother's patronage to become a leader of men in his own right. Outnumbered and outgunned, he led his men from the front and demonstrated great skill. He made best use of his limited resources of cavalry and infantry and, with perfect timing, managed to rout the Maratha line.

In further battles against the Maratha forces he was victorious again – and also started to demonstrate concern for the well-being of his men. He was finally behaving like a grown-up.

By March 1805 Wellesley was back in Britain. He was newly

knighted and, now wealthy in his own right thanks to prize money collected in the aftermath of his victories, ready to take a wife. In April the following year he married Catherine Sarah Dorothea 'Kitty' Pakenham, whom he'd known since his teenaged years back in Ireland. She'd refused him twice before, but now, in middle age, she finally gave in.

'She is grown damned ugly, by Jove,' he told his brother, ever the charmer.

In 1808 Napoleon invaded Portugal and it was now that Wellesley's fate was to begin to become entwined with that of Moore.

Ever since Nelson's victory at Trafalgar in 1805, the Emperor had been made to accept that he was trapped on the continent of Europe. The most he had managed to do in reply was impose his 'Continental System' of blockades – whereby no ship from Britain or any of her colonies was to be allowed into any port under French control. Napoleon hoped this supposed stranglehold would bring him the prize that neither his navies nor his armies had been able to deliver – the surrender of Britain. But since Russia too had so far evaded his grasp, British ships and cargoes were able to enter Europe at will, via the ports on the Baltic and Adriatic Seas. It was all so very tiresome, made up of tit-for-tat decrees and ultimatums on all sides, none of which brought matters to a head. It would cause hardship in Britain before the end, but it damaged the French too by severely reducing their income from Customs and Excise Duty. The rest of Europe suffered as well, missing out on imports from Britain and her colonies, like coffee, cocoa, cotton, sugar and tobacco.

Napoleon would cite the need to tighten up his Continental System as the explanation for his decision to invade the Iberian Peninsula – but really he just wanted to help himself to the fabulous wealth promised by Spain's empire in South America.

But while Spain was the main prize, the real prize, Napoleon set his sights first of all on Portugal. Having anyway secured permission to march his army through Spain, he also approached Prince João, regent of Portugal, and asked him to close his ports to Britain. The British Government, meanwhile, slyly operating behind the scenes, persuaded the Portuguese court to depart the country en masse and take refuge in their colony in Brazil. It was a brilliant coup – in the end the royals, together with thousands of aristocrats and their retainers, boarded ships and high-tailed it down the River Tagus and out into the Atlantic before Napoleon had a chance to turn round.

As angry as he had ever been – which was saying something – Napoleon responded to the British-Portuguese sleight of hand by pressing ahead with the invasion of Spain he had planned all along. But if the Emperor believed the Spanish would roll over like the submissive inhabitants of Naples and Italy he had already placed under his control, he was mistaken.

It's not hard to see why his observations of the country would have led him to believe he was looking at a walkover. Spain was over the hill and on the way out as an international player. The mass of the population were dirt-poor peasants, either completely ignored or treated with contempt by an indolent, self-satisfied court that was rotten and in decline. Napoleon rounded up the royals – King Charles IV, his faithless Queen Maria Luisa, her long-term lover Manuel de Godoy, prime minister and de facto ruler of the country, and the feckless and duplicitous Prince Ferdinand, who had attempted to conspire with the Emperor against his own father – and spirited them all away into exile. He then placed his own brother, Joseph, on the Spanish throne.

For reasons known only to themselves, the Spanish people took great offence at this usurpation and the kidnapping of their royal family. To Napoleon's surprise and dismay, this badly whipped dog of a population rose up on its hind legs and began snapping at him. On 2 May 1808 – the day remembered in Spain as the Dos de Mayo – the people of Madrid rose as one to slaughter every Frenchman in sight. In other towns and cities across the country there were protests, riots and calls for war with France.

Finally turning to Britain for help, they were not disappointed. The British Government was moved by the spirited and decisive action of the people of Spain – as well as feeling the need to tackle the Emperor before he grew any bigger – and quickly set in motion plans to intervene on their behalf.

Sir Arthur Wellesley, recently promoted to the rank of lieutenant general, was sitting at Cork in southern Ireland at the head of a 9,000-strong invasion force. It had not been gathered for the job of tackling the French in the Iberian Peninsula – and had been meant to support British plans to invade Latin America and 'liberate' its people from Spanish rule. But since the soldiers and their transport were already in position, it was a simple matter to alter their course. Given the challenges ahead, it was a modest army, but Britain often did things by halves – heavy on the big picture stuff and light on the details. They set sail on 12 July, bound for the northern Portuguese port of La Coruña – the place British history would come to remember as Corunna.

Sir John Moore had hardly been idle all this while. By 1803 he was back in England – and using his innovative intelligence to help revolutionise the training of soldiers. His willingness to invest in the intelligence of his men – to trust them to think – was behind his development of what eventually became the light infantry and reconnaissance forces we still have today. From now on his officers were taught to observe their men and identify the strengths and weaknesses of individuals. In an age when the officer class kept themselves removed from the fighting men they commanded, this was a major change of thinking. As a further innovation he had his soldiers taught to aim and shoot to kill with rifles – rather than blindly trusting the volley-fire of inaccurate musketry.

In the past the British infantry had been trained to lay down repeated rounds of musket fire towards an approaching enemy. There had been no emphasis on picking out individual soldiers in the opposing ranks – instead the tactic was simply to unleash a hail of lead and hope some of it found a mark. Far from aiming, musketeers were trained to level the barrel in the direction of the foe and then, before pulling the trigger, to look towards the right. This was a move designed to protect their eyes from the flash and smoke of the firing – and clearly did nothing for accuracy.

Moore was a pioneer of a new age – when soldiers would hold their fire until the last possible moment. As well as skilled marksmanship, this new tactic also demanded a different kind of bravery from the rank and file. Instead of blasting away at a still distant army – giving vent to pent-up tension and fear – now they were being trusted to wait and wait ... and wait. The prospect of standing ready, motionless, while thousands of enemy soldiers march steadily onwards, hardly bears thinking about.

It was from the likes of Moore, and the training he helped devise, that we get notions like, 'Steady, lads ... steady ... wait until you see the whites of their eyes ...'

Having fired that one, telling volley of carefully aimed rifle fire, the infantry would take advantage of the mayhem they'd created among the foe by charging across the short distance with levelled bayonets. In short, Moore was one of the first commanders in the British Army to value the 'intellectual soldier' who studied tactics and made a profession out of a job. After decades in which the regular soldier had been nothing more than a routinely abused and disposable scaffold used to fill a scarlet tunic, under Moore's influence he began to exist as a human being in his own right.

The famous historian Arthur Bryant would write:

Moore's contribution to the British Army was not only that matchless Light Infantry who have ever since enshrined his training, but also the belief that the perfect soldier can only be made by evoking all that is finest in man – physical, mental and spiritual.

By the time Wellesley arrived in Portuguese waters there was a whole list of disappointing and worrying events to hear about. The French were making multiple inroads in the Spanish interior, defeating one Spanish force after another. It was hardly surprising. Her generals were superior and used to winning, as were their men, and they were opposed by the armies of a nation that had been presided over for decades by one set of lazy, corrupt managers after another. Spain was a country whose star was setting; France was a nation and an empire on the make and on the rise, led by one of the most talented and ambitious men the world has ever seen.

What was also happening, but which Wellesley so far knew nothing about, was that the Spanish *people* were also rising to oppose the French armies. And then between 18 and 22 July there was something of a miracle. A French army under General Dupont had captured and sacked the city of Córdoba in early June. But as the days and weeks wore on Dupont realised that all across Andalusia the Spanish people were in revolt. Sensing trouble, he pulled out of the city and began a steady withdrawal through the countryside in the face of a rising tide of people power. He was finally cornered and surrounded by a Spanish army led by General Castaños. Along with regular soldiers there were militia and roughly armed peasants – all told, a force much greater in number than that of Dupont. The Battle of Bailén that unfolded during those four days in July finally secured a French surrender. Thousands of French prisoners ended up in prison hulks and Dupont himself was taken. More important than the statistics, however, was the priceless knowledge that the French were not invincible.

Wellesley landed in Mondego Bay and marched his force south to Lisbon. As well as steeling himself for the fight with the French, he was concerned by news that British reinforcements were on their way to the peninsula – and that they would be accompanied by officers who outranked him. General Sir Hew Dalrymple would arrive first, accompanied by General Sir Henry Burrard. Even more intimidating for a man like Wellesley was the news that Sir John Moore – the nation's greatest soldier – was shortly to arrive with yet more men.

Burning with ambition now, and desperate to make his mark before he could be called to heel by his superiors, Wellesley set himself the target of tackling the French alone and at once. He encountered a much smaller force than his own, under General Henri François, Comte de Laborde, in the hills around the towns of Obidos and Rolica, in mid-August. He brought them to battle on the 17th of the month, and although he succeeded in routing his enemy, he lacked the necessary cavalry to mop them up. Before he could find a way to capitalise on his modest victory, Sir Henry Burrard arrived and replaced him as commanding officer.

Convinced that prompt action would carry the day and deliver Lisbon to the British, Wellesley pleaded for the chance to take the fight back to the demoralised enemy. But the older man valued caution over action and ordered his hot-blooded junior to take up a defensive position on a ridge above Vimeiro. There they would await the arrival of the rest of the British reinforcements, due to disembark at the mouth of the Maceira River, west of the village.

It was from this position, on the morning of 21 August, that Wellesley got his first view of the approach of General Jean-Andoche Junot and a rejuvenated French force. Junot was sure his smaller force would be more than enough to drive away the inexperienced British soldiers. But despite savage fighting – finally through the narrow streets of the village of Vimeiro itself – Wellesley's men held firm. The French attacked repeatedly, throwing everything they had at the larger army ranged against them, but were finally broken. By midday it was all over. From a force of more than 18,000 men, Wellesley had lost 720. Junot's army of 13,500 had been depleted by at least 2,000 dead, and they had lost as many as 15 of their guns.

Wellesley was cock-a-hoop and ready to march his men all the way into Lisbon. Ever cautious, however, Burrard said no. They would hold firm where they were until they could be joined by Moore, Dalrymple and the others. And so for Wellesley, for now, the moment was lost.

There was worse to come. Dalrymple duly arrived and backed up the decision taken by Burrard, his second-in-command. Junot, safe behind freshly cut trenches at nearby Torres Vedras, couldn't believe his luck. Far from following up on the victory of Vimeiro – and perhaps hobbling Napoleon's ambitions for the whole peninsula – Dalrymple instead entered into peace talks with the French. What happened next sent shock waves all the way back to Britain.

On 30 August Dalrymple signed a document known as the Convention of Cintra – and forced Wellesley and Burrard to put their signatures to it as well. The French would evacuate their positions and the Royal Navy would transport them – all 26,000 of them together with their arms and everything they had looted from the Portuguese – all the way back to France. Furthermore, there was no stipulation that these French soldiers would refrain from returning to the war. They were free to do as they pleased.

Under protest, Wellesley signed the document, and when news of the arrangement reached London the following month all three men were recalled to London. The resultant inquiry found no fault with any of them – but only Wellesley would fight again. Dalrymple and Burrard were quietly put out to grass.

With Wellesley licking his wounds back home, command of the British Army in the Iberian Peninsula now fell to Sir John Moore. As if the challenge he faced wasn't great enough, an air of optimism had developed back home. Despite the humiliation of the Convention of Cintra, the British people were buoyed up by news of the victory at Vimeiro that had preceded it. Nearly 20,000 more British infantry, cavalry and gunners had been dispatched under the command of Sir David Baird to bolster the war effort. Even Joseph, the Emperor's own brother and erstwhile King of Spain, had been forced to flee Madrid. Suddenly there were high hopes that Napoleon's ambitions for the peninsula were soon to be quashed.

Moore was more than enough of a soldier, however, to know that the reality of the situation was likely to be different. By mid-October he had his men on the move out of Lisbon. His objective was to cross the border into Spain and make for Salamanca, where he would join up with his reinforcements. To do so he had to lead his men through mountain passes 4,000 feet high and across 300 miles of rough terrain. They were cheery enough on that outward leg. The going was hard in the mountains, and since they were in an area devoid of human habitation they had to carry with them everything they needed, but eventually they made it down into western Spain, where the living was relatively easy.

The British people back home were confident of success and now the same mood began to infect their soldiers. The victory at Vimeiro was still at the forefront of their minds, and now they wished for a chance to drive the French interlopers out of Spain once and for all.

How little they knew, or understood, these guileless soldiers now marching across quiet lowlands, populated only by peasant farmers. While they allowed themselves to believe they were marching towards victory against an enemy in retreat, the bogeyman was coming to get them.

Infuriated by his generals' failures, Napoleon had decided he would get the job done himself (as they do say: 'If you want a job done give it to someone busy'). And so it was that the Emperor turned his attention away from his other concerns – Austria rearming herself as though to turn on him and Russia being distinctly vague about her own imperial intentions – so as to play to his real strengths. Fighting was his game, making war, and so for a welcome distraction he turned his fury against the British Army niggling at him down there in Spain.

There were 60,000 French soldiers in the north-east already, loitering behind the River Ebro. Napoleon took his best generals – Lannes, Lefebvre, Ney, Soult and Victor – along with 100,000 additional troops. The Emperor was enraged and only a crushing victory would ease his pain. He brought his fury down upon Spain like a righteous blade. He brushed aside the native forces and drove on to Madrid, taking the city with little trouble on 1 December. Elsewhere, reinvigorated French forces were sweeping all before them. Castaños – the unlikely victor of Bailén – was crushed at Tudela and Moore might have decided to make a run for it then. Instead he struck towards the north-east, hoping to interrupt Napoleon's supply line.

This was beyond brave and into the realm of insanity. Napoleon's *Grande Armée* was grinding through Spain like a juggernaut and instead of running away Moore had turned to dodge between its wheels. But there was method in his madness. Moore reasoned that if he could draw the monster towards him, it would leave the Spanish armies to regroup and fight another day. And so, with winter closing in, Moore embarked upon a great and dangerous game. By sheer skill and audacity he succeeded in bloodying French noses as he skipped and danced across the north-east of the country. At Sahagún on 21 December his cavalry administered a humiliating drubbing to their opposite numbers – but now word reached Moore's ear that Napoleon himself was about to make an appearance.

No British commander had ever faced Napoleon in the field – and none would before Waterloo. Finally accepting that he had pushed his luck as far as it would go, Moore decided on a hell-for-leather run towards the port of Corunna, from where he could evacuate his men by sea. He could not and would not face the Emperor in open battle, and instead he turned his men towards a gap between the approaching armies of Soult, Junot and Napoleon.

Having left their baggage behind them in the aftermath of Sahagún, and with their commissariat soon in complete disarray, the retreating soldiers turned to looting for their survival. As they approached the mountains that stood between them and any hope of safety, the going became harder still – and their hearts hardened along with the terrain. The cavalry and the guards fought a disciplined rearguard action against the French horsemen snapping at their heels, but the rank and file descended into savagery. There were women and children among them too – some of the soldiers' own wives and children, together with the camp followers that inevitably trail in the wake of thousands of men on the move. Babies were born along the way, their mothers giving birth to them among the rocks and snowdrifts; those howling infants that survived the trauma of their entry into the world had then to endure the ceaseless march. As the army climbed higher into the snowbound mountains, so the number of casualties increased. It was a frozen hell on earth.

At the village of Bembibre, on New Year's Eve, the soldiers helped themselves to the local wine and the local women. When the army moved on they left behind hundreds of men too drunk to move, lying comatose amid lakes and rivers of spilled drink. Napoleon, miles behind at Astorgas, broke off from his pursuit that same day. Leaving Soult and Ney with an army

50,000 strong to continue the chase, he returned to Paris for news of the wider world.

Moore was horrified by all that was happening around him, but there was nothing to be done except to keep the bulk of the horde moving towards Portugal and Corunna. Villafranca was next in their path – and every scrap of food was torn from the citizens' hands and looted from their homes, every cask of wine emptied. There was no support for them now from the people they had allegedly come to save. Word of their conduct had spread before them like the virus they were, and as they plunged on through the mountains every door was barred to them, every face turned away. Only when the enemy reached out to claw at them did they remember they were soldiers – and then they turned and fought like the lions they had been trained to be.

By early January they were at last dropping down out of the frozen mountains and by the 11th they had reached Corunna. By now there were only 15,000 soldiers at Moore's command – thousands more had been left behind in the mountains, either dead or taken prisoner by the French.

Devastated by what he had seen, by what his men had become as he struggled to lead them home, Moore wrote:

> I am sorry to say that the army, whose conduct I had such reason to extol in its march through Portugal and in its arrival in Spain, has totally changed its character since it began its retreat. I would not have believed, had I not witnessed it, that a British Army would, in so short a time, have been completely disorganised. Its conduct during the late marches has been infamous beyond belief. I can say nothing in its favour, but when there was a prospect of fighting the enemy, the men were then orderly, and seemed pleased and determined to do their duty.

Though Moore and his army had arrived at the port, the ships to take them home had not. It would be four days before they would make their appearance and now the general had to turn his back to the sea and face the French once more.

On 16 January, while the troops were at last beginning to make their weary way on to the transports that would ferry them back to England, 20,000 Frenchmen commanded by Marshal Nicolas Soult, hero of Austerlitz, appeared on the hills above the town. Unfolding below him was a scene much like that which would be played out on the beaches of Dunkirk in 1940. A beleaguered British Army, harried beyond endurance, had made it as far as the sea. It only remained to be seen whether it could defend itself long enough for its would-be rescuers to do their job.

The arrival of the French was no surprise to Sir John Moore. He'd known they would appear before the end and now he put hastily prepared plans into action. As the French guns opened fire from the ridge and as the enemy soldiers marched in steady lines down the hillsides, Moore's infantry stood ready to meet them. Sir John was ever to the fore, upon a cream-coloured warhorse with black tail and mane. As the French moved towards him in their serried ranks, so he galloped from high point to high point, his cloak snapping in his wake, gauging the attack, shaping the defence. Again and again he was seen by officers and men, all across the battle front, wordless and intent as he strove to deny his enemy and ensure the survival of his men.

The forces finally clashed, and when the French tried to sweep around towards the British flanks, Moore unleashed a reserve force of fresh soldiers. They drove their erstwhile tormentors back with the shining points of their bayonets. Rattled by the reinforcements, the French began to withdraw – only to be cruelly harried by a British rearguard that gamely chased them back up into the hills.

The British force, outnumbered and with nowhere left to

run, was closing in on an unlikely and unexpected victory. But as Moore rode among his men, cajoling, scolding, demanding that they give of their best, a cannonball smashed into his body. Knocked clean out of his saddle, he crashed on to the frozen ground beneath his horse's feet; bad luck and nothing more. The round shot had broken him open like a doll – a gaping hole below his ruined left shoulder and collarbone revealed his lungs.

He was still alive when he was carried away from the field of his last victory.

'I have always wanted to die this way,' he said, as men of the 42nd Highland Regiment bore him down into the streets of the town. 'I hope the people of England will be satisfied. I hope my country will do me justice.'

Having lived long enough to hear the French attack was falling away like melting snow, Sir John Moore died without another word. His sacrifice shone like a glorious jewel within a tarnished setting. As the final moments of the fighting were played out, he was hurriedly buried behind the ramparts of the town. A memorial was later raised over the grave at the orders of Marshal Soult himself.

The embarkation of the men continued throughout the night. As Moore had hoped, the army escaped back to England, safe to fight another day. He had left the door open behind him – and it was Arthur Wellesley who would shortly march back through it. Luck travelled with that son of privilege as always, and remained safely in his pocket all the way to Waterloo and beyond.

Moore's death became a legend, ensuring that the Retreat to Corunna would be remembered as a triumph.

In 1816, it was immortalised in a poem by Charles Wolfe:

> No useless coffin enclosed his breast
> Not in sheet or in shroud we wound him

But he lay like a warrior taking his rest
With his martial cloak around him ...
Slowly and sadly we laid him down
From the field of his fame fresh and gory
We carved not a line, and we raised not a stone
But we left him alone with his glory.

The luck of the Irish

Leaders were hardly immune to personal disaster. Scott would have understood from childhood that the sort of men who set out to change the world were at the greatest risk of being destroyed by it. He would also have known that even the most careful and rigorous preparations could never be enough to cope with every eventuality. The other, greater lesson to be learned from the life and death of a man like Sir John Moore is that all human endeavour depends, at least in part, upon luck.

Sir John was one of the most naturally gifted soldiers and leaders of men who has ever lived. He was intelligent as well as brave. He made careful preparations for every job he ever set himself and made the welfare of his men a priority second to none, even when they let him down. He may well have been a genius. But there on the hills above the town of Corunna he was undone by bad luck.

On 3 January 1902, as the *Discovery* crossed the Antarctic Circle, it still remained to be seen whether or not Scott was a lucky man. From Lady Newnes Bay he went ashore and headed inland, accompanied by Dr Wilson and Lieutenant Royds. Keen to take advantage of any available high ground for a better look at the surrounding terrain, they scrambled up the slopes of the closest of the volcanic peaks. From an unnamed summit they took in their first view of the Great Ice Barrier, its awe-inspiring mass striding away from them as far the eye could see.

Back aboard ship, they set a course alongside the great white cliffs of ice towering 2–300 feet above their heads. They steamed along the Barrier's length for days, marvelling at the very existence of an 'eighth wonder of the world'. While they watched from the deck, icebergs ten miles or more in length and weighing millions of tons were 'calved' from the great mass of it and began their silent journeys towards the north.

You have to keep reminding yourself these men came from a world and a time when hardly a soul before them had dared venture so far south. There had been no television documentaries, and precious few photographs, to forewarn them of them of the sights they would see. What they were looking out at was a world so new and fresh the frost of the dawn of the making of the world was still untouched upon it.

By the end of the month, Scott and his crew were in virgin territory, viewing and mapping parts of the Antarctic coastline never before seen by man. They called the new domain King Edward VII Land, and on 2 February they finally reached an inlet that breached the Barrier and allowed them to steam towards the continent. They went ashore again at the first opportunity and on 4 February Scott made an ascent in a tethered balloon, rising to a height of 800 feet and gazing out towards the Great Ice Barrier and the mountains, glaciers and ice fields beyond. Next up in the Heath Robinson contraption was one Ernest Shackleton, a Merchant Navy man Scott had appointed as third lieutenant in charge of holds, stores, provisions and deep-sea analysis.

Having seen the eastern end of the Barrier, Scott decided they should stop their eastward advance and head back to McMurdo Sound, where they planned to make their permanent camp. On 8 February the *Discovery* dropped anchor in the sheltered waters of a bay towards the southern end of a peninsula jutting out from the foot of Mount Erebus. Here, with the summit of the volcano towering more than 13,000 feet above them, they erected a prefabricated hut they had brought with them. Forever after, polar explorers would refer to the place as Hut Point. There were separate huts too for the scientists' lab work, and also kennels for the huskies.

If all seemed well enough to begin with, it wasn't long before Antarctica demonstrated its capacity to harm the inexperienced and the unwary. In early March a dog-sled party went out under the leadership of Royds – a chance to practise their techniques on the ice and snow as much as anything else. It should have been commanded by Scott but he had injured his knee some days earlier and was not yet back to full fitness. Some of the men wore reindeer fur boots that provided little in the way of grip on the ice, and when a blizzard descended upon them they soon learned how vulnerable they were. As they stumbled blindly through the whiteout, three of them lost their footing and slipped helplessly down a steep, ice-covered slope to within inches of a sheer cliff edge. Able Seaman George Vince was not so lucky and, along with one of the dogs, shot past the rest of the men and out into the abyss. It was a 200-foot drop into the sea below and he was never seen again.

As they struggled to come to terms with what had just happened – and how quickly – they realised another of the party, an 18-year-old steward called Hare, was nowhere to be seen. The survivors struggled back to Hut Point – numb with cold and the horror of what had befallen their experimental expedition. Miraculously, young Hare walked back into the camp two days later, having somehow survived two nights in the open. By his own account, he had simply lain down and fallen asleep. Good luck dictated that the conditions created by the incessant snowfall somehow insulated him against the worst of the storm raging around him. After a day and a half spent dozing peacefully, he simply stood up and walked back to base.

Soon after Lieutenant Royds's near disaster, Scott called a halt to any further trips and the party settled down for 'winter routine'. By now the sun was no longer rising above the horizon at any point during the day and the men spent the hours cleaning the huts, collecting ice for drinking water, maintaining the equipment and generally passing the time as constructively as possible. Through it all, the captain insisted that standards were maintained. On Sundays the officers and men put on the best of their available clothing and attended a church service conducted by Scott, reading from the Book of Common Prayer.

As the weeks and months of darkness slipped by, preparations were made for the sled trips that would justify the expedition as a scientific exercise as well as a voyage of discovery. Increasing familiarity with the ways of the sled dogs caused great anxiety for the men – and in particular for Scott, who had been deeply sensitive to the welfare of animals all his life. For a polite English gentleman, raised to see dogs as lovable pets, the savage politics of the pack were heartbreaking for him to witness. It seemed that if any of the dogs received the slightest show of affection from one of the men – a pat on the head, a casual stroke of the coat – the rest would turn on it at the first opportunity and mete out summary justice. Furthermore, the dogs they had brought were not the best for sledding and generally refused to pull any loads at all unless the men walked in front of them, coaxing them all the way. Scott would eventually form the opinion that dogs were not the answer to the problem of crossing the Antarctic.

On 2 November Scott, Shackleton and Wilson embarked upon a journey south that was supposed to be a dry run for any future attempt on the Pole itself. For the first couple of weeks they were accompanied by a support party, but conditions deteriorated and by the middle of month, the trio were left alone on the ice. The rest of the men returned to camp, dropping dumps of food and fuel supplies along the way for collection and use by the others as they made their painful way back. The dogs were as miserable and disappointing as ever, and had to be destroyed one by one. Reduced to man-hauling the huge weight of their sled, the three men suffered terribly. For part of the remainder of the trip Wilson was snow-blind – but it was Shackleton, youngest of the three at 28, who was most badly affected by the conditions.

It's worth bearing in mind the kind of clothes the men were wearing for their journeys across one of the harshest environments on Earth. Not for them the protection of modern textiles, or Gore-Tex or any of the other developments in weatherproofing that most of us take for granted. Scott and the rest of the British men of the heroic age of exploration wore a few layers of woollen underclothes and jumpers topped by close-weave outer garments of cotton or Burberry. On their feet they wore leather boots with tacks in the soles for grip, and on their heads woollen balaclavas. I wear more than that to take my kids to the park in October. None of it had been tested for the conditions – and they didn't really know how bad conditions could get in any case. It was all about being tough – each man testing himself and desperate that he would not be found wanting.

In spite of it all, Scott, Wilson and Shackleton managed to cross the 82nd parallel and made a final camp at 82 degrees 16′ 33″, by 300 miles the furthest south that any human beings had ever travelled. They were, however, still 420 miles from the Pole, and turned for home on New Year's Day 1903. Shackleton was severely weakened and with every passing day his condition worsened. His breathing was laboured, he coughed blood and his gums darkened – a classic symptom of scurvy. Pulling the sled was beyond him now and he could do no more than stumble alongside it as Wilson and Scott shared the work of three between them – a load of around 250 pounds per man. Eventually, too weak even to walk, Shackleton had to add his own weight to the sled by sitting on it, dejectedly tending a makeshift sail he had erected in hope of easing the burden he had become to his comrades.

By the time they made it back to Hut Point, on 3 February, the experience had taken its toll on the personal and working relationship between Scott and Shackleton, as well as upon the health and well-being of all three. They had nonetheless achieved a major first in the story of polar exploration: they had covered a distance of 960 miles in 93 days and had shown some of what would have to be done to reach the South Pole.

Within days of their return, word reached Hut Point that a support vessel named the *Morning* was just a dozen miles or so away from them across the ice blocking McMurdo Sound. It had been sent jointly by the Royal Society and the RGS – the Presidents of both bodies having convinced themselves an orderly withdrawal from the south was now the best course of action. Scott was to take command of both ships and return to New Zealand with his whole team at the first opportunity. Irked by the suggestion that he should abandon his expedition, Scott was relieved to see that the *Discovery* was completely ice-bound and unlikely to be able to move for months to come. Instead he decided the *Morning* should depart before it too became trapped – taking with it those team members who had had enough. He added Shackleton's name to the list of those who would be leaving. And with that stroke of the pen, one of the great rivalries in the Heroic Era of Polar Exploration was born.

Sir Ernest Shackleton and the Imperial Trans-Antarctic Expedition

The interior of South Georgia was unknown to man in 1916. Captain James Cook had made the first landing on the shore of the island, in 1775, and named the place for King George III. Hunters came soon after, attracted by reports of abundant wildlife, and all but wiped out the population of seals that struggled on to the rocky beaches each year to give birth to their young. By the turn of the 20th century it had attracted whalers from Norway, who made working stations for themselves in the natural harbour they called Grytviken. There they could process their catch before making the long journey home to the other end of the world.

The coastline of South Georgia had become familiar to mariners of the most adventurous sort – notably those like Scott and his men making for Antarctica – but in more than 135 years no one had found the need or the nerve to venture among the mountains and glaciers that loomed behind the shoreline.

In the early hours of 19 May, 1916, three men set out from King Haakon Bay on the south-west of the island, making for a whaling station at Stromness, on the north-east coast. As the crow flies it's a distance of no more than 40 miles, but it was across completely uncharted territory. Who knew what lay ahead of them? And this was to be no sightseeing trip – this was a matter of life and death. Depending upon the success of the crossing were the three men actually embarking upon the journey, three men left behind in a cave at Haakon Bay – and 22 men stranded beneath two upturned boats on a barren, uninhabited rock called Elephant Island, 800 miles away across the Southern Ocean.

They could hardly have been less well equipped for the ordeal ahead, these pioneers. Already physically and mentally exhausted by months *of hardship in the toughest environments on earth, half-starved and frostbitten, they set out wearing worn-out clothes and carrying their food rations in a sock. They had scavenged brass screws from the timbers of the boat that had brought them to the island, and worked them into the soles of their boots in hope of adding a bit of grip, the better to tackle glaciers, cliffs and ice-covered rocks. They carried a primus stove, fuel to cook six meals, 50 feet of rope and a carpenter's adze.*

Three men set out that morning, tramping into the frozen dark with the weight of the world on their shoulders. Their names were Tom Crean, Frank Worsley and Ernest Shackleton – and they were on the last leg of one of the grandest adventures of all time. But as the hours and miles began to fall behind them, each had the strangest and most unexpected feeling. None of them mentioned it at the time – there was too much at stake and no strength left for fanciful talk – but each felt it just the same. As they walked across that barren and treacherous landscape, all three felt the unmistakable, unseen presence of a fourth soul.

Ernest Shackleton was born in County Kildare, in Ireland, on 15 February 1874. The family later moved to London, where Ernest was educated. His father was a doctor – and wanted his son to follow him into the profession – but Ernest was a stubbornly independent boy and joined the Merchant Navy instead, winning his master mariner's ticket in 1898.

A member of Scott's ultimately triumphant *Discovery* expedition of 1901–4, he was humiliated by his leader's decision to send him home early after his near-death during the 'furthest south' march of 1902–3. Taking his dismissal from the team as a personal slight, he developed a grudge for his erstwhile boss that never left him. The characters and personalities of the two men were too different, and their ambitions too much the same, for there to be any hope of repairing the damage. Alpha dogs lead alone.

In April 1904 he married Emily Dorman, a friend of his

sister's, and the couple would eventually have three children together. Like all men of his calling, the ties of family were never enough to keep him at home. Siring children was one thing, but the job of rearing them and loving them was among the many things those adventurers freely chose to leave behind them in their wake.

Shackleton's adventures on the southern continent continued without Scott, and in March 1909 newspapers carried reports that he had made it to within 100 miles of the Pole during his *Nimrod* expedition. It was another tale of awful hardship, and the readers could only wonder at the spirit and determination of such men. Shackleton and his three comrades had barely made it back to their base alive, but on his return to Britain he was awarded a knighthood. It was the best shot at the Pole until Scott and Amundsen would make their respective trips to the place in 1912.

By 1913 Shackleton had conceived of what he called the 'last great journey on earth'. Both Poles had been conquered and now it required imagination to come up with anything else worth doing at the ends of the earth. Shackleton was nothing if not inventive, and came up with a wheeze he called 'The Imperial Trans-Antarctic Expedition'. He was going to lead a handpicked party of men from one side of the southern continent to the other, via the South Pole. As if that wasn't bold enough, he said they would cover the distance of 1,800 miles in just 100 days. He had little experience of, far less expertise in, the use of sled dogs and yet he planned to take 120 of them to spare his men the old horror of man-hauling the sledge-loads of necessary food and kit across the barren terrain. No one had ever contemplated such an undertaking before, but while Scott had been every inch the reticent Navy man, less than comfortable when exposed to the full glare of publicity, Shackleton had something of the flamboyant showman about him.

When it came to raising funds for the trip, he took to the

job like a natural. He needed the modern-day equivalent of around £2.5 million to finance the project, and cheerfully embarked upon the necessary round of glad-handing and public speaking. David Lloyd George, then Chancellor of the Exchequer, provided a fifth of the total from the public purse. The rest was harvested in the form of donations great and small from the people of Great Britain. The largest single gift – something in the region of £1 million in today's money – was received from James Caird, a multi-millionaire jute manufacturer turned philanthropist, from the city of Dundee.

The expedition headquarters were established at an address in Burlington Street in central London, and legend has it that an advertisement was placed in the newspapers that read:

Men wanted for hazardous journey. Small wages, bitter cold, long months of complete darkness, constant danger, safe return doubtful. Honour and recognition in case of success.

Not exactly an invitation to join the Big Brother house then, but it attracted the usual mix of the good, the bad and the ugly. Thousands of men offered their services and Shackleton famously sorted the letters of application into three boxes marked, 'Mad', 'Hopeless' and 'Possible'. Gradually he whittled them down, using his considerable ability to judge the character of men almost at first sight. Three women applied as well, but Shackleton decided the expedition would be challenging enough without the complication of adding a second sex into the mix.

The expedition would take two ships. The main thrust of the voyage would be undertaken by the *Endurance*, a converted Norwegian-built vessel that had already won its colours in the Southern Ocean. She would carry Shackleton and his team to the Weddell Sea, from where they would head off towards the Pole and the eastern coast of the continent beyond. A second ship, the *Aurora*, would sail to Cape Evans, in McMurdo Sound in the Ross Sea, and drop off a team of men tasked with travelling into the interior from the other side of the continent. They would then work their way back towards their ship, dropping supply dumps as they went. Shackleton and his men would collect these supplies and make use of them as they completed the second half of their proposed journey from the Pole back out to the sea.

By June the *Endurance* was in London, being loaded with the mountains of supplies required for such a trip. On the 28th of the month Archduke Ferdinand, heir to the Austrian throne, was assassinated in the Balkan city of Sarajevo and the touchpaper of the Great War was lit. On 1 August, the same day that Germany declared war on Russia, the *Endurance* set sail from Millwall Docks. Shackleton brought the men together on deck and said any and all of them were free to leave the ship and enlist in His Majesty's armed forces, if they so wished. The ship docked in Margate and several members of the team duly took their leave of it, and headed off to war. Shackleton sent a telegraph to the Admiralty saying that he, his ship and all of its supplies were at the disposal of the country. But Winston Churchill, then First Lord, sent back a one-word reply urging the men to go ahead with their odyssey. It read: 'Proceed.'

Taking the message to mean the continuation of the expedition was now a patriotic duty, Shackleton pressed ahead with his final preparations. He stayed behind in England to secure the outstanding funds pledged for the trip and sent the ship and her crew on to South America, where she made port in Buenos Aires, in Argentina. He finally sailed from Liverpool and rejoined the *Endurance* in mid-October. On the way to South Georgia, their last staging post, they discovered a stowaway – a 19-year-old named Percy Blackborrow. Shackleton gave the teenager a severe dressing down, but decided he should be allowed to join the team. Now there were 28 men en route to Antarctica.

On arrival in Grytviken, Shackleton received depressing news from Thoralf Sorlle, one of the leaders of a party of Norwegian whalers working there. He said the pack-ice was further north than usual for the time of year, and in the opinion of him and his men it would be foolhardy to take a ship towards the Weddell Sea in such conditions. Despite the warnings – and advice to delay the trip south – Shackleton would not be put off. On 5 December 1914, while the great nations of Europe set about tearing themselves into bloody pieces, the *Endurance* sailed away from the world of men.

Sure enough, they encountered pack-ice almost at once and by Christmas 1914 they were making no more than a mile an hour on a typical day. At the other end of the world, Allied and German soldiers were putting down their weapons and walking tentatively into no man's land to wish one another a Merry Christmas. It was the last time they would extend such a courtesy to their fellow men. They made time to perform proper funerals for their dead and men from both sides came together, beside at least one grave, to recite, in their own tongues, verses of the 23rd Psalm. What would the men of the *Endurance*, so very far away, have felt if they could have heard the words?

> The Lord is my shepherd. I shall not want. He maketh me to lie down in green pastures. He leadeth me beside the still waters. He restoreth my soul ... Yea, though I walk through the valley of the shadow of death, I will fear no evil ...

Men in danger have a tendency to look beyond what they can see all around them, to reach out for an unseen hand. Those men aboard the *Endurance* were from Edwardian Britain – and relied upon their Christian faith to an extent that is hard for many people living today to imagine, far less empathise with. There is no denying that their belief in a merciful God was a comfort to them.

On 19 January 1915 the men awoke to find they were no longer aboard a ship at sea, but in a no man's land of their own. During the night the pack-ice had completely closed around them; still waters indeed. Despite Herculean efforts in the days and weeks that followed – attacking the ice with picks and saws in an attempt to cut a channel towards open water – they finally had to accept they were stuck fast, prisoners of the floe. There was nothing for it but to wait out the Antarctic winter aboard their stranded vessel.

While the men settled into the routine of monotonous days lived out in darkness, Shackleton remained optimistic. This was only a delay, he told himself and anyone who would listen. The ice floe of which they were now a fixed part was drifting slowly northwards with the currents and prevailing winds. Eventually they would be so far north they would be released from their prison and able to make the journey back to South Georgia. Then, when conditions were right a few months later, they would return to Antarctica and make their crossing of the continent as planned.

Nature had other ideas, however. Deeper into the southern winter, the weather steadily deteriorated, with temperatures dipping to minus 40 degrees Centigrade. Gale-force winds drove the ice, twisting and tormenting it so that the separate floes ground and squealed against one another, making all manner of unearthly sounds. Aboard the *Endurance* the men could only listen while massive forces were brought to bear upon her timbers. The ice screamed and growled and in her agony the ship screamed back.

In mid-October there was a brief respite when she drifted free of the ice. But towards the end of the month, and without making any headway, they became trapped once more. This time the forces became too much for the ship to bear. By the 27th the hull had been pushed, pulled and twisted too far and great torrents of freezing water began to gush through gaping holes in her planking. The men had been manning the pumps off and on for weeks, fighting steadily rising water levels as leaks sprang here and there, but now there was no hope of holding back the deep. The *Endurance* was doomed and three small boats – all that stood now between the men and the imminent wrath of the Southern Ocean – were manhandled off her deck and on to the ice. This was no longer an expedition, a voyage of discovery; from now on the men would be engaged in a simple fight to stay alive.

Priority was given to salvaging as much as possible of the food and other supplies still aboard. The 28 men were now crowded into small tents pitched on the ice itself. The sled dogs had been installed in 'dogloos' erected months before and now had the best of the living arrangements. But all the while the men worked, a grim realisation was dawning in their minds: they could not stay where they were indefinitely. If they wanted to remain alive, they would have to find their way to open water. If they could take to the boats they would have some control over their destinies once more – and could perhaps attempt to reach one of the several small islands dotted around the fringes of the Weddell Sea.

On 21 November the *Endurance* finally exhaled her death rattle, slid beneath the ice and sank, bow first, to the bottom of the ocean. A few days before, some of the men had gone aboard one last time and raised a Union Jack on her mast – and so it was with her colours flying that she went to her grave. Her final departure was nonetheless a terrifying reminder to the men of what was really beneath their feet and added a renewed urgency to plans to take matters into their own hands.

Shackleton, knowing what the loss of the ship might do to the men's morale, sought at once to make them see that their situation was actually quite straightforward.

'So,' he said cheerfully, 'now we'll go home.'

In the short term, all they could do was wait in their tents while the Boss, as they called him, decided quite how that neat trick was to be pulled off. And all the while they waited, the pack-ice was drifting north towards the open ocean. Eventually, Shackleton knew, there would come a day when the solid mass would break up. By that time they might be far beyond islands like Joinville, Paulet, Elephant or Clarence, where they might find sanctuary from the sea. Then they would be adrift on a million square miles of ocean, a thousand miles from civilisation. The time was approaching when they would have to get into the boats and make for land, any land.

Over the next three months, the men embarked upon two attempts to haul their three small craft to open water. The effort was enough to break backs and hearts – the boats were simply too heavy and unwieldy – and both times the men had to give up after covering almost no distance at all. As the food rations began to dwindle, the dogs were slaughtered and eaten one by one. Conditions on the floe were worsening steadily – the ice was breaking up and becoming soft and slushy underfoot – and Shackleton and his officers scanned the horizon desperately for glimpses of navigable water.

The three boats – named the *James Caird*, the *Dudley Docker* and the *Stancomb Wills* after three of the expedition's original benefactors – had been readied for the voyage by ship's carpenter Harry 'Chips' McNeish. Using timber and nails scavenged from the *Endurance*, he had raised the height of the gunwales on the *James Caird* and the *Dudley Docker* to provide greater protection from the expected swells. Supplies of food and other equipment were stowed inside and all that was needed now was the opportunity to put them to the test.

On 23 March the men glimpsed Joinville Island – 60 miles away towards the west at the northern end of Graham Land, a thin finger of terra firma that stretches out from Antarctica towards the rest of the world. But the hellish soup of icebergs and slushy sea separating them from the lonely rock made a crossing impossible, and the three boats remained on the ever-shrinking floe. Now the only viable targets were towards the north-east – Elephant Island or Clarence Island, both around 60 miles away and, 800 miles beyond them, South Georgia itself.

And all the time, the floe they were camped upon was shrinking and breaking apart. Once about a mile across, by the end of March 1916 it was no bigger than a football pitch. From time to time the ice would split – occasionally beneath the men's camp itself. On more than one occasion luckless individuals had been pitched from their tents into the freezing water and only rescued from certain death by the lightning reactions of their colleagues. So getting the boats into the water was no longer a problem: uncertainty now concerned *when* to leave, and *where* to make for once they took the decision to put to sea.

On 9 April, with the peaks of the mountains on tiny Clarence Island clearly visible, the three boats were finally dragged into the sea and the men climbed aboard. Shackleton believed now was their last chance to make for a realistic destination before the vastness of the ocean swallowed them up. Even so, it was an awful thought to leave behind their camp and head off into the most dangerous water on Earth. Shackleton was asking his men to bid farewell to a devil they knew, and to strike out towards a devil they did not.

Their food rations were severely depleted after months of waiting on the ice, and they carried with them only the most essential personal belongings. As long ago as October 1915 they had cast aside almost all of their private possessions. Shackleton himself had made clear the need to be ruthless by throwing away his gold watch and cigarette case along with almost everything else he had brought with him. Scattered behind them or already lost to the ocean were the men's books, letters from loved ones, photographs, clothing and scientific instruments intended for the original expedition. Now carrying little more than their diaries and the smallest of trinkets to remind them of home, they embarked upon the most dangerous stage of their adventure so far.

As well as struggling to man the oars and pull the boats away from their erstwhile home, the men had to take turns fending off looming icebergs that threatened to smash their tiny vessels to pieces. Conditions aboard were appalling by any standards. Even the *James Caird*, the largest of the three boats, was only 22-and-a-half-feet long. The *Dudley Docker* was just 22 feet and the *Stancomb Wills*, little more than a rowing boat to our eyes, less than 21.

Despite McNeish's best efforts to raise the gunwales of the larger two boats, waves regularly came close to swamping them and certainly ensured regular drenchings. The wool and cotton clothes they were wearing were best suited to dry, cold conditions – and had none of the waterproof qualities you would want for sitting in an open boat in the open sea. The men aboard the *Stancomb Wills* – an unmodified cutter – were easily the most vulnerable. But the constant wetness and numbing cold took an inevitable toll on every one of the 28 men. Percy Blackborrow, the stowaway, suffered most and developed frostbite in both feet, but most of the men were quickly mired in physical miseries of one kind or another. Meals had to be eaten cold or hurriedly heated on primus stoves during breaks when they could tie up against some of the more stable ice floes that still crossed their paths. Diarrhoea was commonplace, and the men had to relieve themselves by hanging their bared backsides over the sides of the boats – risking frostbite in the most alarming locations imaginable.

After five days afloat they made it clear of the pack-ice and into open sea. For the first time since the *Endurance* had become entombed, they were able to raise sails and make proper headway.

Even so, many of the men were approaching breaking point. The currents had taken them scores of miles off course and they were soon further from Elephant and Clarence Islands than when they had set out. Months of imprisonment had severely weakened them all and they were in no condition for prolonged exposure to the Southern Ocean in open boats.

Shackleton was skipper of the *James Caird*, and with him aboard was skilled navigator Frank Worsley. It was thanks to Worsley's genius that they were able to make up the lost miles and get back within reach of dry land. On 15 April, seven days after setting out from the pack-ice, all three boats and 28 men made landfall on a rocky beach on Elephant Island. They were the first human beings ever to set foot on that barren, comfortless place – and for the first minutes ashore it must have seemed to them like the promised land.

Any affection for the place was soon swept away. Stable land it may have been, but it was anything but dry. The beach they had landed upon was shallow and could give no real protection from the waves at high tide. Shackleton let the men bed down for a desperately needed rest, but he was already making plans to move them on again as soon as possible. A scouting party identified a second beach some miles away in a slightly less exposed position, and in the early hours of the morning the men piled back into their boats. The journey was short but perilous, and all their remaining strength was required to get themselves and their vessels out of the water and on to 'dry' land a second time.

A relentless gale pummelled them, knocking them off their feet, and they had to upturn the two smaller boats and crawl beneath them to try to find some respite. Worse, though, than the cold, the wind and the exhaustion was the elephant in the room on Elephant Island. The fact they had to face up to was that no one in the world had any idea where they were. Family and friends back home could only assume the men were some-

1. Captain Robert Falcon Scott: the greatest hero of them all.

2.
The Penlee lifeboatmen train with a Navy search and rescue helicopter.

3.
The SAS and the Battle of Mirbat.

4.
The Demons
of Camerone.

5.
The Battle of
Isandlwana.

6.
Blondie Hasler (*front*):
the leader of the
Cockleshell Heroes
trains in a kayak.

7.
A battle-scarred
HMS *Amethyst* after
the Yangtze Incident.

8.
Sir John Moore
and the retreat
to Corunna.

9.
Sir Ernest
Shackleton
(*second from left*)
and members
of the Imperial
Trans–Antarctic
Expedition.

10. The Nez Perces.

11.
Women and
children first:
the Birkenhead
Drill.

14.
The crew of
Apollo 13.
From left to right:
Commander James
A. Lovell, Jr.;
Command module
pilot John L.
Swigert, Jr.; and
Lunar Module pilot
Fred W. Haise, Jr.

15.
The Siege of
Constantinople.

16.
French soldiers at Dien Bien Phu.

17.
The Battle of Britain was the greatest aerial conflict the world had ever seen.

18.
Jacques-Louis David's famous painting of Leonidas at Thermopylae.

where on the continent of Antarctica – more than 1,000 miles away from their present location – and any relief ship that might eventually come looking for them would make for the Weddell Sea. Since no one would have any idea they had had to abandon the *Endurance* and make for Elephant Island – an uncharted, uninhabited rock many miles from any shipping lanes – no one would ever look for them there. Any rescue attempt would have to be mounted by the men themselves.

Shackleton knew all too well that most of them were too weakened, both mentally and physically, to take to the boats once more. In any case, their next destination would have to be South Georgia, some 800 miles away across the fearsome waters of the Drake Passage, and such a lengthy journey was simply too much to ask of so many near-broken souls. He decided that just he and the five strongest men would take the *James Caird* on the final and greatest leg of the journey back to the world. From South Georgia it would be relatively easy to organise the rescue of the rest of the team.

The final choice of crew was Tom Crean, Frank Worsley, Tim McCarthy, Chips McNeish and Jack Vincent. It went without saying that Shackleton would skipper the boat on this most perilous stage of the entire odyssey. After difficult and emotional farewells on the beach, around lunchtime on 24 April 1916, the *James Caird* pushed off into the swell. It's impossible to say whose hearts would have been heaviest – those facing 800 miles of savage Southern Ocean in a 22-and-a-half-foot whaler, or the 22 desperate men left behind. If fate overtook the six, then nothing but a lingering death from exposure awaited their comrades on the rock of Elephant Island.

In truth, the greater part of the burden of the journey to South Georgia fell upon the shoulders of Worsley. He had already demonstrated his skills as a navigator by getting them across open sea to Elephant Island. Now he had to pinpoint another relatively tiny target, and if he missed it, the currents and prevailing winds would sweep them out into the vastness of open sea separating Antarctica from the continents of South America, Australasia and Africa. If Worsley were to overshoot South Georgia, the men aboard the *James Caird* would be doomed, unable to fight their way back against the tides for a second chance.

Conditions aboard were as bad as before. The weather was deteriorating and the men's only protection from the wind and waves was a canvas shelter improvised by McNeish in the days before their departure from Elephant Island. The men split into two teams of three, and while one manned the vessel and tended the sails, the members of the other took what rest they could, huddled in their soaked sleeping bags beneath the canvas. Day after day they fought the sea, pumping and bailing the flooded interior, and cooking meals of seal stew washed down with boiling hot milk.

It was a relentless routine, but enlivened by all the dangers of the Southern Ocean. On 5 May Shackleton saw a bright line on the horizon that he briefly took to be sunlight on the water. Then to his horror he realised it was a towering wave bearing down on the little boat. Most likely caused by the 'calving' of a great iceberg many miles away, it was the tallest wall of water any of the men had ever seen in all their many combined years at sea. It surged towards the *James Caird*, hitting it and picking it up like so much flotsam and driving it forward on a terrifying run. Miraculously, the little boat stayed upright and all six men remained inside it. As quickly as it had appeared, the great wave was gone and the men were safe to continue with their journey.

On 8 May, after 15 days of sailing, the men sighted land for the first time. Against all the odds, Worsley had done it. With sheer skill and perseverance he had hit his target dead centre, and delivered the men out of the emptiness of the ocean. Two days later, after more close calls with mountainous seas that seemed intent on dashing the men's hopes on the very doorstep of salvation, the *James Caird* sailed into the relatively sheltered water of King Haakon Bay.

Although they had performed the miracle of reaching inhabited land, still their ordeal was not over. King Haakon Bay was on the southern coastline of the island and all the inhabited whaling stations were around Grytviken Bay in the north. One last journey, this time overland through the never before explored territory of South Georgia's interior, would be required of the men if they were finally to re-establish contact with humankind.

It was clear, however, that they wouldn't all be making the last leg of the trip. McNeish and Vincent had reached the ends of their tethers, both physical and mental, and would have to stay behind and await rescue. A relatively comfortable base was established on King Haakon Bay – beneath the upturned hull of the *James Caird* – and it was agreed that McCarthy would stay behind to look after the other two. Shackleton, Crean and Worsley allowed themselves a few days' rest – and some welcome meals of fresh meat, caught and cooked on the island – before setting out yet again in the early hours of 19 May. Three tattered vagabonds, ill-clad and with long hair and beards matted by months of neglect, they shook hands with their comrades and headed north. Once again the fate of the many would depend upon the fortitude of the few.

The weather at least was kind to them, remaining relatively calm, but a fog descended so thickly that for a time the trio could hardly see their hands in front of their faces. A close shave, which saw all three come within inches of stumbling into a huge crevasse, persuaded them to rope themselves together. It was in this manner, depending on one another for the safety of every step, that they picked their way towards the mountains separating them from their goal. Time and again they climbed to heights of 4,000 feet or more only to find their way blocked by sheer drops or impassable crevasses. They were driving themselves onward mercilessly, stopping only to cook hurried meals of seal stew before plodding on again. Hours went by and still they could see no end to their troubles. Finally, after more than 30 hours without sleep, they crested a rise and looked down upon the distant but unmistakable shapes of the buildings of the whaling station at Stromness. More miraculous than the man made structures, though, was the sight of tiny figures going about their everyday business. Apart from their comrades, these were the first human beings the three men had laid eyes upon in a year and a half.

After a few more miles of marching, Shackleton, Crean and Worsley presented themselves quietly at the door of one of the buildings. A Norwegian by the name of Anderson found them first and was so shocked by their appearance – and their claim to have walked across the island – that he left them on the doorstep while he went to find his boss.

The man who came next was Thoralf Sorlle, who had entertained Shackleton and his party all those months before. There was no recognition on his face as he beheld the three wild men, who looked as if they'd emerged whole and breathing from some ancient past. Shackleton would later recall their first exchange.

'Well?' said Sorlle.

'Don't you know me?' I said.

'I know your voice . . . you're the mate of the *Daisy*.'

'My name is Shackleton,' I said.

Sorlle put out his hand at once. 'Come in, come in,' he said.

Arrangements were quickly made to collect McCarthy, Vincent and McNeish from King Haakon Bay, but it was not until late August that it was finally possible to return for the 22 men on Elephant Island. Several attempts were made, but the pack-ice drove the rescue ships back each time.

Shackleton, Crean and Worsley were aboard the steamer *Yelcho* when it made the successful trip from Punta Arenas, in Chile, to that desolate rock where the lost souls sat patiently awaiting whatever fate would choose to deliver.

Once they were within sight of the island, Shackleton and Crean climbed aboard a cutter as it was lowered over the side of the ship and rowed over to the beach. When they were close enough to be heard over the breaking waves of the surf, Shackleton shouted out: 'Are you all well?'

Back from the beach came the reply the leader had hoped with all his heart to hear, and done everything in his power to ensure.

'We are all well, Boss!'

The achievement of Shackleton, Crean and Worsley has never been equalled, let alone surpassed. They survived months aboard the trapped *Endurance*, then led 25 men across the Southern Ocean in open boats to Elephant Island, before setting out with their three colleagues to complete a further 800 miles of sea crossing. All of this was done in the worst possible conditions and with wholly inadequate and unsuitable clothing and equipment. And after all that they managed a forced march across 40 miles of uncharted glaciers, ice fields and mountains in the interior of South Georgia in order to bring help to their comrades.

The crew of their support ship *Aurora* had not been so fortunate. Knowing nothing of the plight of Shackleton and the rest of the men aboard the *Endurance*, the 10-man team had battled appalling hardships of their own. Ill-equipped and faced with appalling weather conditions throughout, they had struggled to complete their assigned task of marching into Antarctica's interior to lay the supply dumps for the planned second leg of their comrades' journey past the Pole. Unbeknownst to them, they were risking everything for a journey that would never even be attempted, let alone completed. Three of them died in the attempt, and yet such was the furore that greeted the reports of the survival of Shackleton and his first team that the bravery of the 'Ross Sea Party' was all but overlooked by history.

And so to that fourth soul sensed by Shackleton, Crean and Worsley as they crossed South Georgia. It would be easy to say that three men in such a predicament, weakened by malnutrition and exhausted to the point of collapse, might be subject to hallucinations. It wouldn't be the first or last time that men pushed to the limits of their physical and mental strength have been tricked by their own imaginations as their minds fought for survival.

But the fact remains that while the phenomenon was not acknowledged, far less discussed by the men at the time, both Shackleton and Worsley later wrote about it in their accounts of the expedition.

In *South*, for example, Shackleton noted:

I know that during that long and racking march of 36 hours over the unnamed mountains and glaciers of South Georgia, it seemed to me often that we were four, not three. I said nothing to my companions on the point, but afterwards Worsley said to me, 'Boss, I had a curious feeling on the march that there was another person with us.' Crean confessed to the same idea. One feels 'the dearth of human words, the roughness of mortal speech' in trying to describe things intangible, but a record of our journeys would be incomplete without a reference to a subject very near to our hearts.

There can be no rational explanation for what those men experienced on their march to save their comrades. Crean would later say simply that God had watched over them and brought them home. Maybe he was right. God was certainly absent from the war in France, where millions of boys and men were fighting, killing and dying. There was a time, and that time is not now, when British men took the presence of God for granted. Their belief is part of the explanation for why, and even how, they did the things they did.

The voyage of the *James Caird* and the crossing of South Georgia is, anyway, a story not of gods but of men. Most fitting of all was the comment made by one of the whalers as they gathered around the grateful trio in their club-room on the night they arrived at Stromness. These were tough individuals all, hardened by years of physical labour in the toughest environment on earth, yet every one of them was desperate to shake hands with the pilgrims in their midst.

Out of the tobacco-smoke haze stepped one old man, a veteran of four decades or more on the Southern Ocean. In all his years, he said, he had never heard the like of the tale he'd just had from Ernest Shackleton, Tom Crean and Frank Worsley. It was an honour he said, a real honour to know fellows such as these. And then, having all but run out of words, he gestured flamboyantly at the dazed newcomers.

'These – are men!' he said.

The scale and significance of what they'd done was not lost on the Boss. By the time they had reached that whaling station at Stromness, they had thrown away their stove and adze. Their last obstacle had been a waterfall and the rope, securely tied to a rock at the top, had to be left behind when all three reached the bottom. They brought out of the Antarctic only the clothes they wore. After all, wrote Shackleton:

That was all of tangible things; but in memories we were rich.

In trying to give words to his feelings, he turned to lines by the poet Robert Service in 'The Call of the Wild':

'We had pierced the veneer of outside things,' he wrote.

We had 'suffered, starved and triumphed, grovelled down

yet grasped at glory, grown bigger in the bigness of the whole'. We had seen God in his splendours, heard the text that Nature renders. We had reached the naked soul of man.

In search of a place in the world

Brave, physically tough and resourceful though he undoubtedly was, Shackleton was also a lucky man. He pushed himself and his men to the limits of endurance, and during those moments when they teetered on the brink, he had good fortune to thank for their deliverance as well as his own skills as leader. A different twist of fate here or there might have undone his good works and sent them all to oblivion. But instead Shackleton came home, a deserving hero and a legend of polar exploration.

The survivors of the Imperial Trans-Antarctic Expedition returned to a world changed beyond recognition.

'We were like men arisen from the dead to a world gone mad,' wrote Shackleton.

> Our minds accustomed themselves gradually to the tales of nations in arms, of deathless courage and unimagined slaughter, of a world-conflict that had grown beyond all conceptions, of vast red battlefields in grimmest contrast with the frigid whiteness we had left behind us.

It was 1917 before Shackleton made it back to Britain. He was 42 and officially too old to join any of the armed services. He made numerous offers to get into the fray on behalf of King and Country, but all were rejected. Weakened by all he had put his body through – hard drinking not the least of it – he finally died of a heart attack on 5 January 1922. He was back on South Georgia when the moment came, still exploring, still looking for something out there just beyond his reach. His body was put aboard a ship bound for England, but when word reached his wife, Emily, she had it turned back. If Shackleton had ever belonged to another human being – and that seemed doubtful – it had not been her, or their children. Shackleton's was a vagabond heart and it belonged not at home, but on the journey. He was duly returned to South Georgia and there buried among whalers and mariners in one of the loneliest graveyards on Earth.

Of the rest of his men – both those of the Weddell Sea and the Ross Sea teams – no fewer than 30 joined the fighting of the Great War. By the end of it all, five of them lay dead on the battlefields, drowned in the seas, or lost to illness.

But those fates lay in the future, beyond the imaginations of those who lived out their lives in the years before 1914.

Back on the Antarctic ice of 1904, Scott was coming to the end of his first cradling in those frigid arms. After a second winter on the ice at Hut Point, the *Discovery* expedition came to a close in the February of that year. This time two ships, the *Morning* and the *Terra Nova*, had been sent south by the worried folks back home – and again Scott was infuriated at being ordered to return to Britain. This time there was no escaping the inevitable. By the end of the month all three ships were heading north, arriving back in the harbour at Lyttelton around Easter time.

Scott and the crew of the *Discovery* eventually sailed into Stokes Bay between Southsea and the Isle of Wight at around 11 o'clock on the morning of 10 September 1904. They arrived in Portsmouth harbour later the same day and the ship was instantly surrounded by boats of all sizes, their passengers desperate to catch a glimpse of the men aboard. Boy sailors in the rigging of Nelson's *Victory* added their voices to the cheering.

Like astronauts returning from another world they were hailed as heroes – and their achievements had been immense. They had after all been the first travellers to explore and survey the Great Ice Barrier, first to discover the polar ice cap and first to lay the groundwork that would eventually fix the position of the South Magnetic Pole. During 28 sled journeys they had advanced the studies of marine biology, glaciology and terrestrial magnetism. In so doing they had mapped and surveyed hundreds of square miles of previously unknown coastline. Scott himself had led the team of men that had made the 'furthest south' journey, which almost claimed their lives.

But while the press and the public made a celebrity of Scott of the Antarctic, the still quiet and retiring Navy man struggled to cope with the spotlight now turned upon him. Laurels were heaped on him – the King made him a Commander of the Victorian Order and the French welcomed him into their Legion of Honour. He received gold medals from the geographical societies of nation after nation. Even Shackleton wrote to congratulate him and to welcome him home. The younger man was fully recovered from his ordeal, newly married and making the most of life back on dry land. He told his former leader that while he had no more energy for further expeditions, his heart, 'had ever been turned south'.

Of all the advancements, the one that pleased Scott most was his promotion to the rank of captain and its associated pay rise. He was after all a Navy man through and through. He asked for six months' leave to write up his adventures in a book, and set his heart on dropping out of public life.

What he thought he wanted was peace.

The flight of the Nez Perces

On 21 September 1904 a doctor was summoned to examine the corpse of a Native American man who had died earlier that day on the Colville Reservation in Washington. It was the same month that saw Scott's triumphant return to England.

The Indian was 60 years old and had lived on the reservation since 1885, when the United States Government had seen fit to separate him from the younger members of his tribe. While the braves were sent to a reservation set aside for their people, on land north of the Wallowa River beneath the Bitterroot Mountains, the old man was considered too dangerous to go with them. He might exert his baleful influence over the impressionable youngsters and turn them back to their old wild ways, and so, together with other senior members of the tribe, he was sent instead to Nespelem on the Colville Reservation. It was there that he lived out the remainder of his years, cut off from the blood and the land of his fathers.

The doctor made an examination of the old man's body and was somehow able to record the cause of death as 'a broken heart'.

In the language of his people – a language spoken then by only a handful of human beings left alive on the whole Earth – his name was Hin-ma-tow-ya-lak-ket. To the white men who wrote about him later, he was Chief Joseph of the Nez Perces.

The destruction by white Europeans of every civilisation they encountered in the Americas – North and South – is an old and well-known story. Having crossed the Atlantic Ocean in the wake of Christopher Columbus, they were in no mood to put up with the sitting tenants they found occupying their New

World. Relations were briefly cordial in North America – in the early days when the incomers were still few in number and living space upon the vast new terrain was hardly an issue. But as the 19th century dawned and progressed, and with the immigrants numbering now in the millions, the people referred to today as Native Americans were systematically brushed off the page to make way for a new story.

This is what Europeans have always done, at home and abroad. The ancient history of Europe, as revealed by archaeology, hints at innumerable occasions when one people has roughly displaced – or replaced – another. Part of the misfortune for the present-day white inhabitants of the United States of America is that the victims of their forefathers' actions lived within the age of the camera.

As the centuries and millennia rolled by, waves of new peoples arrived on British shores and muscled their way past existing populations on the way to creating new societies. The Picts gave way to Scots and to Vikings; Britons submitted to Romans, and then to Anglo-Saxons – who in turn fell before the Norman conquerors of 1066. But those vanished peoples survive only as names on a historian's page, and some artefacts in the display cases of museums. In the case of the opening up of the Old West of North America, however, we have photographs of the men and women swept aside.

The stories of people like Lone Wolf, Cochise, Kicking Bird, Standing Bear and Sitting Bull would be heartbreaking enough even if only their names had survived. But seeing the unsmiling faces of those sentinels, who look right through the lens to accuse the world beyond, makes it that much harder to hear about their lives and deaths. This is bad luck for modern Americans. They inherited their land from men and women who committed many wrongs against a people that lacked either the numbers or the technology to truly threaten them. Everyone in the northern hemisphere is descended from invaders like that – but we're mostly spared the discomfort of having to look into the faces of the victims.

There is a photograph of Chief Joseph in the US National Archives, taken when he was still in his middle years. Like the rest of the people of the Nez Perces, he was relatively fair-skinned. The native peoples, scattered in tribal groups throughout the American continent, varied greatly in colour, from almost black to a tone lighter than that of any Portuguese or Spaniard. Contrary to the Hollywood image created by the movie *The Last of the Mohicans*, for example, the men and women of that tribe were light-skinned, with mid-brown hair. The cast was composed, in the main, of members of the Sioux tribe – who bore no resemblance to real Mohicans. Also relatively fair-skinned were the people of tribes like the Blackfeet of Saskatchewan or the Pammas of Brazil.

Chief Joseph has an open face, a wide, handsome mouth and a high forehead. His chin is slightly raised for the camera, challenging. He is made instantly recognisable as an Indian by the long side plaits in his hair and the style of his clothes. In the photograph he is not looking directly at the camera but off to one side, which is probably just as well. His eyes shine with an emotion that is somewhere between pride and sadness, and it looks as though it would have been hard to look him fully in the face.

His father, a chief of the Nez Perces before him, was called Old Joseph. It was Old Joseph who could more clearly remember the days when the whites were considered good neighbours. The members of the exploration party led by Lewis and Clark in the early years of the 19th century were among the first to see the Nez Perces. The encounter was a happy and peaceful one for all concerned – and especially lucky for the whites, who had been close to starvation and suffering from dysentery when they stumbled down out of the Rocky Mountains, into what would become modern-day Idaho, en route to the Pacific coast. The Indians took them into their homes, fed them and cared for them until they had regained their health and strength.

Apparently the whites noticed that some among their hosts wore jewellery, made from shells, in holes pierced through their noses. Since they had heard reports of such 'pierced-noses' from the French trappers and explorers called the *coureurs de bois* – those who run in the woods – they applied the French name to this people they found living by the banks of the Clearwater River: Nez Perces. At the time of that first meeting, the Nez Perces numbered around 4,000 souls in total. They fished for salmon and, in the hunting season, made the tough crossing of the Bitterroot Mountains in search of buffalo. The whites observed that they were outstanding horsemen and that they kept one of the largest herds of any of the native peoples they had encountered so far.

After a few weeks, Lewis and Clark and the rest of their party were strong enough to continue on their westward adventure. A basis for warm friendship had been made, though, and for the next 70 years the Nez Perces would take pride in the fact there had never been bad blood between themselves and the whites.

But the land occupied by the Nez Perces – like every other scrap of mountain, water and valley between the two coasts of North America – fell eventually under the hungry gaze of the incomers. Old Joseph, like others of his kind, did not regard his territory as something 'owned' by him or anyone else. It was just there – a self-renewing source of food, clothing and shelter. Anyone and anything was therefore free to roam across every part of it.

This was a philosophy that had had its day, however noble it may appear when viewed from today's perspective. For all the millennia when the population of North America could be counted in terms of hundreds of thousands, or a few million, there was so much empty land that ownership of it mattered not at all; in fact it was a meaningless concept. But when the land-hungry and the dispossessed of the Old World poured into these formerly empty places in their tens of millions, they brought a lumbering juggernaut of new thinking with them as well. In time they would find a grand name for their unstoppable advance across the land – Manifest Destiny – but in the short term it was a simple land-grab.

When in 1855 the Governor of Washington Territory, a man named Isaac Stevens, told Old Joseph he would have to limit himself and his few hundred people to a clearly defined portion of the land – and accept that the rest of the territory was now 'owned' by the whites – he refused to listen. Old Joseph was just one of the chiefs among the Nez Perces, however, and although he refused to sign up to any treaty formalising the proposed arrangement, there were others who did. As far as the US Government was concerned, therefore, all the Nez Perces had accepted the deal.

By 1863 there were more new people pressing in on the territory west of the Rockies and the hunger for the land was greater again. A new treaty was offered to the Nez Perces. This time they were to give up 90 per cent of the land ceded to them by Stevens's paper of 1855. Among other places sacred to Old Joseph, he was now expected to surrender the land of the Wallowa Valley, known to his people as the Valley of the Winding Waters. Having refused to acknowledge the legality of the 1855 treaty, Old Joseph was doubly enraged at this new proposal.

'The country was created without lines of demarcation and it is no man's business to divide it,' he said. 'Perhaps you think the Creator sent you here to dispose of us as you see fit. If I thought the Creator sent you, I might be induced to think you had a right to dispose of me. Do not misunderstand me, but understand fully with reference to my affection for the land. I never said the land was mine to do with as I choose. The one who has a right to dispose of it is the one who has created it. I claim a right to live on my land and accord you the privilege to return to yours.'

Once again, Old Joseph refused to make his mark on any paperwork. But other chiefs – strangers to the Wallowa Valley in any case – duly signed the treaty and gave away the land.

When Old Joseph died in 1871 his son replaced him as a chief. If Joseph the younger inherited anything from his father, it was the unshakable belief that no one had the right to tell him or his people where or how they might live. Like his father, he refused to acknowledge the 'treaties' of 1855 and 1863, and so when white men came to tell him he must now move his people to the newly created Lapwai Reservation, he ignored them. It was a mark of the intelligence of the man, however, that he also attempted to play the white man at his own game. With a sense that he was entitled to the same legal rights as anyone else living under the protection of the President of the United States, Chief Joseph wrote to Ulysses S. Grant asking that he be allowed to continue living on the land of his ancestors. There was support for the Nez Perces among some sections of the white community too. They, like Chief Joseph, could see the questionable legality of foisting treaties upon a people given no option but to submit. In what must have seemed like a crowning triumph, on 16 June 1873 President Grant ruled that the Wallowa Valley – the Valley of the Winding Waters so beloved by Old Joseph and all his people – belonged to the Nez Perces and was not to be colonised by any whites.

Betrayal of promises was not, however, a character weakness limited to nameless bureaucrats. Within two years of the executive order, the President decreed the Wallowa Valley open to white settlement once more. Now white soldiers returned to the land of the Nez Perces to tell Chief Joseph their time was up and that they must ready themselves and their animals for the journey to the Lapwai Reservation to the north. It was

1877, the year after General George Armstrong Custer's catastrophe at the Little Bighorn at the hands of Sioux warriors led by Sitting Bull and the legendary Crazy Horse, and there was no love left for any Indians in the hearts of most white men.

Tribes the length and breadth of the country were already suffering. The Cheyenne, the Navajo, the Sioux, the Apache, the Arapaho – all of these peoples and more had felt the harsh hand of the US Government and its military.

General Otis Howard was the soldier in charge of clearing the Nez Perces out of the Wallowa Valley and on arrival at Lapwai he sent messengers to Chief Joseph summoning him to a meeting. Together with his most trusted comrades – his own brother Ollocot, Lean Elk, the prophet Toohoolhoolzote, White Bird and Looking Glass – Chief Joseph rode up to the reservation to try to face down the inevitable. But they arrived at Lapwai as emissaries of a world already living beyond its allotted time. What their opponents called their Manifest Destiny – their apparently divine right to rule the Americas – was just the arrival of the future in the world of the past. Chief Joseph and his men were already ghosts, haunting the living.

The meeting was ill-tempered from the start, and Toohoolhoolzote argued so bitterly with Howard that the General had him arrested and thrown into the guardhouse. He was freed once he was judged to have calmed down, and returned to the Wallowa with Chief Joseph and the others to begin the job of preparing their people for exodus. It was May, and at that time of year the livestock of the Nez Perces, horses and cattle, was scattered over many square miles. En route to Lapwai they would have to cross the Snake River, which was still running deep and fast. Despite these complications, Chief Joseph had his people on the move within a few weeks. He had considered his options and understood all too well that he lacked the numbers of fighting men needed to keep the white soldiers out of the Wallowa by force. Better, he thought, to keep everyone together and safe – and to move out of harm's way.

He would say later:

... we could not hold our own with the white men. We were like deer. They were like grizzly bears. We had a small country. Their country was large. We were contented to let things remain as the Great Spirit Chief made them. They were not, and would change the rivers and mountains if they did not suit them.

In the end, matters were taken out of Joseph's hands – not by the white man but by the actions of a handful of his own warriors. Unlike their chief, the prophet Toohoolhoolzote was no longer counselling peace. On the contrary, he wanted a fight to avenge him for the indignity of his imprisonment at Lapwai. And he was able to argue quite persuasively that obeying the white man's orders would give them no guarantee of safety. After all, though they had only covered a few miles, they had already been harried by whites who had stolen some of their livestock while they struggled across the swollen Snake River. After months and years of simmering acrimony, insults and slights felt on both sides, it was one wrong too many. Whipped up into a killing mood by Toohoolhoolzote's words, a few Nez Perces braves slipped away from the rest of the tribe and spilt the blood of the first whites they could find.

When Chief Joseph learned what they had done, he knew peaceful relocation was no longer possible. He also knew his Nez Perces were not the only members of the tribe to have refused to sign the treaties of 1855 and 1863. More so-called 'non-treaty' Nez Perces were encamped in nearby White Bird Canyon, and now, with blood on his braves' hands, Chief Joseph decided to join up with the rest of the fugitives.

The people who gathered together that spring and early

summer by the waters of White Bird Creek were hardly a war band. It is hard to be precise about numbers but there were no more than 700 individuals. Of these perhaps 250 were fighting men, the rest being the elderly, the women and the children. Also there with them was what remained of their material wealth – around 2,000 head of horses. Threatened and outnumbered though they were, there was no panic. Instead there was dignity and resolve – an understanding that the actions taken now must be for the good of the group.

It was there in White Bird Canyon, on 17 June 1877, that the Nez Perces began the fight to preserve some remnants of their way of life. Looking Glass had been chosen as war chief and, with a superior understanding of the terrain, he deployed his slim forces. Using skirmishers to draw forward the horsemen of Howard's 1st US Cavalry, the Nez Perces braves were able to isolate and expose their attackers' flank. Around a third of the cavalrymen, lured into this vulnerable position, were killed within minutes. The rest were forced to flee for their lives. Looking Glass had demonstrated an understanding of guerrilla tactics that would serve them well.

The war had begun, and as the gunsmoke of that first battle drifted high into the sky, Chief Joseph understood what they must do. Gathering his fellow chiefs around him, he told them what they already knew in their hearts: that the Wallowa Valley could never again be home to the Nez Perces. He said too that none among them wanted to see their people herded like cattle into the Lapwai. There was only one option available to them – to follow the lead of Sitting Bull, victor of the Little Bighorn. Sitting Bull and his Sioux people had travelled north, all the way across the border into Canada. Chief Joseph said that since that land was governed not by the US, but by Great Britain, they could not be followed there by the cavalrymen who had fought with them just now. In Canada, the land of Queen Victoria – whom they knew as the Grandmother – they could live their old lives once more, free from persecution.

The other chiefs agreed – or could suggest no better option – and so began the flight of the Nez Perces. From the very beginning it was an unequal contest – and one that captured the imagination of those who heard of its unfolding by means of telegraph communications that crackled across the country. This was not an army on the move but a people, the vestiges of a civilisation made alien in its own homeland.

Howard's men had had their noses bloodied, but were far from beaten. As Chief Joseph led his people towards the Lolo pass through the Bitterroots – a trail they knew well, since it led to their buffalo hunting grounds in Montana – the cavalrymen gave chase. Even slowed down by their elders, their women and children and the horse herd, the Indians were far quicker over the broken, rugged ground than their pursuers. Five weeks later, however, they encountered a fortified defensive position slung across the Lolo trail by soldiers commanded by a Captain Charles Rawn.

After some inconclusive skirmishing over several days, the Indians managed to slip past the enemy and continue on their route north – but they could not know that a third force had been dispatched against them and was closing in fast. Colonel John Gibbon, with 15 officers, 146 troopers, and 34 volunteers, was moving into position to strike. This then had been Rawn's real objective all along – to stall the fugitives and give time for the larger trap to be sprung. By the second week in August Gibbon's men were in place and on the 9th they launched a night-time attack on the Indian encampment.

It was a scrappy offensive, carried out by men who had prepared for the job by drinking whisky. Drunken and badly executed though the assault had been, for some little while it looked as if the element of surprise might carry the night. Instead a Nez Perces chief named White Bird rallied his braves.

The rearguard action he choreographed punished the soldiers severely – and gave time for Chief Joseph to bring order out of the chaos and get the remains of the camp up and moving through the cries of the dying. With the false warmth of liquor and adrenaline now draining fast from their veins, the soldiers lost the taste for the fight. Driven back in disorder, many of their number stumbling blindly into a river, they saw sense and turned tail, back into the darkness. It had been a cruel night for the Nez Perces nonetheless, with many of their women and children lying dead and mutilated across the broken ground.

Just days later the fleeing Indians were attacked once more. This time it was by Howard's cavalry, still infuriated by their drubbing two months before in White Bird Canyon. They were to be humiliated again – this time losing their baggage train and many of their horses as Chief Joseph and his warriors brushed past them in the manner befitting the ghosts they were.

By now their flight had brought them to the territory of the Yellowstone – land designated as North America's first national park in 1872. There waiting for them was General William Tecumseh Sherman, hero of the Civil War and commander of the US Army. How, Sherman wanted to know, was a rag-tag band of fugitive Indians leading his professional soldiers such a merry dance? They were taking their women and children along for the ride, for God's sake, and still they were outwitting and outfighting his men at every turn.

Risen like a phoenix after their destruction at the Little Bighorn, the 7th Cavalry were desperate for the chance to show their mettle and to prove to the General that they would not be found wanting a second time. But although they threw themselves after the fleeing Nez Perces, they failed to pin down the main body. Outriding forces of skirmishers from both sides played cat and mouse with one another, but the fugitives remained elusive to the last. Fighting rearguard actions to cover the flight of the old, the women and the young, they drew red blood from the blue coats time and again as August gave way to September.

By the end of that month Chief Joseph and his people had been on the run for over sixteen weeks. They had travelled more than 1,500 miles from their homes in the Valley of the Winding Waters and evaded the best efforts of 2,000 of the best trained and best armed soldiers the US Army could send against them. They had bested or equalled their enemy at three major encounters and countless other running engagements – and they had done all this while moving and protecting their women and children and everything else of value they possessed.

General Sherman would later report:

> The Indians throughout displayed a courage and skill that elicited universal praise; they abstained from scalping; let captive women go free; did not commit indiscriminate murder of peaceful families, which is usual; and fought with almost scientific skill, using advance and rear guards, skirmish lines, and field fortifications.

It was the least he could have said.

By the end of September Chief Joseph had brought his people to within one long day's march – perhaps 40 miles – of the Canadian border. His people were hungry, and once they had made it across the Missouri River he allowed them to make camp in the Bear Paw Mountains in north-central Montana. They had seen no soldiers for several days and for the first time in a long while they were allowing the fires of hope to be rekindled. Soon perhaps they would be with Sitting Bull and his Sioux in the land of the Grandmother.

After a night spent feasting on freshly killed buffalo, the quiet of the morning was torn apart by the thunder of approaching horsemen. It was a cavalry force commanded by Colonel Nelson Miles and they had managed to place themselves between the

Indians and their promised land of Canada. Disciplined to the end, those of the Nez Perces who were still able to fight took up positions and calmly unleashed a volley of rifle fire into the approaching horsemen. The fighting that followed was intense and brief. The Indians successfully drove off the attackers but with heavy losses on their own side. Among the dead were the prophet Toohoolhoolzote and Chief Joseph's brother, Ollocot.

While Joseph and his surviving war chiefs held their final councils, around campfires stacked high against the aching chill of falling snow and freezing wind, General Howard and his men arrived to surround the Indian position.

In one final skirmish Looking Glass was killed by a single bullet to the head, and Chief Joseph's heart was broken. Some of the survivors, Chief White Bird among them, begged Joseph to fight on. They had come so far, they said. Even if they should die now, it was better than surrender. Chief Joseph did not agree and his mind was made up.

The American journalist Charles Sutherland witnessed what happened, on 5 October 1877. He said the chief appeared on the prairie just as the sun was setting. He was on horseback, his chin lowered to his chest. He was accompanied by just five of his comrades. As he came close he suddenly raised his head, the better to look into the eyes of his tormentors. He held his rifle in one hand and now he straightened his arm out towards Howard, signifying the end of his resistance and of the flight of the Nez Perces.

The speech he made to his captors then has become one of the best known of all statements made by Native Americans of the period. The poignancy and the poetry of it is clear to all – but whether that is down to Chief Joseph or to the soldier who recorded and translated it, will never now be known:

Tell General Howard I know his heart. What he told me before I have in my heart. I am tired of fighting. Our chiefs are killed. Looking Glass is dead. Toohoolhoolzote is dead. The old men are all dead. It is the young men who say yes or no. He who led all the young men is dead. It is cold and we have no blankets. The little children are freezing to death. My people, some of them, have run away to the hills, and have no blankets, no food; no one knows where they are – perhaps freezing to death. I want to have time to look for my children and see how many of them I can find. Maybe I shall find them among the dead. Hear me my chiefs! I am tired; my heart is sick and sad. From where the sun now stands I will fight no more forever.

Later that night, White Bird and a handful of the still rebellious braves crept stealthily through the encircling cordon. A few days later they made it to the camp of Sitting Bull.

For the rest, their surrender led only to greater heartbreak. Instead of being sent to the reservation set aside for them at Lapwai, the 87 men, 184 women and 147 children who surrendered that day were transported to imprisonment on land beside Fort Leavenworth, in Kansas. It was yet another betrayal. Chief Joseph would say later that if he had known Howard would break his word in that way, he would never have surrendered. Many of them died there, perhaps as many as 100 or more, before the remainder were moved to a barren patch of sand and scrub in north-eastern Oklahoma, deep in the set-aside land known as the Indian Territory. The Nez Perces who lived and died there called it 'the hot place'.

When in 1928 Chief Joseph's descendants decided to exhume the old man's body, for reburial on a patch of land back in the Valley of the Winding Waters, they found that his skull was missing. This came as no real surprise, since for years it had been rumoured that some or other person had taken it for a souvenir.

First, women and children

Did Scott know about the fate that had befallen the Indians of North America – some of it taking place during the years of his own childhood and early adulthood? Had any of *their* bravery in the face of impossible odds inspired his own?

In 1887, when Scott was 19, Buffalo Bill Cody brought his 'Wild West and Congress of Rough Riders of the World Show' to Britain. While those refugees from a lost civilisation became a spectacle on one side of the Atlantic, Sitting Bull, last great chief of the Sioux, was still at large in the US. Before his death in 1890, during a bungled attempt to arrest him, would come the rise of the Ghost Dance. While learning the steps, taught to them by a prophet, the surviving Indians would hear that a Christian messiah was soon to walk among them, restoring their lands to them and bringing their loved ones back from the dead.

Also in 1890 would come the final atrocity at Wounded Knee, when more than 250 captive Sioux – warriors, squaws, children, old men and women – would be cut down by the 7th Cavalry and left to die in the snow, four days after Christmas. No messiah for them; no more dancing.

Among the 200-strong company that Buffalo Bill brought to Britain were nearly 100 Indians – many of them warriors and chiefs still wanted in the United States for their part in battles like Little Bighorn. The Wild West, and the way it had been won, was far from unknown in Victorian and Edwardian Britain.

If Scott had taken the time to study anything of the story of the conquest of North America by the white man, he would have learned that sometimes it is futile to surrender. Chief Joseph of the Nez Perces surrendered himself and his people to the US Government – and though it preserved their lives for a while, it hardly brought them any happiness, or even dignity. He acted out of the best of motives – the hope that he might have the chance to find his lost children – but it brought only misery for himself and his people. Part of the lesson of Chief Joseph and the Nez Perces is that sometimes, giving in is not an option.

Scott's two-volume *Voyage of the 'Discovery'* was published in the November of 1905 and received universally good reviews. By now he was a friend of the likes of J.M. Barrie, who had brought his play *Peter Pan* to the London stage for first time just the year before. All about the 'lost boys' – boys who choose never to grow up – and the quest for adventure in a place called 'Neverland', Peter Pan may well have struck a chord with adventurous manly men the world over.

Barrie introduced Scott to the actress Pauline Chase, then starring as Peter Pan, and the two were often seen dining together after the show. There were other women friends as well for this newly famous sailor: there was Mabel Beardsley for one – another young actress and a friend of his sister Ettie, who was also earning her living on the stage by this time.

Mabel was very keen on Scott for a while – and apparently so possessive of him they became quite the talking point among their mutual friends. It was Mabel who lived at 32 Westminster Palace Gardens and who, on that fateful day in 1907, invited Scott to a luncheon party along with her sculptor friend Kathleen Bruce.

Before the fame and the financial benefits of his explorations, women had been an undiscovered country for Scott. He had a loving mother and three loving sisters and doted on them all, but there had never been any women *friends*, no romance. There was his natural shyness for one thing – and from a practical point of view his relative poverty had always left him too poor for entertaining the ladies.

From now on, he was plotting a course towards the possibility of a wife and a family of his own – unfamiliar territory and fraught with dangers. What was required of the roles of husband and father? What does a manly man do when it comes to looking after the women and children?

The Birkenhead Drill

In the late January of 1917 a troopship left the port of Cape Town in South Africa bound for an undisclosed location in France. She was the SS Mendi, a steamship normally used for transporting mail but now chartered by the British Government. Aboard were more than 800 black soldiers of the South African Native Labour Corps (SANLC). They had been recruited from among the great tribes of South Africa – Xhosa, Pondo, Swazi, Basutho, Zulu – and were on their way to a Great War. But instead of fighting in the trenches they would be expected to fell trees, quarry stone, make roads, or work at the docks unloading cargoes of hay, coal, ammunition and other essential supplies. Many of the men had never been to sea before and were on their way to a world that was utterly foreign to them.

The Mendi was crewed by 33 British sailors and the trip north was uneventful for the first few weeks. By the early hours of the morning of 21 February they were in the English Channel, 11 nautical miles off the southernmost tip of the Isle of Wight. Their last berth had been in Plymouth and since leaving there on the 19th they had been escorted by the British destroyer HMS Brisk. The Channel is and was a body of water that demands respect from mariners and, at the height of the war, was being made even more dangerous by the lurking presence of German U-boats. It was bitterly cold and a heavy fog had settled upon the water, making navigation even more problematic than usual. The Brisk and the Mendi had cut their speed to a crawl.

Some time before dawn the troopship was involved in a collision with the SS Darro, a British steamship twice her size. 'Collision' makes it sound like a knock-for-knock accident. In fact the Darro was travelling at full speed and struck the starboard side of the Mendi so hard she almost cut the smaller vessel in two. Freezing water rushed into the jagged tear, filling the hold and instantly drowning hundreds of men as they lay sleeping in their hammocks and bunks below decks. Almost at once the ship began to keel over.

Those men still alive and able to move either threw themselves out into the water or scrambled up on to the open deck. The catastrophic damage to starboard had put all the lifeboats on that side of the ship out of action. Boats were lowered from the port side, carrying away handfuls of men, while others put on whatever lifejackets they could find and awaited the inevitable. The ship continued to roll slowly over into the cold black water.

The crew of HMS Brisk did all they could to help – putting boats into the water and rowing into the fog to pick up survivors – but for reasons no one fully understands to this day, nothing was done by the crew of the Darro. Her captain, Henry Winchester Stump, issued no orders and simply held off while a tragedy unfolded in front of him. The cries of the men in the water, though muffled by the fog and weakened by the cold, filled the night. At a subsequent official inquiry Stump would lose his Master's ticket for a year, which hardly seems like any punishment at all.

But as the panicked men of the SANLC gathered in knots upon the deck of the Mendi a familiar figure appeared among them, walking tall and with arms upraised. He was the Reverend Isaac Wauchope Dyobha and he had words to say to his fellow Africans.

'Be quiet and calm my countrymen,' he told them, 'for what is taking place is exactly what you came to do. You are going to die, but that is what you came to do. Brothers, we are drilling the death drill! I, a Xhosa, say you are my brothers. Swazis, Pondos, Basuthos, we die like brothers. We are the sons of Africa. Raise your war cries, brothers, for though they made us leave our assegais in the kraals, our voices are left with our bodies!'

And there on that sloping deck, as the waters rose to receive them, those sons of Africa kicked off their Army boots and stamped the steps of their death dance and let their voices rise high into the night sky to fly far away from that awful place.

Within 25 minutes the Mendi *was gone, sunk to the bottom of the English Channel. Nearly 650 soldiers and crew were lost along with her, drowned or dying where they floated in their lifejackets – killed by the effects of hypothermia. The Reverend Dyobha was among them, of course. It is still one of the worst disasters to have taken place in British waters.*

The loss of the Mendi *has been remembered longest in the oral histories of the South African tribes. It was reported in some newspapers at the time, but is a story largely lost to the world. Among the tribes they still say that news of what had happened reached Africa before the white men had time to write it down. The men's voices had been carried home with their spirits. Much later, there were commemorations and memorials. In life the men of the SANLC had been thought inferior to white soldiers – unfit to fight and die alongside them. Only in death were they accorded any respect.*

The sea is the graveyard for countless brave men. It has neither memory nor malice and yet time and again it has demanded unimaginable valour and courage from those who would ride upon it.

Some 65 years before the tragedy of the SS Mendi *another troopship had sailed between England and South Africa – in the opposite direction. For the events of 1914–18 were not the first to bring the white man together with the Xhosa, the Basutho, the Pondo, the Swazi or the Zulu for the atrocity of war; far from it.*

This time there were around 700 souls aboard – officers and men bound for the Cape Frontier War. There were also women and children, families of some of the officers. She was the HMS Birkenhead.

By the 1850s the armies of the British and of the Boers had been at war, off and on, with the people of the Xhosa tribe in the Eastern Cape of South Africa for as long as anyone could remember. Squabbles about rights to land had begun in the late 1770s between the Dutch and the amaXhosa, and then gradually escalated into full-blown battles. The British allowed themselves to be swept up into the fight – as the British invariably do – and now after several decades there was still no end in sight. Historians have given numbers to these wars and by 1852 the British forces in the Cape needed reinforcements for their continuing efforts to secure victory in the eighth round.

In January 1852 the iron-hulled, ocean-going paddle steamer HMS *Birkenhead* – one of the first of her kind – left Portsmouth with fresh soldiers bound for what they called in those days 'the Kaffir Wars'. The ship was something of an oddity, fully rigged for sail but gaining most of her forward propulsion from two huge paddle wheels mounted amidships. She'd been launched in 1845 in Birkenhead on Merseyside from the famous shipyard operated by the Laird family and, at just over 200 feet long and weighing 1,400 tons, was originally designed to be a powerfully armed frigate. But the Admiralty saw her as something between a ship of sail and a ship of steam, and since they couldn't quite decide what to do with her, simply consigned her to service as a troop carrier. Her captain was Robert Salmond, RN, and his family had been sending its sons to the sea since the time of Queen Elizabeth I.

She journeyed first to Cove of Cork, in southern Ireland, where she collected more soldiers and horses. As far as fighting men went, these were as green as could be. Most had signed up just weeks before, to escape the long-drawn-out horror of the potato famine that had blighted Ireland throughout the 1840s, and had had precious little in the way of training by the time they clumped awkwardly up the gangplanks and on to the deck of the *Birkenhead*. Perhaps they had notions of finding adventurous new lives in far-flung places; more likely they were just attracted by the prospect of three square meals a day.

From Ireland they headed south, and to war. The largest single draft aboard consisted of 66 men of the 74th Regiment, later to become part of the Highland Light Infantry. They were commanded by the strapping six-foot-three-inch figure of

Lieutenant Colonel Alexander Seton, a 38-year-old Scotsman. As it turned out, he was imbued with more than enough sense of discipline to provide a share for every man aboard. He had been ordered to South Africa to replace Lieutenant Colonel Fordyce, who had been killed in action, and as the senior military figure aboard the *Birkenhead* it would be his job to whip those raw recruits he had inherited into some sort of recognisable shape.

It is hard to come up with accurate figures but it seems likely that well over 600 men had filed up the gangplanks by the time the *Birkenhead* departed for South Africa. There were also women and children aboard, though again the loss of muster rolls makes it impossible to say how many. It wasn't unusual for officers to take their families on campaign with them at that time – and perhaps the presence of women and children improved the atmosphere aboard the ship for the several weeks of the journey.

Seton made good use of the time afforded him as the ship headed south. On deck the men were put through their paces – drilling, exercising and learning what it was to be a soldier in the Army of Queen Victoria. He also worked at overcoming the divisions between the different regiments aboard and sought to establish something amounting to *esprit de corps*.

The *Birkenhead* made stops at several African ports along the way, and during the last week in February they arrived in the port of Simon's Bay, near Cape Town. They were just two days from their final destination of Port Elizabeth, in Algoa Bay. Some time in the afternoon of the 25th, fully loaded with fresh water and other supplies, they set out on the final leg of the trip. Captain Salmond was now under orders to cover the last few miles as quickly as possible, but still he was relaxed and unconcerned. The sky was of the clearest blue when they departed and there was only a light wind. The conditions were perfect. He was as experienced as any man of his rank in the

Royal Navy and he expected the next two days to go off without incident of any kind.

The *Birkenhead* was making about eight or nine knots, her steam-powered paddle wheels pounding rhythmically upon the waves and driving her steadily south-east. To make the fastest time possible, she was hugging a line just three miles out from the South African shore. So close in, there was always a possibility of grounding on some or other uncharted sandbank, and so an experienced sailor was using a lead weight, on the end of a long line, to measure the clearance between the hull and the seabed. There were lookouts stationed fore and aft, officers on the bridge and sailors on watch all around. Captain Salmond was so reassured by his own precautions he had gone below to sleep.

Just before two o'clock in the morning of 26 February a sailor's voice broke the silence of the night. It was the leadsman, reporting the depth as he had been doing for the past many miles: 'Sounding 12 fathoms,' he said. There was nothing to worry about and all was well.

Minutes later there came another reassuring voice, another part of the night-time routine aboard ship: 'Four bells, sir,' said the sailor, telling the duty officer it was the halfway mark of the Middle Watch.

No sooner had that officer given his reply of 'Strike them,' than the *Birkenhead* ran full-tilt on to a submerged reef of rock. They were in an area known generally as Danger Point, but the rocks with which they had collided were not marked on any chart. It was just bad luck.

All of that was meaningless detail now. The ship had grounded so hard, her paddle wheels continuing to push her forward even after the initial impact, that her bow had been ripped wide open between the forepeak and the engine room. The sea poured into the hull, instantly flooding the sleeping quarters of scores of the men. Most of them were drowned where they lay.

Captain Salmond, thrown from his bed by the impact,

appeared on deck moments later, half-dressed. Shocked he may have been, but he was also an old Navy hand and quickly into action for the sake of his ship, his crew and his passengers. He was barking orders left and right – ordering his men to assess the damage and report back to him. He dispatched others to round up the women and children and bring them up on deck at once. Distress rockets arced across the night sky. They'd been loosed out of force of habit, but there was no help to be had within miles.

As quickly as Salmond had made it on to the deck, Lieutenant Colonel Seton appeared too, dressed in his night clothes but with his sword belted around his waist. The peaceful sleep of minutes before was more distant now than home, and here he was, surrounded by confused and injured men who needed him as never before. Half naked, dazed, barefoot and frightened, the survivors of that first impact were crawling up on to the deck and counting themselves lucky to have lived so long. Some of them were terribly injured, but there was nothing to be done for them now.

Salmond's crewmen needed help with the pumps and Seton immediately placed 60 of the able men at the captain's disposal. He gathered his officers to him then and told them that all hope lay with their ability to maintain order.

The manner in which he chose to do that – the words he chose and the tone of his voice – were the measure of the man and of the army that had made him: 'Gentlemen – would you please be kind enough to preserve order and silence among the men and ensure that any orders given by Captain Salmond are instantly obeyed,' he said.

No sooner had Seton finished than the captain called for help to lower the lifeboats. Sailor and soldier alike united for the job – but found to their dismay that the chains and winches had either been painted over or left to rust, stopping them working. Only three boats out of an available eight could be lowered – two eight-oared cutters and a gig. What was instantly obvious was that there was to be no salvation for most of the people aboard. They were at least three miles from land and would be going into water known to be thick with sharks, including Great Whites.

Although he never actually used the words, 'Women and children first,' Seton made it clear to everyone aboard just who would be taking up the first places in the available boats. The officers' families had been safely rounded up and were now ushered aboard one of the cutters. Wives cried out for husbands and children for their fathers, but there was nothing else for it. Nothing like this had ever been done before, aboard a naval vessel or any other. Previously when all hope was lost, it had been every man for himself. But here aboard the *Birkenhead* the past was erased and the future shaped. The young officers and men of the 74th and the other regiments were about to set a new standard.

Seton selected a young ensign of the 74th, 19-year-old Alexander Cumming Russell, to take charge of the women and children's cutter and see it to safety. Fearing the worst, Seton then positioned himself at the foot of the gangplank leading aboard the little boat and drew his sword. He was ready to repel any would-be boarders – but not one man stepped out of line.

Instead they remained where their officers had told them to be. Some in night clothes, some half-dressed in their uniforms and some naked, they had come to order. Shoulders back, eyes front and chins up, they looked into the starry southern sky while the women and children were rowed away from the *Birkenhead*.

The places in the remaining serviceable lifeboats were filled using the system the Army has always called 'Funeral Order' – youngest first – and these too were lowered into the sea and rowed clear of the ship.

Thinking he might move his vessel off the rocks that had holed her, Salmond ordered the engines to be put into reverse. If they could get out into open water, he thought, perhaps the buoyancy trapped in other parts of the ship would keep her afloat. As it turned out, the effect of his plan was catastrophic. A second rip was torn through the iron plates of the hull and now seawater gushed into the engine room as well. The fires heating the boilers were immediately extinguished by the deluge and smoke and steam billowed up on deck from below. With that final hope dashed, Salmond issued an order to have all the horses led into the sea. The terrified animals were blindfolded before being manhandled out of their stalls and into the water. But although it had been thought they might strike out for land, most were quickly drowned or taken by sharks, their whinnies and screams serving as a foretaste of what might be to come.

Some time then the *Birkenhead* broke her back upon the reef. She started to lean crazily, but still Seton called for order from his officers and men, willing them to hold their places. And there they stayed, neatly in their lines as the deck bucked and slid beneath them. The ship's funnel finally gave in to the forces of gravity and snapped off at its base. It tumbled down on to the deck, killing or maiming a group of soldiers and sailors as they worked to try to free another of the lifeboats.

Captain Salmond had climbed up into the rigging – either to try to stay clear of the water or to find a better place from which to address the soldiers. From his perch he shouted at them to get into the water now and swim towards the lifeboats.

'Save yourselves while you still can,' he called. 'Those of you who can swim – jump overboard and swim towards the boats. It is your only hope of salvation.'

Hearing him, Seton raised his sword above his head and

shouted out to his soldiers. He knew what must be done, what must be endured, and his voice cracked with the emotion of it all: 'You will swamp the cutter containing the women and children,' he cried. 'I implore you not to do this thing and I ask you all to stand fast!'

Not a man broke ranks, though the deck rose beneath them and only the sea and the sharks awaited. The officers took up the call too – urging their men to hold the line. And so they did. Green youngsters they might have been when they boarded the *Birkenhead*, but they were men now. Their last remaining duty was to preserve the lives of the women and children and that was what they were going to do.

As the water rose around them, and while the women, children and youngest of the soldiers looked on from the little boats, the officers and soldiers shook hands with one another and said goodbye. One man's voice rose above the din of the ship's dying: 'God bless you all,' he said. 'God bless you all!'

Captain Wright of the 91st Regiment, who made it away from the wreck and lived to fight another day, said later:

The order and regularity that prevailed on board, from the moment the ship struck till she totally disappeared, far exceeded anything that I had thought could be affected by the best discipline; and it is the more to be wondered at, seeing that most of the soldiers were but a short time in the service.

Every man did as he was directed and there was not a cry or a murmur among them until the vessel made her final plunge. All received their orders and had them carried out as if the men were embarking instead of going to the bottom of the sea; there was only one difference, that I never saw any embarkation conducted with so little noise or confusion.

Quickly now the ship began to slip beneath the waves. Soon only the top parts of her masts and rigging were visible and pockets of men clung there before their strength failed them and they disappeared. For many of those in the water, time was short. Sharks circled for a while and then, emboldened by numbers, began to move in for the kill. Men cried out as the great fish closed on them and plucked away one after another. Who could have imagined such a thing? Hundreds of impoverished young men, who had left behind a country blighted by famine in hope of a better life, ending up as food for sharks. In spite of all that irony and agony, not one made a move for the three lifeboats standing off many yards distant but still within reach.

Driven beyond endurance by what they were witnessing, however, the women in the cutter commanded by Ensign Russell eventually insisted it be rowed back towards the struggling men. None of the soldiers would reach out to accept the help being offered to them, none would disobey his orders. One family spotted their father and called out to him. He too refused to approach, but Ensign Russell jumped into the water and helped the man to take his place in the cutter. Seeing the husband and father reunited with his family, the teenager struck out for shore. He was taken by sharks before he had made 20 strokes, and disappeared from sight.

He was not alone. In all more than 430 men died that morning. Captain Salmond was killed when one of the ship's masts fell on top of him. Lieutenant Colonel Seton was last seen among his men, but perished along with most of them.

Every single woman and child was saved.

There were other miracles too: one young officer managed to swim the three miles to the shore and, when he clambered gratefully out of the surf, found his horse standing there waiting for him. Some hours later, the schooner *Lioness* came across one of the lifeboats and took the survivors aboard. She carried on until she reached the scene of the tragedy and her crewmen managed to pull some more survivors out of the water. Fewer than 200 had lived to tell the tale of the *Birkenhead*.

News of the loss did not reach Britain until April – but the reports from the survivors ensured a place in legend for the officers and soldiers who had given their lives for the sake of the few. When the King of Prussia, Frederick Wilhelm, later the first German emperor, was told of the event, he ordered that an account of it be posted in every barracks of his army. This, he said, was the standard of behaviour he expected from his men.

By their actions, Seton and his men changed maritime protocol for ever. The cry of 'Women and children first' is more properly described as 'the Birkenhead Drill'. This then is their memorial and their greatest monument.

Half a century later, Kipling immortalised the greatness of it all in his poem, 'Soldier an' Sailor Too', which he dedicated to the Royal Marines:

> To take your chance in the thick of a rush, with firing
>   all about,
> Is nothing so bad when you've cover to 'and, an' leave
>   an' likin' to shout;
> But to stand an' be still to the Birken'ead drill is a damn
>   tough bullet to chew,
> An' they done it, the Jollies – 'Er Majesty's Jollies – soldier
>   an' sailor too!
> Their work was done when it 'adn't begun; they was
>   younger nor me an' you;
> Their choice it was plain between drownin' in 'eaps an'
>   bein' mopped by the screw,
> So they stood an' was still to the Birken'ead drill, soldier
>   an' sailor too!

The last word on the matter comes from a history of the 74th. The action taken by the men during the *Birkenhead* tragedy, it said:

> ... sheds more glory upon those who took part in it than a hundred well-fought battles.

For England's sake and duty

I first read about the Birkenhead Drill in one of my mum and dad's copies of the *Reader's Digest*. The story featured in one of the magazine's regular sections under the heading 'Drama in Real Life' – 1,500 words usually given over to accounts of hapless kids falling down wells on their parents' farms in the Australian outback, or hunters in Africa cornered by rogue elephants or man-eating lions. But this story about a Victorian shipwreck was different. For a start, there was no happy ending – which was usual from the pages of 'Drama in Real Life' – and furthermore, the way those soldiers had behaved in their final moments was no accident.

I'd recently seen the film *Jaws* for the first time as well, so treading water in a shark-infested sea was particularly easy for me to visualise that year. In particular, I remembered the monologue by Robert Shaw, Captain Quint of the *Orca*, about most of the crew of USS *Indianapolis* being eaten alive by sharks after they delivered the Hiroshima bomb in 1945.

That was another true story, but those American sailors had been lost in the open sea beyond sight of land and with no hope of rescue. The soldiers from the *Birkenhead*, on the other hand, were within swimming distance of three lifeboats, albeit lifeboats packed with women and children. Most of them were just young – teenagers some of them, probably. They didn't know those women and children personally, didn't owe them anything – so why had they sacrificed themselves to save them? Why had they chosen grisly death over a chance at life? How had they found the strength to do such a thing? I thought about it for weeks.

Scott might well have imagined it was a quiet life he was after – but events conspired to shape his destiny in a different way. As part of the quest for normality – and the resumption of his Navy career – he'd joined HMS *Victorious* as flag-captain in August 1906. Soon afterwards, while on duty in the Mediterranean, fate ensured his path crossed again with that of Sir Clements Markham. The old man made it quite clear to Captain Scott that the further exploration of Antarctica was the patriotic duty of Englishmen – if any flag were to be raised over the South Pole it must be the Union Jack.

Duty is an old-fashioned concept now, as outmoded as the wearing of caps and standing up when a lady enters the room. Boys and men hardly ever talk about it – and when they do it's only to describe the allocated time spent by soldiers in Iraq or Afghanistan: a *tour of duty*. But there was a time when duty was an unavoidable responsibility. If you were born male, you had a duty to live up to that birthright and not let the side down. Nobody chose duty. It just arrived along with an Adam's apple, a deeper voice and the need to shave.

For Captain Robert Falcon Scott, duty was everything. When an elder of the tribe like Sir Clements Markham had to *remind* you of your duty, you were already perilously close to resigning as a male, let alone as a manly man. There was no choice in the matter of duty – no opt-out clause and no alternative. It wasn't like choosing home economics instead of physics, or a letter from your mum instead of cross-country running. When those soldiers of the *Birkenhead* went into the water, and as the big fish circled ever closer, they knew it was right and proper that the women and children were safe in the boats. By staying put and accepting their fate they weren't just obeying orders. They were doing their duty.

In Scott's world, examples of duty – and of duty *done* – were all around. If you needed reminding, you only had to look back into the recent past.

The Thin Red Line and the Charge
of the Light Brigade

As World War II in Europe entered its closing stages in 1945, Roosevelt, Stalin and Churchill met in the town of Yalta, in the Crimea, to discuss the coming spoils. During a break in the talks Churchill asked Stalin if he might be allowed to visit a nearby battlefield. Stalin gave his permission and Churchill was taken to a valley near the harbour town of Balaclava on the Black Sea.

As recently as the previous year the area had been the scene of savage fighting, when the last of as many as 100,000 Soviet troops had died fighting uphill against heavily fortified German positions. The whole place was peppered with ordnance – both spent and unexploded. Between 1942 and 1944 something like 10 tons of high explosive were detonated for every square metre of ground there. Today the place is given over to vineyards that produce a good-quality sparkling white wine – and still the soil is thick with shell fragments, bullet cases and pulverised human bones.

It wasn't the latest horror that interested Churchill, however. Instead he wanted to cast his historian's eye over the site of a cavalry charge that had taken place over some of the same ground nearly a century before. Churchill was no stranger to the tactics of cavalrymen – as a 24-year-old he had taken part in the British Army's last ever cavalry charge at a place called Omdurman, during the Sudan campaign of 1898 – and believed he had conducted himself with all the sangfroid required of an Englishman. 'I never felt the slightest nervousness,' young Winston told his mother afterwards. 'I felt as cool as I do now.'

With such experience under his belt, he wanted to look over terrain described by the poet Tennyson as 'The Valley of Death'. For here near Balaclava were the scenes of two moments immortal in all the history of war – performed during the most famous few hours of chaos *ever deliberately unleashed by fighting men. Madness and heroism, futility and flair, quixotic dash and monumental stupidity – all of that and everything else besides was there, in the Thin Red Line and the Charge of the Light Brigade.*

During the middle years of the 19th century, great European powers circled like vultures around the ailing Ottoman Empire. Left behind by the industrialisation of Russia and the nations of the West, it had long since ceased to wield the power and influence of its glory days. Under the reign of Suleiman I – Suleiman the Magnificent (1520–66) – its territory had stretched from Persia to Morocco and from the Austrian border to Yemen. But during the 18th century its control and influence had begun slowly and steadily to evaporate in the heat of industrial revolution elsewhere.

Already picking at the living flesh was Tsar Nicholas, who saw in the 'sick man' an opportunity too tempting to resist. Russia's southward expansion via the Bosphorus had always been blocked at Constantinople, modern-day Istanbul. By swallowing the right parts of the Ottoman Empire, he knew, his Black Sea Fleet could make its way through that narrow waterway, past the Dardanelles and out into the rich pickings of the Mediterranean. For as long as the old empire was in its weakened state, Europe's back door was effectively open.

Britain and France had other ideas, however. The prospect of Russia making uncontested land-grabs on Europe's eastern extreme – and then sending her ships south and west – was hardly one they relished. Subtle (some might say underhand) diplomacy by all parties eventually ran its course. The Russian Black Sea fleet surprised and destroyed the Turkish fleet at its base at Sinope and her troops were sent across the Danube. The time for talking had apparently passed, and Britain, France and Russia, together with their various allies, stumbled into what some historians have described as the first 'world' war.

Of all the protagonists, Britain had the least business making war on a modern adversary. Since the final crushing of Napoleon at Waterloo in 1815, Britain had exercised her aggressive side only on tribal peoples in territories like India and southern Africa. The British Empire had begun to grow during this time – but as a by-product of trade. That part of the globe coloured pink grew larger in those years not because Britain wanted to conquer, but out of a desire to harvest the riches of the wider world.

Fighting and conquest were really the least of it. As a result, in the years following the Napoleonic era Britain's Army sank into the decline of neglect. In India the necessary fighting was conducted not by the British Army as such but by the privately maintained forces of the East India Company. In southern Africa, Britain's adversaries came armed only with spears and shields. The British Army had a more clearly defined role as a police force than as a weapon for extending frontiers and by the 1820s it numbered no more than 80,000 men. By the end of the 1840s the strength was up to 100,000, but when the need arose for a force capable of tackling Tsarist Russia, in 1854, it wasn't just a question of numbers.

The six British divisions that boarded ships for transport to the Crimea – five of infantry and one of cavalry – were handicapped first and foremost by a lack of back-room organisation. Since 1815 the whole infrastructure of the British Army had either been allowed to atrophy or been cut away altogether. Gone was the wagon train, the means of supplying an army fighting in far-off places. Gone too was the staff office, that part of the Army whose job it is to keep abreast of the whole nature of warfare – most crucially, what the other guys are doing. What was left of the organisational framework could be described as a bugger's muddle. Control was spread across more than a dozen different Government departments, whose various duties overlapped.

Just as bad was the perpetuation of the tradition that favoured class over training and ability when it came to career advancement. The British Army of 1854 was one that still looked down its nose at the 'intellectual' soldier who had bothered to study his craft and learn the lore of tactics and intelligent command. During the Napoleonic Wars, Sir John Moore and his ilk had begun the process of modernising the Army to take account of ability, but during the peaceful years that followed Waterloo the momentum of change was lost. In the 1850s, therefore, rank was still something you bought and the upper classes knew, without having to think about it, that the ability to lead men to victory was a product of breeding, nothing more and nothing less.

To make matters worse, the Duke of Wellington, the Iron Duke who had destroyed Napoleon and freed Britain from decades of nightmare and fear of invasion – had been the anti-quated system's strongest supporter. He had died in 1852 but the shadow he cast over the Army was as persistent as it had been during his lifetime. The problem, of course, was that the Iron Duke had been one of the greatest military geniuses of his own or any other age. If there were deficiencies in the way the Army ran its affairs under his command, then it mattered not a jot. All the time he was in overall charge, his daring and vision had been enough to transcend any obstacle and disguise any shortcoming of the tools he used to get the jobs done.

But the Iron Duke was gone now, and the first question that had faced the Government, as war with Russia loomed closer, was who to place in command of the British force. Europe had been at peace since 1815 and the Army's senior figures had pursued their trade elsewhere, if at all. The commander-in-chief, Lord Hardinge, was nearly 70 and far too old for the job of leading an army in far-off, foreign climes. Several of the other tried and tested warhorses, veterans of India and elsewhere, were older still. In the end the top job went to Lord Fitzroy James

Henry Somerset, 1st Baron Raglan. Given his CV, he had nearly been the obvious choice in any case.

At the outbreak of the Peninsular War in 1808, just five years after his father bought him a commission in a cavalry regiment at the age of 15, young Somerset was made aide-de-camp to one Arthur Wellesley. By the time Wellesley was created Duke of Wellington after his narrow but vital victory at the Battle of Talavera the following year, the pair were firm friends as well as colleagues. The relationship would remain close for the rest of the Duke's life.

During the fighting at Waterloo, Raglan's right elbow was shattered by a French musket ball. The arm had to be amputated below the shoulder – without anaesthetic and with knife and saw – but he made not a sound until the surgeon tossed the severed limb into a basket.

'Hey, bring my arm back,' he said. 'There's a ring my wife gave me on the finger.'

The wife who had given him the ring was none other than the Iron Duke's own niece, and Raglan was the Iron Duke's man. He was 66 years old when Britain went to war with Russia – clearly knocking on a bit himself – and was placed at the head of a set of divisional commanders that could hardly be said to inspire confidence.

Sir George de Lacy Evans, in charge of the 2nd Division, was the best of them. He was 67 years old, but a decorated soldier who had seen celebrated action in Spain, India and America. The Duke of Cambridge, the Queen's own cousin, led the 1st Division. He was young at least – just 35 and one of only two of the divisional commanders aged under sixty at the start of the war – but had never taken battlefield command in his life. The 3rd Division was led by Sir Richard England, who up until that time had made no impact of note on the story of the British Army, and the 4th by the unremarkable Sir George Cathcart. The 5th and last infantry division was commanded by Sir George Brown, whose reputation was primarily that of a vicious disciplinarian whose men feared rather than respected him.

The portents for disaster were most glaringly obvious in the Cavalry Division. Overall command was given to George Charles Bingham, 3rd Earl of Lucan. He had all the necessary pride and sense of grandeur required to carry off the role of commanding the Army's mounted men – but little else. His birthright and wealth had enabled him to buy his way into the highest levels (he had once purchased the command of the 17th Lancers for the rumoured sum of £25,000), but his active military experience was minimal. If the 54-year-old was known for anything at all, it was snobbish arrogance. Under his command, the 17th Lancers had become an over-dressed, over-disciplined and decidedly unhappy body of men. It did not bode well.

On the bright side, Brigadier-General James Scarlett, a man respected and trusted by his men, commanded the Heavy Brigade. On the dark side, the Light Brigade had at its head a man even more comprehensively loathed than Lord Lucan. James Thomas Brudenell, 7th Earl of Cardigan, was another strutting fop whose family name – and family money – had secured him a status he could never have obtained any other way. Though he was now in command of the Light Horse, he had no experience of leading men into battle. Rather more worrying than any of this, however, was the state of Cardigan's personal relationship with his divisional commander. The two men were brothers-in-law but Lucan had split acrimoniously from his wife Anne, Cardigan's sister. The separation had happened years before but Cardigan bore a seething grudge.

Weaknesses at the top of the pyramid of command hardly eased or improved the lot of the men at the bottom. In the middle years of the 19th century the enlisted men of the British Army were as poorly regarded by their leaders as they had ever been. Life in the ranks still beckoned only to those who had nowhere else to go – the poor and the wretched, men routinely described as the dregs of humanity. They were brutally disciplined and poorly paid and yet in time of war they were the people depended upon by the very society that despised them. The Iron Duke himself once said: 'I don't know what they do to the enemy, but by God they frighten me!'

And yet for all the shortcomings and outright failings, these were the men – rich and poor, empowered and oppressed – of whom legends were about to be made. Immortality would be assigned to them not because of who or what they were, but because of what they were about to do.

A site on the Dardanelles peninsula was the base of operations originally proposed for the British, but an advance party concluded that the available site was poorly supplied with fresh water and, in any case, too far from the Black Sea. If you're going to embark on a bit of good old-fashioned posturing, you want your opponent to be close enough to see you flexing your muscles. Scutari, across the Bosphorus from Istanbul, was chosen as the alternative.

It was here that the British forces came face to face for the first time with their French brothers-in-arms. Right away they saw that their allies were far better supplied with the accoutrements of war. In particular they noticed that the French medical supplies were wholly superior to anything on their own side.

Lord Raglan's opposite number was the proud and ambitious Marshal Armand-Jacques Leroy de St Arnaud, and almost at once the Frenchman sought to have himself placed in command of the Turkish forces as well as his own. Raglan demonstrated his talent for diplomacy by persuading St Arnaud that all three armies should retain a degree of independence from one another, and it has to be said that despite their differences the French and British fighting men at every level demonstrated a willingness to work together.

From their base at Scutari, the British moved up first of all towards the Black Sea port of Varna. This was at the request of the Turkish commander, Omar Pasha, who wanted both French and British troops to be on hand to help force an end to the Russian siege of Silistria on the River Danube. Austria, on her own account, had already massed troops on the Transylvanian border, and in the face of all that opposition, Russia pulled her forces back into the motherland.

Instead of stopping at that point, short of any bloodshed and with Russia seemingly acknowledging her neighbours' consternation about her expansionist behaviour, the Allies pressed on. The principal objective remained the Russian naval base at Sebastopol on the Crimea, and in all likelihood Britain would never have stopped short of an outright assault on the city. Russia had to be put in her place, and the Black Sea Fleet had to be tackled.

During the third week in September a combined Allied force of British, French and Turkish infantry and cavalry numbering around 60,000 men landed on a wide, shallow bay at a place called Kalamita on the Crimean coast. Sebastopol was two days' march away to the south-east and the huge army began its lumbering advance on 19 September. On the morning of the following day they found their way blocked by the River Alma and a Russian force of 40,000 men, commanded by Prince Alexander Menshikov, deployed on high ground above them. The battle that followed was a victory for the Allies – but, in every way that mattered, an inconclusive one.

The fighting began at 1.30 p.m. with an artillery bombardment – and when the French advanced on the right they drove the Russians in front of them so quickly they brought *themselves* to a halt for fear of losing touch with their British comrades.

On the left, the British had embarked upon a full-frontal assault of strongly defended Russian positions in hope of supporting the French, but found themselves bogged down by heavy fire. It was largely the strength and commitment of the Highland Brigade, commanded by Brigadier-General Sir Colin Campbell, that maintained the British sense of purpose and kept the advance moving. By around 4 p.m. the Allies had broken the Russian front line along its entire length, and were in position up on the plateau to turn the retreat into a rout. But Lord Raglan passed up the chance of outright victory – and perhaps an early end of the war. Fearing that the Russians were retreating in good order – and that his own forces might be drawn into a trap – he decided against unleashing his own cavalry. The Russian forces lived to fight another day and the Allies were faced now with the prospect of following them all the way to Sebastopol and besieging them there. Raglan's caution would cost him dearly.

While the Allies considered their options – notably how best to approach Sebastopol – the Russians used the time to prepare the defences around their city. The work was overseen by Lieutenant-Colonel Franz Edward Todleben, a military engineer of genius, and in short order he repaired and strengthened the city's perimeter. By the time the Allies arrived, his work was complete and six great bastions faced the attackers – the Quarantine, the Central, the Flagstaff, the Redan, the Malakoff and the Little Redan. It was a cordon to strike fear and trepidation into the hearts of any would-be attackers.

Some historians have insisted that had Raglan and St Arnaud taken the initiative and chased their foes back towards the city in the heat of the Battle of the Alma, the main prize could have been taken before Todleben had time to get the job done. Instead the Allies faced the prospect of an army dug in on the motherland with nothing to do but fight to the death.

After waiting at the Alma long enough to bury their hundreds of dead and dispatch the wounded to the misery of hopelessly inadequate field hospitals back at Scutari, the Allies began their march towards Sebastopol on the 25th. Rather than tackle the place from the north, the commanders marched their men around towards the south of the city and by 26 September they were at the harbour town of Balaclava. It was from here that St Arnaud was placed aboard a ship to carry him back to Constantinople. He had been sick from the start of the campaign and by now was dangerously ill. He would die before the sea journey was over.

French command was now in the hands of General François-Certain Canrobert – known to the British squaddies as 'Bob-can't' – and he insisted on a further delay in fighting until he could get his heavy guns into position for the assault on Sebastopol. More waiting for the men, more time for the Russians to prepare the welcome for their guests.

Word of the victory at the Alma reached Britain by the start of October. But along with that happy news came a report of the conditions being endured by the Queen's wounded soldiers at Scutari. It was a tale of misery, disease and, most gallingly of all, inadequate medical provision. Why, asked the British public, were Her Majesty's troops being so neglected after spilling their blood on her behalf? Among those who stepped up in response – not to answer the question but to try to ease the suffering – was one Florence Nightingale. A trained nurse, she rounded up a team of women and set out to see what could be done. History has shown that her methods became part of the short-term problem. Failure to understand the nature of disease and the importance of hygiene meant men would continue to die, and in even greater numbers. But in the long term her actions paved the way for the eventual review of the medical care of fighting men.

Such improvements were still a job for the future. The immediate task for Menshikov, safely ensconced at Sebastopol, was how to cut the Allied supply lines. He knew the port at Balaclava was vital to the British. Every boot and jacket worn, every morsel of food and drink consumed, every bullet and shell fired, came through that harbour from Royal Navy ships. Now Balaclava was the objective for the Russians themselves and Menshikov marshalled his forces for an attack designed to cut the British throat.

On high ground above the harbour town were British, French and Turkish soldiers. They were calling the high points 'Canrobert's Hill' and 'Causeway Heights' and had created a linked series of redoubts from which to defend them. On 25 October a massed Russian force numbering 25,000 infantry and accompanied by cavalry and heavy guns advanced towards the Allies. When the first news of the action began to filter through to Lord Raglan, he refused to believe the scale of it and carried on eating his breakfast. By the time he had wiped his chin and set off to work, the Russians were grinding their way through the defenders up on Causeway Heights.

Historians used to say the Turkish soldiers were the first to crack under the pressure – as though they quickly turned tail and fled. Nowadays it's acknowledged they fought and died where they stood, until a quarter of their number were cut down. Only then, after more than an hour of bloodshed, did the remainder begin to waver under the seemingly unstoppable advance, before withdrawing from their positions.

As the Russian infantry advanced and their cavalry hovered on the wings looking for their opening, they reached the Fedioukine Valley and the 93rd – the Sutherland Highlanders – under the command of 61-year-old Sir Colin Campbell. Here was a soldier who had fought and led with distinction in India and by rights should have been far higher up the chain of command in the Crimea. He had lacked the cash and the connections to secure his advancement, however, and perhaps it's just as well. For it was here in the Fedioukine that his moment came – his chance to show just who he was – and he drew a line that will be remembered as long as soldiers fight.

Lord Raglan and his staff were approaching the fray now, and from where they stood could see Campbell and his High-landers, together with a few hundred Turkish soldiers and British men of other regiments, up on the Heights. They could also see, thundering towards the British position, a massed force of Russian Horse. Surely, thought Raglan, an infantry force could not long stand in the face of cavalry in such numbers. He sent word to Lord Lucan to dispatch the Heavy Horse in support of the foot soldiers. But for now they could only watch as the Russian horsemen bore down on Campbell and his men.

The military textbooks made it clear that infantry survived best in the face of such an attack if they formed up four ranks deep – or better yet, in squares. But up on the slopes of the Fedioukine Valley, Campbell had neither the time nor the incli-nation to issue either order.

'I did not think it worthwhile to form them four deep,' he said later, cooler than cool. And he was right.

Instead he had his men form up in a line just two deep, armed with their French-designed Minie rifles, bayonets fixed and shoulder-to-shoulder. His Highlanders were at the centre, giving backbone to the formation, while the rest of the British soldiers and the Turks made up the left and right of the line. Mounted upon his horse, Campbell rode along the ranks to remind them what was at stake and what he expected of every man: 'Remember, there is no retreat from here,' he shouted. 'You must die where you stand.'

'Aye, Sir Colin,' replied John Scott, Campbell's aide-de-camp. 'Needs be we'll do that.'

Such was the stuff of which those men were made, and it caught the eye of war correspondent W.H. Russell, covering the war for the *Times* newspaper. He watched as the Russian horsemen galloped onwards: 'They dashed on towards that thin red streak, topped with a line of steel,' he wrote – a phrase misquoted almost ever since to give 'the thin red line' of legend.

'As the Russians came within 600 yards, down went that line of steel in front and out rang a rolling volley of Minie musketry.'

The cavalry advance was staggered, galled by the steel and the lead and the stubbornness of those bearded Highlanders. Some of the horsemen broke away towards their left, hoping to get around into the flank of the footsoldiers. But there was to be no success there either. Campbell wheeled part of his force around to the right, the better to face the encircling horse, and unleashed another rolling volley from even shorter range. Horses and riders fell. Not content with halting the cavalry, knots of the Highlanders now stepped forward, ready to make their own advance into the ranks of horsemen halted in front of them. It took another immortal line from their commander to pull them back into line.

'93rd!' he roared. 'Damn all that eagerness!'

The defence was holding against all the odds but Lord Raglan knew, as did Campbell, that the thin red streak could hardly be expected to hold back the Russian advance for ever.

General Scarlett's Heavy Horse, having found their way through orchards and vineyards that had blocked their advance, burst into view now on the slopes beneath. The 800 British horsemen, sabres in hand, were outnumbered four to one by their foes and, to make matters worse, were approaching from below. As before with Campbell's infantry, it was drill that made the difference in the end. While the Russian cavalry massed into position above them ready to engulf the inferior numbers below, they could only watch as Scarlett took the time to order his men into the perfect alignments befitting British fighting men. Content that all was as it should be, Scarlett ordered the attack and led from the front. Plunging into the packed mass of the enemy, he received five different wounds, while his aide-de-camp Lieutenant Elliot collected 14. The fighting was so claustrophobic, with men and horses hemmed in on all sides, that there was no room to use the sabres with the thrusting motion for which they were designed. Instead the men of the Inniskilling Dragoons, the Scots Greys and the Dragoon Guards had to hack and chop like butchers. After fewer than ten minutes of this horror, the Russian cavalry broke and fled.

It was an astonishing victory – first the defiance of the Highlanders, then the uphill charge by the Heavy Horse. While Raglan dispatched a rider with the three-word message of congratulation: 'Well done, Scarlett,' elsewhere on the field the unfolding wonder had been watched by less charitable eyes. Waiting with his Light Horse, still denied any chance to show his own mettle, Lord Cardigan could only look on with envy at the exploits of Scarlett and his men. When would *his* moment come?

As things turned out, he didn't have to wait for long. From his position on high ground, Raglan could see the charge by the Heavy Horse had caused disarray among the Russian forces – but the enemy were still in possession of the Causeway Heights. When he saw Russian soldiers moving forward to try to drag away the abandoned British guns, he resolved to throw the Light Horse into the fray.

A junior officer had already pleaded with Cardigan to order a charge towards the rattled enemy horse on the Heights. But Cardigan refused, and would later claim his orders from Lucan were to hold his position until infantry had been brought into position to support any mounted advance.

Raglan was beside himself with impatience at the apparent failure of the Light Horse to follow up the success of the Heavies. A new order was scribbled down. It read:

Lord Raglan wishes the cavalry to advance rapidly to the front – follow the enemy and try to prevent the enemy carrying away the guns. Troop Horse Artillery may accompany. French Cavalry is on your left. Immediate.

The note was handed to the hot-headed and arrogant Captain Louis Nolan – an officer known to dislike both Lucan and Cardigan. A rash decision it may have been, to entrust such a message to such a contrary figure, but it was widely understood that Nolan was the best horseman and best able to reach Lord Lucan in the shortest time.

In the event it took Nolan just a quarter of an hour to deliver the note. Lucan was horrified by it. While Raglan's more elevated position enabled him to see the enemy and the guns on the Causeway Heights, Lucan and Cardigan were on lower ground and had no such view. The only guns they could see were those of a heavily manned battery at the head of the valley, to the north. To make matters worse, those guns were protected by batteries of riflemen on both sides of the valley.

When Lucan suggested that such a move made no sense and would serve no function, Captain Nolan shouted out: 'Lord Raglan's orders are that the cavalry should attack immediately!'

'Attack, sir?' said Lucan. 'Attack what? What guns, sir? Where and what to do?'

Dripping with contempt, Nolan made a vague gesture out towards the valley.

'There, my lord! There is your enemy! There are your guns!'

It seems unbelievable that a junior officer would talk to his superior in this way – or that Lucan would accept what he was being told without seeking clarification. But so it was, and now he issued orders to Cardigan to attack the Russian guns at the head of the valley. Just to make sure no one was in any doubt, he trotted over to Cardigan himself and made clear what was expected.

The two implacable foes considered one another for a moment. Here towards them came a moment greater than anything that had divided them in their lives so far. Cardigan accepted the order but pointed out to his commander that the Russians had a defended battery across the valley floor and rifle batteries on both flanks.

'I know it,' said Lucan. 'But Lord Raglan will have it.'

More to himself than to anyone listening, Cardigan murmured: 'Here goes the last of the Brudenells.'

Then he turned to his men and gave the order to advance. As the 676 men of the Light Brigade began to trot towards the guns, Captain Nolan reappeared and galloped across their front, shouting something at Cardigan. Rather than returning to Raglan as he should have done, Nolan had apparently stayed behind to join the attack – a clear breach of protocol. No one is quite sure what inspired him to try to tell Cardigan something new. Had he finally understood that Lucan had issued orders to attack the wrong guns – and that he must do something to avert disaster? Or was he intent simply on urging the Light Brigade forwards? We will never know. Many yards before reaching Cardigan, a Russian shell burst close to Nolan and a shard of steel ripped into his chest, killing him instantly.

High above, Raglan looked on in mounting horror as he realised what his Light Brigade was about to attempt. Instead of pursuing the retreating Russian cavalry away from the Causeway Heights as he wanted them to do, they were trotting towards certain destruction in a valley Tennyson would later describe as 'the jaws of hell'.

In parade ground order the 4th and 13th Light Dragoons, the 17th Lancers and the 8th and 11th Hussars, all resplendent in their toy soldiers' colours, began to pick up the pace. None wavered, none held back. As they came into range of the Russian riflemen on either side of the valley, all hell was let loose upon them. The defenders could not believe what they were seeing and assumed the British cavalrymen were drunk. But drunk or sober, they became the targets for a withering hail of fire. On they came, at a steady trot, while the heavy guns to the front opened up on them as well. By the time they approached the gun battery itself they were entirely surrounded by fire. Men and horses were being cut to pieces all around. Survivors would report being splattered with the blood and brains of comrades, horses disembowelled beneath them. One rider was seen to be decapitated by an artillery round but his body stayed upright in the saddle, his lance still held level for the charge for many yards before he was finally unhorsed.

Perhaps the gun battery and the riflemen were so taken by surprise they were slow in getting into action – maybe lingering disbelief at what they were seeing slowed their reactions. In any case, the charge succeeded in reaching the guns. Once in among the gunners, the cavalrymen did as they had been trained with lance and with sabre. Then with nothing more to do – and with the massed Russian cavalry waiting to receive them behind the guns – the Light Brigade wheeled around and faced the return trip. Astonishingly, by the end of it there were 195 men still in their saddles. Of the rest, 107 were killed outright, 187 were wounded and 50 were unaccounted for. Somewhere between 400 and 500 horses were dead or had to be destroyed. Cardigan survived – and would later give an account of the event to the House of Commons. For now he was content to leave the field, returning to his yacht in the harbour at Balaclava to drink a bottle of champagne before going back to bed.

The Light Brigade, however, was destroyed. They had raised the reputation of the British cavalry to the highest possible levels, but their sacrifice had done nothing to further the Allied cause in the Crimean War.

With all hope of outright victory now squandered, the British and French soldiers had to settle down for a winter siege. Winter gave way to spring and then summer, and all around were dead and dying. The British forces in the Crimea would lose over 18,000 men before the end – 1,700 or more to the fighting and the rest to disease. In September 1855 the Russians evacuated the city and began negotiations for peace. The Treaty of Paris that ended it all was signed in February 1856. The fighting and the dying amid the stink of corpses had made no difference. The bright uniforms of the British and French were sullied in a way that would never come clean again.

What would be remembered, though, above all else, was that insane charge into the Valley of Death by the Six Hundred.

The French General Pierre-François Bosquet had been among the startled witnesses.

'C'est magnifique,' he said. 'Mais ce n'est pas la guerre.'

It was magnificent, but it was not war.

We're following the leader

Duty and patriotism were woven through every fibre of Captain Scott's character – that much has never been doubted. But it's worth remembering he was only human as well. News was soon circulating that Ernest Shackleton had been making noises about heading south once more. In December 1906 he wrote to a friend:

> What I would not give to be out there again doing the job, and this time really on the road to the Pole.

By early the following year the newspapers were reporting that Shackleton was definitely planning another attempt – what would eventually become the *Nimrod* expedition, which won him a knighthood – and it's easy to imagine that it was this as much as anything else that got Scott moving again. Another alpha dog sniffing around his territory – and Scott certainly believed he had made his proprietary mark on the continent – was bound to put his hackles up. From then on, the game was afoot.

But 1907 brought Scott a distraction of a quite different sort. From his first meeting with Kathleen Bruce, he had been besotted. She was the girl for him, and he was soon writing letters to his mother telling her so. Though slower off the mark than her suitor, Kathleen was eventually convinced that Scott was a man in possession of a first class honours degree in Manliness. She had found the father of her children. They were married on 2 September 1908 in the Chapel Royal at Hampton Court.

By January 1909 she was pregnant, and utterly convinced

she would have a boy. She wrote to her husband saying he should throw up his cap and shout triumphantly.

But there in the background for Scott was the presence of Shackleton. Neither of the men ever publicly acknowledged the great rivalry between them, but it was there just the same. The Americans were getting in on the act (Commander Robert Peary would make his controversial claim to have reached the North Pole in April 1909), so too the Norwegians, but it was Shackleton's efforts and ambitions that drove Scott hardest.

In March of that year the newspapers were full of the younger man's achievement of reaching to within 100 miles of the South Pole. The threat posed to Scott's pride by the possibility of being usurped in a domain he considered his by right was finally too great. By September he had published his plans to reach the South Pole and claim it as a prize for Great Britain. On 14 September, Kathleen gave birth to the son she had always wanted. They named him Peter Markham Scott.

For the return to Antarctica, Scott originally wanted the *Discovery*. She was unavailable, however, having been chartered by the Hudson Bay Company, and a replacement vessel would have to be found. In the end he settled on the *Terra Nova*, the 187-foot-long Norwegian whaling ship that had been one of the two relief vessels sent to recall Scott from his *Discovery* expedition in 1904.

There was also the question of funds to pay for it all. For Scott, the necessary round of public speaking and thinly disguised begging was as hard to swallow as it had been the first time around. He needed about £40,000, just less than £2 million in today's money, and in the end more than half of it came from the British Government. As before, much of the balance was made up by public subscriptions great and small. Young Oxford graduate Apsley Cherry-Garrard joined the team after donating £1,000 to the cause. The same sum was received from a captain of the 6th Inniskilling Dragoons, by the name of Lawrence E.G. 'Titus' Oates.

Even before he went public with his intention to head south for the second time – and this time to make the Pole his target – veterans of the *Discovery* expedition were drawing close to Scott once more. Not just those from 'officer class', like Edward 'Teddy' Evans, his second-in-command, and Dr Edward Wilson, head of the scientific staff, but also men from 'below decks' like chief stoker William Lashly, Tom Crean and Edgar 'Taff' Evans felt bound to serve with him again. There was no shortage of fresh volunteers either. Scott established an expedition head-quarters in London's Victoria Street and within days of the advertisements going out, the first of about 8,000 applications duly arrived.

Scott lacked Shackleton's showmanship and confidence in front of the general public, but men were drawn to his side nonetheless. Those who came to know this quiet, generally good-natured man also came to love him. In that way of all great leaders, he inspired loyalty just by being himself.

He was of course, from a long and illustrious tradition of inspirational Navy men.

The Battle of Trafalgar

Napoleon Bonaparte died in exile on the island of St Helena, in the South Atlantic, on 5 May 1821. A coffin was made for him from the timber of a mahogany dining table and lined with scavenged lead. It was carried on the shoulders of men of the 66th Regiment and laid in a stone-lined grave cut into the side of a peaceful valley beside a spring he had loved, beneath a willow tree.

When in 1840 his countrymen were granted permission to exhume the remains for a second burial in Paris, they found it a difficult job. As much effort had been put into imprisoning the late Emperor in death as in life. It took a team of labourers more than 10 hours to return the coffin to the light of day, but when it was opened all were amazed to find the body so well preserved it was as though he was still lying in state. The face was instantly recognisable and peaceful, the hands beautiful. He was taken home then, surrounded by much pomp and ceremony, and lies now in an elaborate sarcophagus beneath the dome of Les Invalides.

Napoleon had surrendered to the British on 15 July 1815, after final defeat at the Battle of Waterloo just a month before. The Duke of Wellington had called his victory 'the nearest-run thing you ever saw in your life', but it ended the career of the greatest warrior Europe had yet seen. And so when Napoleon climbed aboard the British warship Bellerophon *– a warship that had itself taken part in two legendary encounters of those Napoleonic Wars – her sailors were dumbstruck. Here among them at last was the tyrant, the monster they had learned to fear in childhood. What they saw was a plump little man who smiled at them and doffed his small cocked hat as he addressed their captain: 'I have come to throw myself on the protection of your Prince and laws,' he said politely.*

The Emperor had been the most formidable foe imaginable. He had placed the shadow of his hand right across Europe and his ambitions – not to mention his abilities – had seemed without limit. But by the time his dreams were finally brought to an end on the field of Waterloo, in modern-day Belgium, less than eight miles from the city of Brussels, he had already been taught the limits of his aspirations. What he had been made to learn, above all else, was that he was landlocked. Whatever he might achieve with his armies on mainland Europe, he knew that he and they would never be going anywhere else.

'If it had not been for you English, I would have been Emperor of the East,' he told the Bellerophon's *captain, Frederick Maitland, over dinner that evening. 'But wherever there is water to float a ship, we are sure to find you in our way.'*

Napoleon had finally been beaten at Waterloo – that much is certainly true – but his ambitions had been hobbled 10 years before. England's greatest hero, Lord Horatio Nelson, had completed that particular job of work on the afternoon of 21 October 1805 in the sea off the south-west coast of Spain, not far from the city of Cadiz, at a place called Cape Trafalgar.

Nelson was born in 1758, three miles from the sea in the Norfolk village of Burnham Thorpe. His father, Edmund, was the local parson – a man of modest means but occupying that particular stratum of society that traditionally sent its sons to be trained as naval officers. When at the age of 11 young Horatio – or Horace as he preferred to be known – said he wanted to go to sea, it was easily arranged. His uncle, Maurice Suckling, brother to his mother Catherine, was already a captain in His Majesty's Navy and more than happy to take his nephew with him.

Horace had been a sickly baby – so frail in fact his parents had had him baptised when he was only 10 days old, just to be on the safe side – and then hardly the sturdiest of boys. But despite all that, he showed promise as an officer right from the off. By 17 he was an acting lieutenant and by 20 had been promoted to captain – first of the brig *Badger* and then of the 32-gun frigate the *Hinchingbrooke*. He saw active service in the Americas, during the War of Independence, before being put on patrol duty in the West Indies. During that time he met and married the widow Fanny Nisbet, but the letters exchanged between the pair suggest it was a relationship of mutual respect rather than passion.

By the end of the 1780s they were back in Norfolk, living a quiet life while Nelson awaited his next ship. In 1793 he was made captain of the 64-gun *Agamemnon* – the vessel he would ever after describe as his favourite. War with France broke out again within weeks of his new assignment and for the next 12 years until his death, Nelson's star was usually in the ascendant – and his eagerness to fight put him in harm's way again and again.

In 1794, during a siege of French fortifications at Calvi, on the island of Corsica, he was blinded in his right eye. In February 1797 he was commanding the *Captain* as part of a fleet led by Lord Jervis when they encountered the Spanish fleet off Cape St Vincent. The battle that ensued was a sensational victory for the British, and at the height of it Nelson elevated himself to stardom by personally leading boarding parties to capture two Spanish warships in quick succession. In July of the same year, during a disastrous attack on the island of Tenerife, a musket ball smashed his right arm and elbow. He suffered the amputation with all the equanimity expected of a gentleman.

By 1798 Napoleon Bonaparte had declared that Europe was too small to provide him with enough glory – and Nelson was put in command of the fleet to find out precisely what the great general had in mind. The expedition culminated in the Battle of the Nile, a masterstroke choreographed by the British commander, in which the French were comprehensively crushed and Napoleon had to abandon his army to its fate in Egypt.

Hero though he already was both to the Navy and, increasingly, to the British people, Nelson was always able to put himself in jeopardy – and not always aboard warships or in the shadow of enemy forts. During 1798, still married to Fanny, he embarked upon his affair with Lady Emma Hamilton, herself a married woman. Having infuriated his superiors, he was briefly recalled to England. But he was already a personality too large in the imagination of the public to be kept out of action, or the limelight, for long.

Historians look back upon this period and call it 'The Age of Nelson' – and it was. But it was also the time when the Royal Navy itself had come of age. Their systems worked and the service had become one for which victory was second nature, almost routine. Nelson was surrounded by other men of greatness like Cuthbert Collingwood, William Cornwallis, Adam Duncan, Samuel Hood, John Jervis and Augustus Keppel – and much of what he achieved was made possible by this atmosphere of success in which he came to maturity.

It's almost traditional to imagine that life aboard the great ships of the line in the 18th century was one of unimaginable hardship, enlivened only by the occasional horror of a full-blown battle. But while it would certainly be a shock to most of us, it's important to remember that for the mass of the population in the 18th century, life was unimaginably hard by our standards whether lived at sea or on land. The great warships required a crew of 800 men or more, and conditions aboard were of necessity cramped and lacking in any kind of luxury, but they gave men something to belong to and to fight for. Food rations were usually plentiful – if repetitive – and crews understood that the conditions demanded stiff discipline if the ship was to function as a successful fighting unit. The press-gangs were still in operation, plucking civilians out of their lives and spiriting them away to the sea without the chance to say goodbye to family, but in effect this was no more than the system of conscription that would survive well into the 20th century.

Men like Collingwood, Cornwallis and Nelson ruled by example rather than by fear, in any case. They impressed their men with their skill, ability and personal bravery – and along the way they inspired genuine admiration and fondness. In the case of Nelson, of course, it was love. Some quality of his personality enabled him to reach people of every station, and the attentions he paid, the many little kindnesses he extended to those around him, won him adoration that lasted all his life.

Despite the disaster of Egypt and the Battle of the Nile, Napoleon too remained a rising star, by sheer force of will. In the December of 1799 he was made First Consul of the new French Consulate, and the following year crushed the Austrians at the Battle of Marengo. The nations of Europe were finding it easier to make peace with him than fight him. But always beyond his clutches was Britain – on the far side of that frustratingly narrow, yet impossibly wide 'ditch' of an English Channel.

Britain made its own peace with France – the Peace of Amiens – in March 1802. Napoleon saw to it, however, that it was an unhappy interlude and spent the time preparing for his own further aggrandisement. The peace came to an end, as it had to eventually, in the May of 1803, and Napoleon at once unrolled his plans to add Britain to his empire. Soon an army 160,000 strong was gathering on the French coast. It would fall to the Royal Navy, and to Nelson, to make sure those men would come no closer.

Looking out from Dover with a good telescope and a good eye it was possible to see the encampment of *la Grande Armée* – the Grand Army – spreading like mushrooms in the green fields. In harbours and ports the landing craft for the troops were being assembled. Menacing though these preparations were, the cool heads of the Admiralty understood one fact –

something that was certainly known to Napoleon as well: it was impossible to bring an army across the Channel without control of the sea.

The Royal Navy's initial solution to the problem was to keep the enemy ships trapped in all their harbours between Brest in the Bay of Biscay and Toulon in the Mediterranean. If they couldn't get into the open sea, they couldn't cause any trouble, far less clear the way for an invasion. The fulfilment of this objective was an achievement unequalled by seamen before or since.

While Nelson was given the task of monitoring the enemy navies in the relative calm of the Mediterranean, the job of hemming the French fleet, under the command of Admiral Ganteaume, into their base at Brest went to Cornwallis.

There is no one alive today who could begin to explain how Cornwallis and his men kept their fleet on station in those waters for month after month. The skills required to maintain mastery of the great timber ships of the line are long gone and will never be recovered. The conditions off the coast of Brest are challenging today for lone yachtsmen wishing only a safe passage. But the skills of navigation and seamanship required to keep an entire fleet of great ships of the line in position, static among those restless currents and ceaseless onshore winds, beggars belief. Whenever the French sailors looked out, in fair weather or in foul, the British ships were there. That great blockade remains a unique accomplishment, testament to the skills of a lost world.

When Napoleon finally lost patience with it all and ordered the fleets of France and Spain to sail first to the West Indies in a feint, and then back to the Channel to attack the British, he was acting out of pure petulance. Even the most ardent Bonapartist would have to admit that Napoleon was a land mammal. He may have crowned himself Emperor in December 1804, but the golden circlet he placed upon his own head conferred no understanding of the ways of the sea. He thought it was all about force of numbers – that the commander of the largest fleet would carry the day. He was wrong, of course, and Nelson would shortly show him why.

Towards the end of March 1805, Admiral Pierre-Charles Villeneuve reluctantly brought his fleet out of Toulon and made for the West Indies as he'd been instructed. Nelson chased him there and then followed his trail back across the Atlantic without ever managing to bring him to battle. The British Admiral returned to England, to spend some time with Emma.

Collingwood was on station off the coast of Cadiz when Villeneuve appeared. The Vice-Admiral had only a few ships and so simply stood away to allow the French ships access to the harbour. For the British sailors it was a depressing moment. It looked as though they would now begin yet another autumn and winter watching nothing happen at yet another enemy harbour. But Napoleon had reached the end of his tether and Villeneuve, believing he would shortly be replaced by his unhappy Emperor in any case, would shortly make one last roll of the dice.

Word of the French fleet's arrival at Cadiz was sent to England, and to Nelson, aboard the frigate *Euryalus.* Her captain, Thomas Blackwood, delivered the news to Nelson himself.

It was before dawn but Nelson was already up and dressed: 'I am sure you bring me news of the French and Spanish fleets and I think I shall yet have to beat them,' he said.

Blackwood left then, to inform the Admiralty. But Nelson was right. After just three weeks at home with his family, he had to leave and make his way to Portsmouth and the *Victory.* He joined the fleet off Cadiz on 28 September and, with all his famed diplomacy, gently replaced Collingwood in overall command.

The long game of cat and mouse came to an end at dawn on 21 October. As the sun rose above Cape Trafalgar the players stepped out on to the stage. To the astonishment of the watching British ships, Villeneuve's 33 sail emerged into open water.

Aboard the *Royal Sovereign*, Collingwood could hardly have seemed less impressed. When his servant entered his quarters just after daybreak he found his master shaving, just as he did every day.

'Have you seen the French fleet?' asked the Admiral, scraping more stubble from his chin with a slow, steady hand.

'No sir, I have not,' came the reply.

'Well, go and take at look at them,' said Collingwood. 'And in a little while you'll see a great deal more.'

While the sun balanced on the horizon, Nelson's ships began the ponderously slow business of forming into the two divisions he had ordered. Although a heavy swell was rolling in from the ocean, there was precious little wind and for many hours to come every movement of the fleet would be in slow motion.

Throughout the British fleet the men were piped to breakfast as usual. As the morning wore on, and the approach towards the enemy continued, the officers were to be seen in full dress uniform – the more conspicuous the better as far as British gentlemen were concerned. In time of battle it was the duty of officers to show their confidence and their bravery by taking up highly visible positions in full view of the foe. This was an era when nailing one's colours to the mast demanded both bravery and a certain flair.

Audible above the roll and wash of the waves was the sound of bands playing upon the decks of warship after warship. There was almost an air of celebration already, before a shot had been fired. Still the treacle-slow advance continued. For men on the open decks it was bad enough, but at least they could look at the scene around them and take in the sight of the distant French and Spanish fleets. But for those waiting below in the gloom of the gun-decks it must have been next door to intolerable. The wind was blowing no more than two or three knots and the fleets were closing upon each other at a speed slightly less than that required for a leisurely stroll. Men took turns to peer through the gun-ports and craned their necks to try to gauge the distance still to be travelled.

Aboard the *Victory* Nelson's simmering excitement was palpable. If Collingwood was the living embodiment of sangfroid, then the Lord Admiral seemed ablaze with the thrill of it all. He entered every battle convinced he was certain to die – and today was no different. But his fatalism seemed to thrill him, freeing him from fear and driving him always towards the place where he felt the greatest danger lay. He had made his personal preparations in any case. That very morning he had added a codicil to his will asking that Emma Hamilton, and their daughter Horatia, be looked after by the nation in the event of his death. Into his journal he had written a prayer in which he offered up his life to the God he felt observed and judged his every move.

At around 11.30 a.m., fairly fizzing with boyish enthusiasm and desperate to be in the thick of the fray, he called his flag lieutenants to him.

'I will now amuse the fleet with a signal,' he told them. 'Suppose we say, "Nelson confides that every man will do his duty."'

The officers around him hesitated a moment, before one of them pointed out that since neither 'Nelson' nor 'confides' nor 'duty' were in the standard code book, they would have to be spelt out letter by letter. To save time, wouldn't it be better to start the signal with 'England expects'?

Nelson agreed at once and the most famous battle signal ever made or read was hoisted to the *Victory*'s yards and mastheads.

It's hard to know just how generally understood his signal was by the sailors who saw it. Better perhaps if he'd stuck to his guns and insisted on 'Nelson confides'. For those thousands of men waiting on the ships around him, upon decks cleared of belongings and piled deep with sawdust to soak up their blood, were not fighting for their country. Here on the swell off Spain's south-west coast, England was far away. They would fight and die for Nelson, because they loved him.

Aboard the *Royal Sovereign* Collingwood only remarked, 'I wish Nelson would stop signalling. We all know what we have to do.'

After a short while the flags of 'England expects' were pulled down and replaced with 'Engage the enemy more closely'. This last would remain in place, limp for want of wind, until it was finally shot away.

In the end it took over six hours for the two fleets to come within firing range of one another. Collingwood led his own division of 15 ships from the front. As recently as July of that year the *Royal Sovereign* had been fitted with a brand-new copper bottom that gave her a smooth turn of speed unmatched by any other ship in the fleet.

Immediately to her stern were two 74s, *Belleisle* and *Mars*, then the 80-gun *Tonnant* and behind her the *Bellerophon*. Next in line came *Colossus*, *Achilles*, *Revenge*, *Polyphemus*, *Swiftsure*, followed by the three-decker *Dreadnought*, Collingwood's old flagship. Bringing up the rear of this leeward division were *Defiance*, *Thunderer*, *Defence* and lastly the 98-gun *Prince*. But Collingwood's new flagship had pulled well clear of the rest and was alone when a roar of guns ripped away the quiet of the morning, just a few minutes before noon.

From a range of 1,000 yards the French ship *Fougeaux* had unleashed a full broadside towards the *Royal Sovereign*.

The ships of the combined fleet were laid out before the approaching British in a gigantic, concave arc. Collingwood and the rest were therefore sailing into the enemy's open arms and for 20 hellish minutes the *Royal Sovereign* was helplessly exposed to broadsides not just from the *Fougeaux* but also from every other enemy ship within range, perhaps as many as five of them. Collingwood coolly ordered his men to lie down on the decks while the round shot tore at the rigging above their heads.

Finally the distance was closed and the crews aboard the trailing British ships could see that the *Royal Sovereign* was making for the steadily closing gap between the *Fougeaux* and the *Santa Anna*, flagship of the Spanish Admiral, Ignatius d'Alava.

Nelson looked on proudly as his old friend showed them all how the job was to be done.

'See how that noble fellow Collingwood takes his ship into action,' he cried. 'How I envy him!'

The *Royal Sovereign* unleashed a full broadside of her double-shotted port guns as she passed close by the Spaniard. Round shot fortified with wooden caskets of musket balls blasted through the *Santa Anna*'s hull, killing and maiming hundreds of her men and destroying a dozen and more of her guns. The rigging of both ships became entangled and they disappeared within the great clouds of smoke from their firing. For the next quarter of an hour at least, Collingwood's ship fought the Battle of Trafalgar alone. Soon she was engaged with five enemy ships simultaneously, the firing so intense that round shot were seen colliding in mid-air and flattening against one another like mud pies before falling uselessly into the waves. Others flew (or were deflected) beyond their intended targets to cause death and damage aboard ships nearby. With elegant understatement Collingwood would say later: 'I thought it a long time after I got through their Line before I found my friends about me.'

Gradually – as fast as the murmuring wind would allow – more great ships of the British line joined the fray. *Belleisle* was next, second in Collingwood's leeward division and commanded by Captain William Hargood. Once engaged, *Belleisle* remained stuck in the thick of things for the duration of the battle, taking on first the *Fougeaux* and then being attacked by ship after ship until her predicament was no better than that of the *Royal Sovereign*, whom she'd come to aid. Finally she came alongside the Spanish 80-gun *Argonauta*, and was able to take her as a prize – but not without the loss of almost a quarter of her men. Heavy though it was, her death toll was far from being the worst aboard the British ships that day.

Steadily the pre-battle formations gave way until each ship was engaged in its own private war. This was no more than Nelson had expected – this was the way of things in battles at sea in the 18th century. What the Admiral also knew, however, was that his captains were the finest the world would ever see and needed no help to make the right decisions. He shone brightest of all during the last dozen years of his life, but he was among a dazzling galaxy of stars. When Nelson said he expected every man to do his duty, it was with absolute confidence. Once battle was joined, each captain fought alone – and within minutes nearly 60 ships were engaged in a hellish dance contained in a single square mile of sea. Nelson had asked for and predicted a 'pell-mell battle' and that was what he got.

Now it was the turn of the *Victory*. She came within range of the French and Spanish guns around 20 minutes after the *Royal Sovereign*, and enemy round shot were soon finding their mark. John Scott, Nelson's secretary, had been among the first aboard the flagship to die, almost cut in two by a cannonball as big as his head. As custom dictated, Nelson was pacing back and forth on the quarterdeck accompanied by his friend, and captain of the *Victory*, Thomas Hardy. A round shot passed so close between them that the air of its passing tugged at their clothes hard enough to briefly wind both men. Another shot shattered her steering wheel and now 40 men had to control her direction by man-handling the tiller on the lower gundeck.

She passed through the enemy line behind the *Bucentaure*,

Villeneuve's flagship, blasting her with the double-shotted carronade on her foredeck as she did so. The 68-pound ball topped with a barrel containing 500 lead balls blasted through the glass windows of *Bucentaure*'s stern and down the entire length of the ship. Moments later she gave the Frenchman the benefit of a full broadside of double- and even triple-shotted guns. The wave of iron swept away 400 men or more at a stroke, along with dozens of her guns. In an instant the French flagship had effectively ceased to exist as a fighting unit.

Nelson and Hardy were not to have it all their own way of course. The French warship *Neptune* poured lethal fire into her, felling men and causing mayhem. But still *Victory*'s gunners kept their cool, still the powder monkeys – little boys – dashed from gun to gun with their cartridges while blood sloshed around their ankles. When the French 74-gun *Redoutable* came into view, the *Victory* was able to let her have a full broadside from her starboard, while her larboard guns raked the hull of the massive *Santissima Trinidad*, largest warship of the age.

Unable to do much to prevent it, *Victory* then rammed into the side of the *Redoutable* and careered along her side until both ships were lying together, facing in the same direction. The gun-crews aboard both ships continued the drill of loading and firing, loading and firing – blasting one another's hulls from point-blank range.

Aboard the French ship, Captain Jean-Jacques Lucas was determinedly preparing his men to board the British ship. He had around 200 of his crew on the open deck, armed with muskets, cutlasses and anything else that came to hand. But the fact was that both ships were drifting helplessly now and it was in this condition that they fetched up in front of the British 98-gun *Temeraire*, commanded by Captain Eliab Harvey.

The *Redoutable* was a sitting duck. She was also smaller than the *Temeraire*, her deck some feet below that of her foe. Seeing his chance, Captain Harvey gave the order to fire and his broadside brushed Lucas's would-be boarding party off their deck in a mist of blood and bone. All three blood-soaked hulks then drifted down on to the French *Fougeaux* until all four warships were locked together, one huge ocean-going abattoir.

Great moments in war come about by luck as often as by design – and the turn of events now handed Captain Lucas one last opportunity for which he had prepared. Stuck in harbour for months as he had been, along with the rest of the fleet, he'd had no way of training his men in the arts of gunnery or seamanship. Rather than waste the time completely, he'd had them practise their musketry. While the British Navy scorned the use of such weapons – reasoning quite rightly that their use could never take an enemy ship – the French found it useful to station musketeers and snipers in their rigging. From their lofty aspect they could pick off targets on enemy decks and make life thoroughly unpleasant for those below them. And so it was that a French sailor so armed, high in the tangled rigging of the *Redoutable*, looked down on to the quarterdeck of the British ship alongside and spotted the prize of all prizes.

Nelson was unmistakable. His battle honours and decorations, faded and stained by constant wear but still instantly recognisable, would have marked him out in any case. Then there was the ruined arm, worn tight across his chest. The sniper took aim and fired. The round entered the Admiral's chest below the collarbone and smashed down through his body, lodging in his spine. Nelson's slight frame crumpled to the deck. It was a mortal wound.

Hardy dropped beside his friend.

'They have done for me at last,' said Nelson. 'My backbone is shot through.'

He was carried below deck.

Perhaps Hardy tried to remain optimistic. Nelson believed he was about to die every time he went into battle – and thought every wound he received would be the end of him. After all, this was England's greatest hero and around him was unfolding his greatest victory. Surely he could not die now? Not this day of all days?

While the hero was being carried, as gently as conditions would allow, down into the semi-darkness of the *Victory*'s cockpit, the battle raged on. Now as never before the superiority of the British crews – and in particular the British gunners – made all the difference. Napoleon had believed that since his sailors spent all their time stuck in harbour, they were being kept fresh for the inevitable fight. In fact the opposite was true. The men and ships of the combined fleet had simply been rotting where they lay – the ships deteriorating and their crews along with them. The British by contrast had become tougher with every day spent at sea. As they worked either to keep their ships on station in the Channel to confine the enemy to port, or chased him around the Mediterranean in a bid to bring him to battle, they became the most efficient seaborne force that ever was.

All of this would be revealed in stark relief at Trafalgar. For a start, the British gun-crews proved at least three times as fast as their opponents. The greatest compliment that can be paid to the gunners on the other side was that they stayed at their posts, facing up to the savage efficiency of the men ranged against them.

The French and Spanish captains would routinely strike their colours and surrender once their ships had been dismasted or otherwise disabled. This thought never even occurred to the British commanders. Instead they fought on through it all, blithely ignoring the damage to their ships and the deaths of their men. Collingwood spent the duration of the fighting aboard the *Royal Sovereign* making jokes with his officers and munching on apples. The behaviour of the officers and crew of the *Belleisle* was also typical. Shot to pieces though she was, her decks running with the blood of her dead and dying and her masts completely shot away, her men found an ensign and fixed it to a pike that could be lashed to a mast stump. In this way they were able to keep fighting while Captain Hargood, cheerful and beaming in the midst of it all, paced the decks while eating a bunch of grapes.

'The ship is doing nobly,' he said to his captain of marines.

By the time Hardy was able to go below and visit his friend, he was able to report the capture of '12 or 14' of the enemy fleet.

He could also assure him that not one of the British ships had struck its colours – that all were still in action, of one kind or another.

'I am a dead man, Hardy,' said Nelson softly. 'I am going fast. It will be all over with me soon.'

Those men not engaged in the fighting gathered around their lord, as he lay propped up on bedding packed against the massive oak beams of the hull. Every shudder of the woodwork must have pained him terribly, and there was next to nothing that could be done to ease his suffering. Still he clung to life, indeed long enough to hear Hardy's assurances that the day was theirs.

Some time between four thirty and five in the afternoon Nelson died. It's hard to know the truth of the moment, since more than one man witnessed it and remembered it differently. Most famously, and fittingly, the *Victory*'s chaplain, the Reverend A.J. Scott, recorded that as he was bent over the dying man, gently rubbing his chest to lift some of the pain, Nelson murmured: 'Thank God, I have done my duty.'

He said it over and over, almost too softly to be heard. Then at last: 'God and my country.' And with that he was gone.

Not a single British ship was lost at the Battle of Trafalgar – though many were terribly mauled. Nelson's death brought to 450 the total of officers and men lost on our side. There were also as many as 1,200 wounded, many of them horribly.

This toll paled somewhat in comparison to that recorded aboard the ships of the combined French and Spanish fleet, which lost 4,500 dead and 2,400 wounded. As many as 7,000 of their officers and men had been taken as prisoners.

For Napoleon, Trafalgar ended any hopes of crossing the English Channel and invading Britain. But his soldiers were already engaged elsewhere. On 20 October, the day before Nelson's triumph, the Emperor defeated the Austrians at the Battle of Ulm. On 2 December he would achieve his most luminous and towering victory at Austerlitz against a combined Russian and Austrian force. In 1806 he would crush the Prussians at Jena and Auerstedt, and in 1807 his armies would inflict the same upon the Russians at Eylau and Friedland.

But thanks to Nelson, Britain was and always would be safe. Napoleon would attempt to strangle us with his 'Continental System' of economic blockade – but his battles to enforce it would lead to the Peninsular War in Portugal and Spain that began his final undoing. In 1812 he would hopelessly overstretch himself in Russia, losing half a million men in the process. Then would come defeat at Leipzig in 1813, his abdication and his exile to Elba the following year – before his final return and the Hundred Days that brought him to Waterloo and destruction. In many ways, the rot set in at Trafalgar – making it the most significant battle of the Napoleonic War.

That victory had been achieved by a British Navy at the absolute peak of its powers, when so many of its captains and senior officers were incapable of anything but winning.

But there is no avoiding the fact that it was above all else the achievement of one man. One man destined to be the best of all.

As Lord St Vincent said: 'There is but one Nelson.'

A long way from home

'Thank God, I have done my duty.' The words still ring out clear. It's hard to read them without involuntarily straightening the spine a little, maybe sticking out the chin a touch. The leaders who live longest in the imagination are those who, seemingly without trying, win not just the obedience and loyalty of their men, but their love as well.

Scott was one of those, but in his case he was, after all, offering opportunities that you just don't see in the papers nowadays. Imagine having the chance to throw up your day-job and join an expedition aiming to go somewhere no human being has ever been before. That kind of break won't come along again unless, when they finally shoot for Mars, they make seats available to the general public.

Shop-workers, clerks, office boys, railwaymen, students and factory fodder – they all sent desperate letters of application to the office in Victoria Street pleading for the chance to risk their lives in the name of patriotic duty. There were professionals too, of course – hoping their skills would give them an edge – doctors, sailors, soldiers, civil servants. Officers from the armed forces, senior men some of them, wrote to say they would swab the decks or tend the horses, just for the offer of a place. (Cavalryman Titus Oates caused quite a stir when he stepped aboard the *Terra Nova* for the first time. Scott had taken him on to look after the ponies intended for some of the sled-hauling duties – and the sailors in particular had been looking forward to judging the mettle of the man they would come to know as 'The Soldier'. So it was with some amazement that they beheld the character in the tattered raincoat and crumpled bowler hat that climbed the gangplank and stepped cheerfully down among them.)

On 1 June 1910 the *Terra Nova* left London bound for Cardiff, where she took delivery of 100 tons of free coal as well as £2,500 raised by public subscription. Scott was so impressed and so personally touched by the show of support and generosity from the people of Wales, that he vowed to make their capital city the first port of call for the *Terra Nova* on her way home from Antarctica.

As before with the *Discovery*, Scott remained behind in Britain to tidy up the last of the financial details and sent the *Terra Nova* and her crew onwards to South Africa. On 16 July, with all the paperwork finally squared away, he set sail aboard the mail steamer *Saxon*, accompanied by Kathleen, who had decided to leave nine-month-old Peter behind in England and stay with her husband for as long as possible. At Cape Town, Scott replaced Wilson as captain of the *Terra Nova* and sailed for Australia.

As soon as the ship arrived in Melbourne, Scott was handed a telegram. Sent by the Norwegian explorer Roald Amundsen, it was brief and to the point.

'Am going south,' it said.

Scott can hardly have been thrilled at the news, but he kept any anger or disappointment from the men. Back in Britain, the news would be greeted by open criticism of the perceived interloper. As far as anyone knew, Amundsen's interests had always been focused on the Arctic. But Peary's triumph in 1909 had brought an end to the Norwegian's dreams of glory at that end of the world. Without a word, he had quietly altered his plans and sailed for Antarctica ahead of Scott. Amundsen was in debt – having raised funds for a dash to the North Pole – and in order to recoup his losses he would need a spectacular result elsewhere. Now the quest for the South Pole had turned into a race.

For now, Scott had to concentrate on his own preparations.

There was still fundraising to be done – in Australia and then in New Zealand. Regardless of whatever anxiety he might have felt about the latest developments, he knuckled down to the tiresome job of exploiting any and all opportunities to raise last-minute cash.

Finally, in the afternoon of 29 November, came the time for last farewells. Whatever words were shared by Kathleen and her husband at the end are not known – since they were said in private earlier in the day. As she wrote in her diary later: 'I decided not to say goodbye to my man because I didn't want anyone to see him look sad.'

Around 4.30 p.m. the *Terra Nova* cast off, making for Antarctica at last. Trouble and hardship were not long in joining them. On 2 December a vicious storm blew up, severely testing the ship and the men. They were already riding low in the water thanks to the sheer bulk of supplies aboard, and mountainous waves driven by near-hurricane-force winds threatened to overwhelm them completely. For two days the men were embroiled in a desperate fight to keep their ship afloat. Eventually coal dust became mixed with the seawater, creating a sludge that put the automatic pumps out of action. By the end, a chain of men – Scott included – were up to their chests in freezing water, using buckets to bail out the *Terra Nova*'s hold by hand.

Fighting for their lives in the great Southern Ocean, they felt they were the loneliest men, aboard the loneliest ship in all creation.

Moonwalkers and Apollo 13

It's now 37 years since human beings last walked on the surface of another world. Only 12 have ever done so, and Gene Cernan and Jack Schmitt were the last. Between 11 and 14 December 1972 they lived on the moon. They drove 21 miles across it in their lunar rover and collected hundreds of pounds of moon rock. They took in the view that only 10 other men had ever beheld – planet Earth from solid ground elsewhere. From time to time they lay down inside their lunar module, and slept while the home planet rose and set in a black sky.

Command module pilot Ron Evans was the third member of the crew. Not for him the small steps of man upon that surface – instead he remained in orbit 60 miles above, ready for his colleagues' return. On 7 December, en route to the moon, one of them had snapped the photograph of planet Earth known as 'the blue marble' – now among the most famous images in history. It reveals the home planet for what it is – a vulnerable ball suspended in infinity. Apollo 17 achieved the sixth lunar landing in three and a half years and it went like clockwork.

When Cernan and Schmitt blasted away from the moon on 14 December it was just 69 years – less than a lifetime – since another American had made the first-ever powered flight. Orville Wright, watched by his brother Wilbur, flew 120 feet across the sky above the beach at Kitty Hawk on 17 December 1903 (when the first Boeing 747 'Jumbo Jet' was unveiled 65 years later its wingspan alone was twice as long as that first flight). On 20 July 1969 Neil Armstrong and Buzz Aldrin had landed on the moon for the first time, having flown the best part of 240,000 miles. It seemed technology and aspiration knew no bounds.

A billion people around the world watched the first moonwalk by the Apollo 11 astronauts that day – when television sets were rarities by today's standards. Armstrong's first words from the surface are etched into the memory of the world. It was hailed as the greatest achievement in human history and it seemed, at that moment, as though the exploration of the universe was just about keeping on walking, more small steps and giant leaps.

But by 1972 the American people had become too accustomed to seeing their fellow citizens at work nearly a quarter of a million miles from home. They'd seen 12 of their countrymen walk on the moon and that was enough. It was no thrill any more, the space race was won and the US Government had pulled the plug on further lunar landings. The world had moved on.

JFK, the president who'd made the moon his nation's inspiration for more than a decade, had been dead for nine years. His brother Bobby was gone too, and Martin Luther King. It was two years since the deaths of Jimi Hendrix and Janis Joplin, not to mention the break-up of the Beatles. Americans were more concerned with their war in Vietnam and what President Nixon's men had been up to in the Watergate Building. The time for moonwalking had come and gone.

Long forgotten too was the adventure of another three-man crew of astronauts – who'd reached out for the moon but found it exceeded their grasp. While they failed to reach their destination, their journey proved all the greater for falling short of the goal.

In December 1910, as they fought for survival in the towering seas between latitudes 50 and 70 degrees south, Captain Scott and the crew of the Terra Nova had felt they were aboard the loneliest ship in the world, and they were. But for a handful of days in April 1970 the loneliest men in the history of the world so far were Jim Lovell, Jack Swigert and Fred Haise, the crew of Apollo 13.

In a speech he gave in 1961, President John F. Kennedy told the American people it was time to send one of their own to walk upon the moon – and then return him 'safely to the Earth'. If that wasn't enough of a challenge, he pledged to see

it done before the end of the decade. He'd been elected in
November 1960 after a campaign in which, among other things,
he'd promised the American people superiority over Russia in
the fields of space exploration and missile defence.

When he set his nation the target of the moon that day, he
made it sound as if it should be done because it was a dream
deserving of being made real. It's hard to imagine what dream
any of our leaders could pledge themselves to today in order
to match JFK's: maybe a trip to the sun, or to the constellation
Orion. Whatever else he did or didn't do, JFK knew how to
shape a dream. In truth, though, he was unnerved by the advances
Communist Russia had made into the new frontier of space
and he was desperate to close the gap.

Sputnik I, the first manmade satellite, had launched in 1957.
On 12 April 1961 Yuri Gagarin completed the first manned
mission into space. American Alan Shepard followed him into
the new domain on 5 May, when he managed a 15-minute
suborbital flight in the cramped capsule of the Mercury *Freedom
7*. Shepard had shown his class – not least because of the calming
influence he'd had upon a nervous ground crew and Mission
Control during the long wait for ignition. He'd been strapped
into the claustrophobic cabin for four hours, but elsewhere
other men were unhappy with the weather and the feedback
they were getting from their machines. Finally Shepard's quiet
voice came over the radio.

'Why don't you fellows solve your little problems,' he said.
'And light this candle.'

And so they did, and the world turned and Shepard flew.

But everyone on that world could see that a two-horse space
race had begun and America was running second. There was a
cold war on as well – or at the very least a cold peace – and
JFK needed to show his people there was something they could
beat the Russians at. What followed was the most extraordinary
demonstration yet seen of the power of imagination and

ambition when coupled to near-limitless wealth. By the end it would cost the American people $24 billion – $100 billion in today's money – using as much as 5 per cent of the annual federal budget.

It was also a demonstration of how desire can persuade ambitious men to turn a blind eye to inconvenient truth. By the end of World War II the Americans had acquired the services of Hitler's chief rocket scientist, Wernher von Braun. The Allies knew the development of von Braun's V2 rocket-bombs had been dependent upon slave labour. But the benefits to be had from rocket technology were deemed more important than the means used to acquire it, and so the SS officer became an unlikely ally.

According to legend, it's to the summit of the Brocken, tallest of Germany's Harz Mountains, that the Devil summons all his witches on the night of 30 April each year before taking them into the underworld. It's a place of mischief. It was in factories beneath those same mountains that von Braun's rockets were built – and where an unknown number of innocent and uncomprehending lives were used up and thrown away. But when in the last months of the war von Braun guessed Hitler's sun was about to be eclipsed, he betrayed his master and placed himself, and scores of his fellow scientists, into the hands of the Americans. He knew such a move would ensure the continuation of his work, and that was all that mattered. America was delighted to have him. It was the undoubted genius of von Braun, tainted though it was, that eventually gave the US the Saturn V rocket that would propel all the Apollo astronauts beyond Earth's grasp and out towards the unsullied moon.

But the best and worst of times and men often travel together – as though one draws the other. Away from the politics, the dream of travelling into space had reached out, faster than the speed of sound, towards brave men. It reached the ears of the test pilots at Edwards Air Force base – men who risked their lives every day in the bright cloudless skies high above California's Mojave Desert. Here was home to men who were already legends. King of kings was Captain Chuck Yeager, who had broken the sound barrier in the Bell X-1 rocket plane on 14 October 1947 – but who would never sit in a space capsule. He had no college degree and so lacked a minimum requirement for the job of spaceman. (It's said he felt flight in a space capsule – deprived of the means of actually *flying* it but travelling instead as a kind of glorified passenger – was beneath an aviator's dignity. It was Yeager or someone close to him who dismissed the Mercury astronauts as 'spam in a can'.)

But the credo of the test pilots was about being the best. Author Tom Wolfe described their essential quality as 'The Right Stuff', in his book of the same name, and defined it as the instinctive ability to always do the right thing at the right time. The men selected for the Mercury Program in 1959 didn't try to be good, they simply were good.

It was also about unspoken personal bravery – of the sort Shepard showed in 1961 when he told his ground crew to get on with their job. Wolfe recounts an anecdote thought to have come out of the Korean War. A young pilot in a dogfight found an enemy MiG locked on to his tail and preparing to fire. Radio channels were kept clear for all but essential tactical communications – but the youngster was filling the airwaves with his shouts and cries, begging to be told how to save his skin. In a break in his transmission another flyer cut in and told him: 'Shut up – and die like an aviator.'

Such was the way of the flyers, and it was this hard, straight edge they brought to the race for space. The first of them, the so-called *Mercury 7* of Scott Carpenter, Gordon Cooper, John Glenn, Gus Grissom, Wally Schirra, Alan Shepard and Deke Slayton were fêted as champions selected for mortal combat – much like gladiators, or Spartan hoplites. These were the men who stepped up in the days before deep space flight was even possible, far less taken for granted, and for that reason, perhaps, they were the bravest of them all – whether they had to fly their ships or not.

By the time Mercury had run its course, NASA – the specially created National Aeronautics and Space Administration – had learned how to put men into Earth-orbit and bring them back alive. More astronauts followed ready to slip the surly bonds of Earth and by 1963 the Gemini Program, successor to Mercury, was teaching them to dock vehicles in space. Jim Lovell, the man who would later command Apollo 13, was among them.

The Apollo Program had been running since 1962 and began to send men into space in 1968, but not before the dream of the moon had claimed its first lives. On 27 January 1967 the crew of Apollo 1 – Gus Grissom, Ed White and Roger Chaffee – were in their command module conducting launchpad tests. Their official flight designation was AS-204 (it would be renamed Apollo 1 later, as a mark of respect) and they were scheduled to be the first of the Apollo astronauts to fly. All three were strapped into their seats, wearing full flight suits and helmets, when a technical fault caused a fire inside the module. It's estimated that all three were dead within 17 seconds, although it's hard to imagine how anyone can be certain about such a thing. It still sounds like a long time to be strapped inside a fire.

In December 1968 Apollo 8 became the first manned flight to finally break free of Earth's gravity and head for someplace new – the moon. Aboard were Frank Borman, William Anders and Jim Lovell. During their flight they orbited the moon 10 times in 20 hours before returning safely home. These then were the first men to fly above another world and it does all seem like too much to believe. The further we get from that decade, when such things were briefly made possible, the easier it is to imagine none of it ever really happened. We don't even have Concorde any more. Will our children believe it was once commonplace to fly across the Atlantic in three and a half hours, faster than a bullet from a rifle, let alone fly on top of a rocket to the moon?

It's worth remembering that 1960s Britain was in third place behind Russia and America in the space race. There were even plans for manned flight. In 1971 we launched our first, and only, satellite into orbit. Called Prospero, it's still up there, feebly cheeping its signal to anyone who'll listen. We dropped out of the space race because our politicians decided Concorde and supersonic air travel was a better investment. Britain stands alone as the only country in the world to have successfully launched one satellite into orbit, and then stopped. At the Scottish National Aviation Museum, near the village of East Fortune, in East Lothian east of Edinburgh, the Black Knight and Blue Streak rockets that once spearheaded our space programme are permanent exhibits. In a final twist of irony, they've recently had to make room for the Concorde that displaced them once before. They're all museum pieces now, even Saturn V.

You couldn't make it up. No wonder the world's biggest conspiracy theory claims man has never been to the moon and that the film of the Apollo 11 landing was a fake directed by Stanley Kubrick. NASA had to learn *everything* that was required of space flight: not just how to get to the moon, but even how to *train* to get to the moon. Everything about it was new and being imagined and invented from scratch. But perhaps if they were really going to fake the moon landings, Grissom, White and Chaffee wouldn't have had to burn to death.

Apollo 11 blasted off from the launchpad at the Kennedy Space Center on Merritt Island in Brevard County, Florida, at just a couple of minutes after 9.30 a.m. local time on 16 July 1969. The Saturn V rocket that lifted them clear of Earth's gravity was a wonder to behold. There's no other way to describe it. The first of its kind had carried Lovell's Apollo 8 into space as well. In all, 32 Saturns would take to the air and not one of them would fail. The Saturn V stood 363 feet tall, less than a foot shorter than the dome of St Paul's Cathedral, and was made up of 3 million parts. Every one of the components in that impossible maze of technology, inside a cylinder taller than a 30-storey building, had to work first time in order for the rocket to function properly – and they did, every time. The Vehicle Assembly Building – the VAB – in Florida, in which the Saturns were put together like the world's most exciting toys, also has dimensions that are too much to take in. Although technically a single-storey building, it stands 525 feet tall. Inside it encloses 129,428,000 cubic feet of space, and the people who've worked inside it insist it has its own weather system. When the conditions are just right clouds form, up towards the ceiling.

On the final descent to the moon's surface, Armstrong was at the controls of the lunar module, a fragile bird of a thing appropriately named Eagle. They overshot the planned landing site, finally touching down into the dust with just seconds' worth of fuel to spare. If Yeager had ever been right about astronauts being spam in a can, it wasn't true by 1969 and Apollo 11. Armstrong had needed every ounce of his undoubted brilliance as a test pilot to put the Eagle safely on to the surface. And while he and Aldrin prepared for their first steps, 60 miles above them their command module pilot, Michael Collins, was embarking upon his own odyssey. For the first time a man would travel alone into the blackness of the moon's dark side. The moon does not rotate, keeping the same face always towards the Earth. When Collins hurtled into that nothingness he was more alone than any human being had ever been.

Apollo 13 blasted away from the launchpad at the Kennedy Space Center a couple of minutes before quarter past two in the afternoon of 11 April 1970. Its 42-year-old commander, Jim Lovell, from Cleveland, Ohio, was already the most travelled human being in history. He'd spent more than 570 hours in space, travelling a distance of around 7 million miles. As this latest journey got under way he became the first astronaut to make four journeys into space. He'd joined the US Navy in 1952 and flown jets in the Korean War before being selected for the space programme in 1962. In the official NASA photographs taken before Apollo 13, wearing his flight suit, he has on his face the vaguely bashful and startled expression of someone who can't quite believe his luck. He was generally considered easygoing, but those closest to him detected the competitive spirit that would elevate him to the status of mission commander.

He'd been back-up commander for Apollo 11 – Armstrong's understudy – and if things had gone as NASA originally planned, would have been the skipper of Apollo 14. As it turned out, the powers that be felt Apollo 13's scheduled commander, Alan Shepard, needed more time to get back up to speed after a long lay-off following surgery for Menière's disease. Shepard and his team were therefore ordered to swap with Lovell's. Fate had played her hand, and now Lovell and his men had Apollo 13. In a further twist, they faced a last-minute change of personnel. Ken Mattingly had been training as the command module pilot, but with just days to go before the scheduled launch he was found to have been exposed to German measles. While Lovell and Haise had had the disease in childhood, and so could be expected to remain healthy during the flight, Mattingly had not. He was duly bumped out of the line and replaced by Jack Swigert.

Born in Denver, Colorado, the quiet and unassuming 38-year-old Swigert had obtained his private pilot's licence by the age of 16. He'd flown jets in Korea and joined the space programme in 1966. Apollo 13 would be his one and only space flight.

Fred Haise was the youngest of the three, just 36 years old. He was from Biloxi, Mississippi, and had been a NASA test pilot at Edwards. Like Swigert, he joined the space programme in 1966 and before the twist of fate that put him on Apollo 13 he'd been back-up lunar module pilot for Apollo 9. He had the same role for Apollo 11, making him understudy for Buzz Aldrin. As good luck would have it, he'd made a point of becoming an expert on the design and use of landing modules. It was knowledge that would shortly matter a great deal. No one made Haise acquire this detailed understanding of the craft that would soon mean so much to him and his two colleagues. He had done it for himself and by himself. This is presumably part of what it means to have 'the right stuff'.

The launch of Apollo 13 went well – although superstition had been running high. For a start, there was that fateful mission number. Second of all, Lovell's wife Marilyn had lost her wedding ring before the flight took off. 'Til death do us part. The loss was featured in the 1995 film *Apollo 13*, starring Tom Hanks, and although at first thought to be a fiction added into the plot for dramatic effect, Lovell admitted later that it had actually happened.

Days one and two of the mission unfolded much as planned. One of the engines had cut out a couple of minutes early – no harm done, though, and Lovell and Co. might have been entitled to think that that had been their inevitable hiccup. At 55 hours into the flight they began a scheduled television broadcast for the folks back home. Lovell's tape recorder, floating around the command module, played 'Aquarius' from the musical film *Hair* as well as 'Also Sprach Zarathustra', the theme from *2001: A Space Odyssey*. They were making it look easy, commonplace.

Shortly after the broadcast came to a close, the good times ended for Apollo 13. A warning light had come on back at Houston, telling the technicians that pressure was dropping in one of the onboard hydrogen tanks. This was nothing particularly worrying in itself, and Mission Control simply told the crew of Apollo 13 to turn on a set of cryogenic fans and heaters. This was a routine action known as 'stirring the tanks'. There was nothing at all routine about what happened next.

All seemed well enough for about another minute and a half, and then Lovell, Swigert and Haise heard a loud bang – not the kind of noise an astronaut wants to hear while he's floating inside a tin can, 200,000 miles from home. Looking outside, the astronauts could see evidence of an explosion – exposed wires, missing panels – and some sort of vapour or gas streaming into space.

Back at Mission Control, they already knew something bad had happened. For two whole seconds, Apollo 13 had gone quiet – as all radio transmissions from the ship had switched off. In the momentary silence, Swigert had spoken into the void.

'Okay, Houston,' he said. 'Hey, we've had a problem.'

Once the radio came back on, gentleman Jim Lovell repeated the gist of the line, but with a change of tense.

'Okay, Houston,' he said. 'We have a problem.'

No panic and no swearing. Cars have been parked with more anxiety.

What they couldn't know then – but what an inquiry would establish later on – was that there'd been a short circuit inside one of the tanks when the crew attempted the 'stir'. Teflon insulation around an electrical motor on an internal fan was damaged and a small fire broke out, eventually causing an explosion that blew apart one of the ship's oxygen tanks and damaged the other. What all this meant was that the command module was now bleeding to death. The vapour they saw venting into space was the gas they depended on to keep themselves and the onboard systems alive. When the oxygen tank exploded, part of the panel covering it had blown off and hit the radio transmitter on the side of the capsule – hence the two-second-long radio blackout noticed by Mission Control.

When you hear about events like these – matters of life and death – it's tempting to assume the necessary decision and actions were being taken and made by men of our dads' age: proper grown-ups. But the ones who looked after the astronauts during the space flights of the 1960s and early 70s were hardly men at all, more like boys. The scientists and technicians now staring into computer screens and preparing to deal with whatever had just happened to Apollo 13 had an average age of 26. Gene Kranz was Director of Mission Operations until 1994. When Armstrong and Aldrin walked on the moon in 1969, he was 35 years old.

'I was the old man,' he said.

The screens and readouts were telling Mission Control that the command module, *Odyssey*, erstwhile home for the three astronauts, was dying. If urgent action were not taken, Lovell, Swigert and Haise would die along with it. Mission Control ordered the three men to go through the routines required to 'power down' – switch off the module. Until the men on the ground could figure out how to bring it back to fully functioning life, the crew would have to find somewhere else to live.

Apollo 13 the movie has the three men shouting at each other at this point, trying to figure out if one of them is to blame for what has just happened. The truth aboard *Odyssey* was less dramatic but more impressive by far. Instead of panicking, they went about their assigned tasks quietly and calmly. With all power off inside the command module, the temperature dropped uncomfortably low. It was dark in there too, and it was at this point in the drama that the crew moved into the lunar module.

Despite there being barely enough room to turn around inside *Aquarius*, far less swing a cat, it would have to be their temporary home; their fragile life-raft in an ocean of black. Apollo 13 was supposed to be about a moon landing. That target was gone now, along with the contents of the command module's oxygen tanks.

By then, in 1970, landing on the moon had been accomplished twice. After Armstrong and Aldrin, Apollo 12's Pete Conrad and Alan Bean had repeated the trick. Facing the crew of Apollo 13 was something quite new. They had to find a way to stay alive and get back home after just about everything that could go wrong had gone wrong.

Having watched those two moon landings, the viewing public had lost interest in the space race by the time Apollo 13's astronauts were showing them weightless tape recorders. But as news of the accident was transmitted, people around the world suddenly found a new reason to be enthralled by events unfolding high above their heads.

On 14 April, Apollo 13 made its loop around the moon. Lovell was looking down at a familiar view, but for his fellow travellers it was all new. As they passed around into the dark side, they were a long way from their intended lunar orbit. In fact their unintended but now unavoidable path meant they were all of 200 miles above the moon's surface. For as long as that long, lonely loop continued, they were further from home than any human beings before or since.

Down on the ground the 26-year-olds were trying to find solutions to a set of problems that no one had ever imagined before. At Kennedy Space Center in Florida and Mission Control in Texas, two teams began simulating the conditions controlling the astronauts' lives. Every solution was tested on the ground to prove it worked before any instructions were transmitted to *Aquarius*. In simple terms, there were two tasks:

1. How to keep the three men alive.
2. How to repair the crippled spacecraft to the point where it was capable of bringing them home.

But while hundreds of men scurried around trying to find answers, three men were jammed shoulder-to-shoulder inside a fragile bubble of air. They were more than four days from home and their life raft, *Aquarius*, was only designed to keep two men alive for 48 hours. While on the dark side of the moon, the astronauts were ordered to fire the lunar module engines to speed up their return. This was not what the engines had been designed for – they were only intended for use in getting to and from the moon's surface – but the frightening move was executed perfectly by Lovell. The three were now 12 hours closer to home.

Kennedy Space Center engineers found a way to use the lunar module's electrical system to recharge that of the stricken command module. Others came up with a way of using some of the men's drinking water to double as a cooling system. Easily the most pressing problem was the atmosphere inside the module. With three of them breathing the same limited air, the level of deadly carbon dioxide was rising fast. Even this challenge was safely met. A filtration system cobbled together from plastic jotter covers, cardboard and anything else known to be aboard *Aquarius* was assembled on the ground before the instructions for its assembly were sent to the crew.

It's claimed the biggest television audience in history witnessed their eventual return. On 17 April, after five days, 22 hours and 54 minutes, *Aquarius* was spotted falling safely towards Earth, suspended beneath its massive parachutes. It splashed into the sea just off Samoa, watched by millions of television viewers and the crews of the US Navy flotilla sent to intercept it. The voice of commentator Walter Cronkite, the world's most believable man, cracked with the emotion of the moment.

Jim Lovell never ventured into space again. For a while after Apollo 13 he was in charge of the 'backroom' scientists monitoring the moonwalks of other men. He retired from NASA in 1973. Jack Swigert left the same year and was executive director of the Committee on Science and Technology for the House of Representatives until 1977. He ran a successful campaign for election to Congress in 1982, but died of cancer before he could take office. Fred Haise was scheduled to be commander of Apollo 19, but after Apollo 17 no more men ever flew to the moon.

We're still waiting.

Enemy at the gates

Terrifying though the prospect of sinking in the Southern Ocean undoubtedly is, surely there's a special horror about the idea of being lost in space? As long as you come to die somewhere here on Earth, at least your body remains where it belongs – on the planet that made it. Someone might even find your bones some day, with your wallet rattling around in your ribcage, and let your descendants know you turned up in the end. But to die in the vacuum of space, doomed to drift in nothingness for all eternity, now that's truly being lost. When the day comes when they're offering free flights around the Solar System, I'm not going.

The crew of the *Terra Nova* had no Mission Control looking after their welfare. Not for them the welcome sound of a distant, disembodied voice offering calm suggestions for solutions to life-threatening problems and equipment failure. Instead they were alone in a way that's hard to imagine from the perspective of a world full of mobile phones and satellite communications. Help for their situation had to be found aboard ship and they would have to do all the hard work themselves. In the end, it was good humour and unbreakable spirit that saw them through. Scott remained in the thick of the action throughout – matching the pace of the toughest and fittest men aboard as they passed the buckets hand to hand.

In a letter to his wife, describing the trials and tribulations of those two days in December, Wilson wrote, in all seriousness: 'I must say I enjoyed it all from beginning to end.'

Eventually the winds dropped, the ocean calmed down and the men had the chance to get the worst of the sea water out without fear of the level being constantly topped up. The pumps were soon repaired and the men cheered as the machines took up the job once more. During the worst of the storm, two of the ponies were killed and one of the sled dogs was lost overboard. Scott, sentimental about animals right until the end, found their deaths hard to take.

Any joy about weathering the storm was short-lived. The pack-ice met them at a latitude much further north than usual for the time of year and for the last three weeks of December the *Terra Nova*'s engines had to be fed worryingly large volumes of coal to enable her to force a way through. They were making for Cape Crozier – a location Scott had noted during his first expedition. It offered a sheltered landing beach and proximity to the Great Ice Barrier – and therefore access to the most direct line of attack towards the South Pole.

For now, though, they were little more than prisoners of the ice – a warning of the fate awaiting Shackleton and the rest of the crew of the *Endeavour*. Scott fretted and worried, pacing the deck of the *Terra Nova* like a bear in a cage or shutting himself away in his cabin to fill his journal with his concerns.

'We are captured,' he wrote. 'We do practically nothing under sail to push through, and could do little under steam, and at each step the possibility of advance seems to lessen.'

The ship finally cleared the pack-ice on 30 December but there was disappointment ahead. A party of men were put aboard a small boat and sent out to take a closer look at Cape Crozier. When they returned they reported that the conditions in the bay were impossible, the waves too strong for any attempt at a landing. Instead the ship had to continue on towards McMurdo Sound, destination of the *Discovery* all those years before. A campsite was chosen in a bay that Scott now renamed Cape Evans, in honour of his second-in-command, and the men began the heavy work of unloading their kit and moving it ashore across a mile or more of frozen sea.

Scott was back, but now he had it all to do. He knew Amundsen was out there somewhere, eyeing the last prize of its kind anywhere on the planet, and he felt he carried the expectations of the entire British people on his back.

Before him were the as yet invincible defences of Antarctica. They had been challenged before and each time had proved too great, too strong, too far. Where could Scott look for inspiration for the challenge of a lifetime? How was he to storm these barricades?

Constantinople

In the middle years of the 15th century prophecy walked the streets of Constantinople hand-in-hand with Christianity. God's will was in all things — of that, its people were in no doubt — but belief in a future already written was just as strong. The question was how to foretell that future, how to read the signs that were all around. Emperor Constantine I had made the city his capital in AD 330 and built for his people a heaven on earth, a new Rome on seven new hills. Once upon a time this Byzantine Empire had reached and encircled the Mediterranean Sea; at its height the capital had been home to half a million souls. By 1453 the golden days were long gone, the empire pushed back nearly to the city walls. Soon the infidel Turks would be knocking at the gates. Another Constantine was on the imperial throne now — Constantine XI. Would his reign bring salvation and a return to the triumphs of his namesake? Or would his time complete the circle and bring all things to a close — Alpha and Omega; the first and the last? It had all begun with one Constantine — would it end with another?

The city known once as Constantinople is today Istanbul, capital of Turkey and the only metropolis in the world that straddles two continents. The waters of the Bosphorus keep Europe and Asia apart here — the opposing shores flirting dangerously with one another behind their families' backs, like Romeo and Juliet.

As it turns out, that narrow parting is the deepest cut of all. It's the place where East and West were finally divided — yet where Islam and Christianity came close enough to kiss. The story of what happened here during the spring and summer of 1453 is part of the story of how our present was made.

The city occupies the tip of a peninsula. Two bodies of water – the Sea of Marmara and the Golden Horn – meet to form the apex of a triangle, pointing roughly east. The base of the triangle, towards the west, is traced across the neck of the peninsula by the great defensive wall of Theodosius. Built in the 4th century to keep out the barbarians, it's still largely intact today. A series of massive arched gates, as imposing in the 21st century as they were 1,000 years ago, cuts through it towards the interior.

As is true of all great cities, the modern façade of Istanbul is marbled with veins of history running all the way back to beginnings so distant they're impossible to recall. By our standards, with today's new houses guaranteed to last just 40 years and the significance of 'Millennium projects' already receding into memory, the chronological scope of the rise and fall of Constantinople is breathtaking.

The Roman Diocletian unwittingly laid the foundations when he established himself as emperor in another city, Nicomedia, in AD 284. It was he who created the 'Tetrarchy'. Ruling as emperor in the east with Galerius as his Caesar, he left the west to Emperor Maximian, with Constantius Chlorus as his deputy.

True to his Roman faith Diocletian ordered the persecution of Christians. But when Constantius Chlorus died at York in AD 306 he was succeeded by his son, Constantine I. Constantine shared the rulership of the empire with Licinius – until he defeated him in battle in AD 323 and proclaimed himself sole emperor with a capital named after himself, at Constantinople.

It has never been clear just how 'Christian' Constantine really was in private life – but he certainly added Christian symbolism to his battle insignia and tolerated, if not encouraged, the new faith among his subjects. The roots took hold and in AD 573 the Emperor Justinian dedicated the Church of St Sophia as the living heart of the city's religious life. It had taken just six years to build and yet it was a crowning masterpiece of vision and architectural skill. None who visited the building in the Middle Ages seemed able to find words to describe it back home. A mosque now, it has the same power to enthral today as when it was new.

Theodosius succeeded his father Constantine – and at his own death in AD 395 split the empire between his sons. After the fall of Rome to the Ostrogoths in AD 476, Constantinople became the single centre of the Roman Empire. The Christianity that crystallised there in the east, beneath the overarching dome of St Sophia, was a dark and lustrous jewel. Its power to beguile was its greatest strength and its final weakness.

Soldiers ranged along Constantinople's defensive walls in 1453 had their first sight of an approaching army during the first days of April that year. On Easter Sunday – the most important day in the Christian calendar – the faithful had gathered as usual in the churches. The people of the city believed the Virgin Mary was their greatest and surest shield. Down the centuries they'd called for her in times of need. With would-be raiders snapping at them from beyond the walls, they had gathered to carry icons bearing her likeness through the streets. She had never failed them before in the face of the heathen, and surely, when the stormclouds ranged around them seemed darkest, she would not fail them now.

While the common people looked to a woman in heaven for salvation, one man on Earth bore overall responsibility for turning back the tide of Islam lapping at the walls. But Constantine Palaiologos, in Christ true Emperor and Autocrat of the Romans, supped from a poisoned chalice. His predecessors had in the main presided over centuries of erosion of an empire that had once inspired respect and awe in all who knew of it. Misrule by many of them, accompanied by civil wars, petty jealousies, corruption and sloth, had presented Constantine XI with an inheritance few would want. The lands and territories were almost all gone. Though he bore the title of emperor, his empire was so landlocked within that of the Ottomans that he was little more than a vassal of the Sultan. Only the impenetrable defences of the city – walls and treacherous seas – prevented the *coup de grâce*.

Yet within Constantine XI shone the brightness of a bygone age of empire. Chroniclers of the time describe a straightforward and trustworthy man who inspired lifelong loyalty in those around him. He was at heart a soldier and a patriot, imbued with a sense of duty to ensure the survival of his people and their way of life. By the time of the siege of 1453 he was 48 years old and in spite of all he had seen – the continued tarnishing of what Constantinople had once been – he was resolute. As he looked out over the battlements of the Wall of Theodosius he knew that his fate and that of his city and his empire were one.

These were dark days indeed for Constantinople and what little remained of the Byzantine Empire. The foe advancing towards them now was led by the 21-year-old Muslim Sultan Mehmet II. He had summoned his fighting forces from around his Ottoman Empire and they had come in numbers that seemed impossible to Constantine and his Christians, huddled behind their ancient defences. Contemporary estimates of the Muslim force range all the way up to figures that can only ever have been inspired by fantasy. But the more reasonable counts still beggar belief. Historians today find it acceptable to imagine an army of 200,000. Clearly much of this is accounted for by servants, retainers, camp-followers and the rest of the hangers-on with an appetite for the scraps left by medieval armies on the move. But still around 60,000 of these are thought to have been fighting men – a combination of infantry and cavalry in roughly equal proportions.

This was not a purely Muslim force, either. Thousands of

Christians were there too, under the banner of the Sultan – some pressed into service from conquered lands and some mercenaries from countries across Europe – and their presence burned the hearts of those they had come to subdue. Inside the city walls, preparing themselves to face this multinational horde, were perhaps 8,000 men. Fewer than half of them could be considered part of what we would recognise as a trained, organised army and there was scant hope of reinforcements.

Although those defenders were desperately outnumbered, they were behind defences that had withstood more than 20 sieges in the past 1,000 years. Hard though it might be to believe, the greater challenge was that faced by Mehmet and his would-be invaders. It was they who had the steepest climb ahead – and the toughest of the enemies ranged against them, greater than the walls and the sea, was time. From the moment a siege begins, its commander is fighting a battle to maintain the morale of his men and to build and sustain momentum in the face of an immovable obstacle. Those inside the defences had nowhere to run – they were in place for the duration and fighting to defend family and home. Those without were always just one disappointment away from deciding to turn and head for *their* homes far away – either individually or en masse. The commander of a siege holds his army like water in his cupped hands.

More than anything, more than territory or ethnic distrust or greed (though these and more were part of the mix), this was a struggle between two faiths. In the 15th century the two great monotheisms were Christianity and Islam, two religions with a common root and as many ties to bind them as to separate. But familiarity breeds contempt. When the Christian populace of Constantinople looked out at the Muslim army preparing to besiege them, they were watching the build-up to the climax of a struggle as old as Islam itself.

According to the faithful, the Prophet Muhammad himself

laid claim to the city in AD 628 in a letter sent to the Byzantine Emperor Heraclius, on pilgrimage to Jerusalem. Heraclius had crushed the forces of Persia and recovered from them the True Cross, most sacred of Christianity's relics. As he arrived at the city, on his way to return the relic to the Church of the Holy Sepulchre, he was handed a letter. It read:

> In the name of Allah the most beneficent, the most merciful: this letter is from Muhammad, the slave of Allah, and his apostle, to Heraclius, the ruler of the Byzantines. Peace be upon the followers of guidance. I invite you to surrender to Allah. Embrace Islam and Allah will bestow on you a double reward. But if you reject this invitation you will be misguiding your people.

Persia's king of kings had received much the same letter, but neither man took up the offer. From then on Constantinople was a target for the forces of Islam – and as the decades and centuries passed without success for the pretenders, the target became an obsession.

The triumph of Muhammad the warrior had been to unite the disparate, nomadic Arab tribes under the banner of Islam. Here was a portable faith that could be easily carried by wanderers. Forged by it into a single blade, they cut a swath through the sedentary civilisations they found beyond the limits of their desert homelands. Muhammad died in AD 632, but his mission drove relentlessly onwards. In the years to come Muslim Arab forces would sweep through Persia and the Middle East, across North Africa and into Spain. Cities fell to them and people bowed down, but not Constantinople.

In AD 669 the Caliph Muawiyah brought his Arab army – and by now an Arab navy as well – to within sight of the city. In the following years he besieged the place again and again, using his ships to maintain a stranglehold and keep his men supplied with the stuff of war. But in 678 the Christians struck back

– and with such awe-inspiring effect that they were to secure for the coming centuries the belief that the Christian God himself had determined to protect this city of his faithful. Out on to the Sea of Marmara sailed a force of Byzantine galleys. Straight towards the Muslim fleet they came and, once in among them, unleashed what appeared to be the hand of a righteous God. Observers saw strange apparatus on the bows of the Christian ships and from it spewed what could only be described as liquid fire. The Arab ships were consumed, their crews burned alive as the sea itself caught flame wherever the flames touched. Traumatised and destroyed, the Arabs lifted their siege. The survivors dragged themselves back home as best they could through a winter storm that further harried them. The Arab land army too was destroyed by Christian forces taking advantage of the demoralised state of their foe.

The weapon that had achieved all this was the medieval equivalent of a flame-thrower – Greek fire. Naturally occurring crude oil was mixed with pine resin and stored in cylinders kept pressurised with hand pumps. Once forced out of a nozzle, the sticky fuel was ignited by small flames and directed anywhere its user wished. It's hard to imagine the impact – the shock and awe – such a technology must have had upon unsuspecting 8th-century mariners armed at best with crossbows, and the magic of its manufacture was among the most closely guarded of all the secrets within the walls of Constantinople.

A second Arab siege 40 years later also failed spectacularly, and with much loss of Muslim life. But it was in 1402 that the city was handed its final and most legendary reprieve. Sultan Bayezit I demanded the city bow down to his will – and declared that he was, after all, the greatest ruler in the world. Word of his boast reached Timur the Lame, the last great Mongol Khan and known to the West as Tamburlaine. Believing that he and not Bayezit was the supreme ruler, he brought the pretender to battle on the field at Ankara and utterly destroyed him. For centuries thereafter there persisted the legend that Bayezit was kept, for the next 20 years until his death, in a cage pulled behind Timur's dogs. In any event, Constantinople was saved.

It must have seemed to those proponents of Jihad – holy war – that this city with its elemental defences of stone, sea and fire would never fall to them. By the time Mehmet and his great army loomed over the city like the promise of bad weather, the Muslim dream of taking Constantinople for Islam was seven centuries old. Think about that. Imagine a wish sparking among us today like a flame – and being kept burning until some time in the 28th century. What kind of wish would that have to be?

The city walls stood as defiant as ever – but the flame of Jihad burned brightly in their shadow. This latest contender, Mehmet, was Bayezit's great-grandson and as determined to take the city as any Sultan or Caliph before him. In 1452 he began to make the final moves towards what he believed was his destiny and his purpose upon the Earth. He made his plans carefully and well.

Utterly isolated on the land, Constantinople was by now a city that depended upon the sea for its survival. Ships brought everything from food supplies to the munitions of war, and Mehmet understood that domination of the waterways was key to any hope of conquest. He already had a castle on the Asian side of the Bosphorus, in Anatolia, built by his great-grandfather towards the end of the 14th century. But with jaw-dropping efficiency he now organised the construction of one on the European side. Between April and August 1452 the 'Throat Cutter' was built – complete with walls over 20 feet thick and 50 feet high. Constantine and his Byzantines could only look on with wonder and dread at this demonstration of logistical prowess. Stone cannonballs from Mehmet's artillery could be sent hurtling across the Bosphorus from either side, into the hulls of any ships daring to try to pass through the straits without his permission.

What Constantine needed was help from the Christian West. As he saw it, any differences between the 'Orthodox' Christians of Byzantium and their 'Latin' Christian brothers and sisters in Rome should be set aside for the greater good of the Church. There had been attempts over the years to heal the Great Schism of 1054 – when the family had torn itself apart over the details of their beliefs – but hardliners on both sides could find no real forgiveness in their hearts. The divide separating Rome from Constantinople was much greater than the Bosphorus, and would not be bridged.

Good news, slight though it was given the scale of the threat, came in January. Towards the end of that month, two Genoese ships arrived from the Mediterranean carrying 700 armed men. Their leader was the charismatic and experienced warrior Giovanni Giustiniani Longo, who had chosen to weave his fate into that of the city. A handful of others answered the call and made their way through the gates into the last redoubt of Christian empire in the East, but as 1453 dawned Constantinople stood alone in the face of the holy warriors of Islam.

The city's population placed unshakable faith in two shields – their religion and their wall. By the time spring approached, however, both were compromised. Divided from their brothers and sisters in Rome by blinkered stubbornness on both sides, they were cut off from the mighty military resources of western Europe. Faithful prayers bring comfort but armoured knights have a more straightforward application in time of siege. Worse still, time itself had caught up with the Wall of Theodosius.

For 1,000 years it had been beyond the limitations of any military technology brought to bear upon it. Attackers first of all faced an outer ditch – the fosse – brick-lined and 60 feet wide. Those who made it across ran then into the shadow of the outer wall, 25 feet high and manned by soldiers raining down arrows, crossbow bolts, boulders, Greek fire and anything else that came to hand. Beyond that first wall lay a level terrace

60 feet wide – a killing field for the use of defenders on both the outer wall and now the inner wall. This final obstacle was the greatest of all – 40 feet high and, like the outer wall, reinforced with massive towers – providing huge advantage for those manning its battlements.

Massed armies, longbows and crossbows, great siege engines, catapults and trebuchets – all had been tried and all had broken upon it. But lumbering in the wake of the army that approached the city this time was a weapon that would test the ancient defences anew. In the years and months before this latest campaign, Mehmet had commissioned and assembled some of the greatest heavy artillery pieces the world had yet seen. The wall had been tested before by primitive Arab cannons – in the time of Mehmet's father, Murat I – and had passed with flying colours. In recent years, however, the technology for producing both gunpowder and the guns themselves had come on apace. One of the pieces hauled laboriously through the Thracian countryside towards Constantinople in the spring of 1453 was nearly 30 feet long, with a barrel big enough for a grown man to crawl inside and hunker down in. The black powder the gunners carried now was greater too – more powerful than anything that had been brought to bear upon the city's land walls before.

In the face of the juggernaut Constantine held firm. He was more than enough of a soldier to understand how grave was the threat facing his city – but like the soldier he was, he prepared to fight. He put Giustiniani in charge of the walls – repairing any gaps or weak points, sealing the gates, destroying all bridges across the fosse and seeing to it that the available fighting men were dispersed along its length to the greatest effect.

Cut off from supplies coming via the Black Sea and the Bosphorus, Constantine had sent ships to the Greek islands of the Aegean to collect whatever foodstuffs were available. Like

Mehmet, Constantine too had heavy artillery, and gunpowder and shot were stockpiled in the arsenals. Another ancient defence was set in place once more – a massive chain stretched across the mouth of the Golden Horn between Constantinople on one side and the Venetian city of Galata on the other. Now no enemy ships could enter that waterway in hope of breaching the walls on the less stoutly defended north-east side of the city.

Easter Sunday came and went, taking with it countless muttered prayers to the Virgin. It wasn't salvation that arrived next day but the enemy, filing on to the rolling terrain beyond the walls in endless procession. Where before there had been one city, now there were two – one of stone and one of canvas. As dictated by the Islamic code of war, messengers approached as far as the fosse and said the city would be spared the customary three days of sacking if it would surrender now. The response was polite but curt: there had never been nor ever would be any surrender by the Christians of Constantinople.

By the second week of April, Mehmet's guns were in position, ranged in batteries in front of perceived weak points in the Wall of Theodosius. On 12 April they opened fire for the first time – and to devastating effect. According to eyewitnesses whole sections of the wall were flattened like grass. A structure that had defied all comers for a millennium – which was, to the medieval world, as permanent as a mountain range – had finally been made vulnerable.

Effective though the guns were, the heat and force generated by firing them put almost unbearable stresses on the bronze of the barrels. To avoid the risk of them cracking – or even exploding – they had to be allowed to cool down for an hour or more after every firing. While Mehmet fretted and paced behind the guns, demanding to know why it was taking so long, Giustiniani used the breaks in the bombardment to effect hurried repairs. Inadvertently he stumbled upon the perfect remedy. The earthen ramparts he used to plug the gaps proved far more resistant to the heavy guns than any wall of stone. While stone shatters, heaped earth absorbs the cannonball and its impact.

Unable to smash the walls down quickly enough, Mehmet turned his attentions to rushing the gates. He had his men attempt to fill in the fosse – using any materials available – but withering fire from the defenders on the outer wall turned such work into a suicide mission. The corpses of the attackers were piled high. Miners were set to work then, digging tunnels towards the walls. They hoped to light fires beneath the foundations and cause their collapse – but again the would-be invaders were thwarted. Behind the battlements and fighting on the Christian side was a Scot called John Grant. He was an experienced soldier and had faced the threat posed by tunnelling many times before. By listening for the telltale sounds of digging – and watching for ripples on carefully placed bowls of water – he could detect the vibrations of the miners at work. By digging their own tunnels from above, the defenders could break in on the enemy miners – and then it was hellish hand-to-hand fighting in the near darkness to drive them off.

Behind the walls the emperor moved among his people. Tirelessly he patrolled the battlements, urging his soldiers on when fatigue was their greatest foe. He prayed with them in their churches, he waited with them through the hours of darkness and he fought with them through the days. Survivors would say later he was always visible, always with some or other knot of defenders as they stood in the face of the rising tide.

Mehmet looked next to the sea in search of the crucial breakthrough. While his gunners blasted, his infantrymen struggled and died hopelessly at the fosse and his miners scrabbled in the dirt and the dark, his ships set sail. Commissioned and built for the campaign, this fleet of galleys was yet another innovation Mehmet could bring to bear against the Christians.

He sent them now against the Byzantine ships defending the chain across the Golden Horn – but while more numerous than the defenders, the Muslim seamen were less skilled. Warfare waged at sea is something learned and passed down over centuries, and for men of the desert there was much knowledge to be acquired before they could tackle a people who had sailed trading ships on the world's oceans for generations. It seemed Mehmet was to be thwarted on the sea as well as on the land.

During those first weeks of the siege it seemed the city would hold out as it always had done. Mehmet flung more and more men and ships into the fray – probing for weaknesses on every face of the defences – and still the defenders defied him. Galled by the failure of his ships, he gazed again towards the mouth of the Golden Horn where that ancient chain barred his path. And then it came to him – if he could not go through it, he would go *around* it. Towards the end of that month of frustrations he set his engineers the task of moving his galleys over land until they could be eased into that crucial waterway at a point beyond the obstruction. As news spread that Mehmet's galleys were now behind them, and in among them, panic spread through the city's inhabitants.

Even this breakthrough was not enough. Still Constantine held the line and now deployed his defenders on to the new front of the sea wall overlooking the Golden Horn.

But although the city was bearing the burden of the siege, it was taking a terrible toll. There hadn't been enough defenders in the first place and their numbers were being winnowed by every attack, every bombardment. Those still alive faced their greatest battle, against fatigue. Rest and sleep were hard to come by for an army with no reinforcements. And here then was the rub. Worse than the fighting and the thunderous bombardment – worse even than the tiredness – was the erosion of hope. This was a people besieged. All they would ever have for the fight was here with them now. Nothing more and no one else was coming to their aid.

There were Muslim breakthroughs too – when the attackers would make it through some or other breach and grapple for a foothold within the walls. Then the fighting was in the streets and lanes, through the houses themselves. This was killing and dying face to face by sword and axe. Many times the Muslims came and every time they were cut down to the last man – their mutilated bodies hung later over the battlements by the defenders in a show of bloody defiance.

April had given way to May and still the stalemate dragged on. For Mehmet every passing day made it harder for him to maintain the resolve of his army, great though it undoubtedly was. Every failure dulled his soldiers' appetite for the siege and as May progressed he, like Constantine, was reaching crisis point. Seeing that final victory – the realisation of his destiny – might be slipping through his fingers, he called for one last great effort.

In Constantinople there were rumours and portents all around. Some said a Christian army was on its way from the west – others feared an ancient prophecy that said the empire would begin and end with a man called Constantine.

In the end the fate of all turned around a gate left unbarred. On 29 May, with fighting raging at points all around the city, a company of defenders returned from a sortie beyond the walls. Once inside and no doubt befuddled with fatigue, each thought another had the job of securing the door behind them. And in that moment a handful of the enemy surged through – living long enough to raise the Sultan's banner from a tower before each was felled. The damage was done. Word spread along the walls like a licking flame.

Inhabitants of the city looked up and saw the dread colours snapping in the breeze.

'The city is fallen,' they cried. 'The city is fallen!'

Elsewhere, Giustiniani fell badly wounded. This man who had emboldened all around him had been hurt before in the fight – and had recovered to fight and lead once more. This time his spirit was broken and he called to his followers to take him now to one of the ships in the harbour still readied for flight. After weeks of stubborn resistance, the defence began to collapse like wet sand before an incoming tide.

Hearing word of the rout – then seeing it with his own eyes as men around him broke and thought about following Gius-tiniani – Constantine cried out to the remnants of his army, urging them to hold fast. It was too late. The thrilling sight of their banner flying within the walls brought the Ottoman forces on like a wave. Where before the defenders had fought to turn them back, now they ran. Thousands of enemy soldiers were inside the defences within minutes and this time they would not be denied.

And what of Constantine at the last? It is a legend that has survived to tell his fate. Muslim and Christian alike looked up from the mud and blood of the last square feet of the Byzan-tine Empire and saw him high on the battlements. He cast off the last remnants of his imperial garb, stooped and freed a sword from the dead hand of a defender. Then as the thousands watched he leapt clear of the walls, out and down into the enemy horde. In that frozen moment he had jumped clear too of the tainted legacy of the many lesser emperors who had gone before him. In that space between the earth and the sky he was a good soldier.

Mehmet would later parade a head upon a lance, saying it was that of the fallen emperor. No confirmed trace of the remains of Constantine XI – Constantine Palaiologos, in Christ true Emperor and Autocrat of the Romans – was ever seen again.

As had been promised weeks before – and as the custom of medieval armies dictated – the city was plundered and its population of 50,000 taken as slaves. At the great Church of St Sophia, work was got under way almost immediately to turn it away from Christ and towards Allah. Hardly a building survived the onrushing wave of the Muslim soldiers.

In time, Mehmet would rebuild the place – seemingly intent on making it a city of wonders once more. Muslim observers would be stunned at the result – a place neither entirely of Islam nor of Christianity, but one man's attempt to recreate something he had never seen.

In the wider world, it was the image of the murderous, marauding Turk that was fixed. A Christian empire had been erased and one of Islam completed. The future of a world split between the two had begun.

Old age and guile beat youth and enthusiasm

The greatest defences can be overcome. Ancient fortresses can be made to yield and to give up their secrets. But luck is always part of the story, good and bad. The most careful preparations might not cover every last detail. The bravest and most ruthless execution of well-laid plans may not be enough to carry the day – without luck. In the end it so often comes down to a pass left unguarded, a door unbolted.

While mindful of the fact that his fate – and that of his companions – could never be entirely in their own hands in such a dangerous and unpredictable place, Scott set great store by studious attention to every last detail of his plans. He was determined to address in advance as many of the likely challenges as possible – and to do so, he developed an open mind about new technologies.

For one thing, his past experiences in the Antarctic had turned him against the use of animals. Squeamish about their harsh treatment in cruel conditions from the first, nothing he had seen during the *Discovery* expedition of 1901–4 had made him change his mind. He knew dogs were used routinely in Scandinavia and throughout the Arctic Circle, but nothing he had seen for himself persuaded him to rely on anything with four feet. He knew too that Shackleton had taken ponies with him aboard the *Nimrod* and that most of them had had to be slaughtered on the ice as they were overcome by the conditions one by one. Scott never hardened his heart enough to see dogs and horses as beasts of burden, and when they suffered, he suffered with them. He had brought ponies and sled dogs aboard the *Terra Nova* almost because convention seemed to demand their presence on the ice. But he was a man with an eye to the future and to progress and he had another technique in mind for hauling equipment.

He had learned about experimental motor tractors being developed by an English engineer. Most interesting from Scott's point of view was their use of a basic 'caterpillar track', a steel band that enabled them to climb and drag themselves over obstacles in a way that wheeled vehicles could not. In 1908 he had sent *Discovery* veteran Engineer-Lieutenant Reginald Skelton to the French Alps to carry out tests on the prototype. By the time Scott was making definite plans for the *Terra Nova* expedition he was open to the possibility that the tractors might make all the difference, pulling huge loads over the worst terrain without the need to cause suffering to either man or beast. This was the future.

On arrival in Cape Evans, three motor tractors were among the first pieces of equipment to be unloaded from the ship. The first two were put to work at once and quickly showed their potential by pulling tons of material across the ice towards the camp. But a portent of disaster – and of the danger of discarding the lessons of old wisdom in favour of new – came when the third and largest of the machines was being unloaded and moved into position. While a team of men prepared to man-haul it away from the ship prior to putting it to work with the other two, the ice cracked and gave way beneath it. Before anyone had time to react, it sank in 100 fathoms of water. Writing about the event in his journal, Scott described the loss as a 'disaster'.

The rest of the unloading and early preparations went off without incident, however, and he eventually shrugged off the initial shock of the loss. He was sure of his men and sure of his plans. They would overcome the challenge posed by the Antarctic and achieve the last great victory of the age. In a letter to Joseph Kinsey, the expedition's fixer back in Lyttelton,

New Zealand, Scott wrote: 'They are a fine lot all round. I could not wish for better.'

A fine new hut was erected as the base of operations – 50 feet long by 25 feet wide by 9 feet high. Inside it was subdivided into two – a wardroom for the officers and scientists and a mess deck for the men. Scott would object even to the use of the word 'hut' to describe the structure, since in his opinion it was the finest building yet constructed in the polar regions. There was a linoleum floor inside and the roof was covered in waterproof rubber. The double-thickness walls were insulated with bags of seaweed and sacks of volcanic sand were used as draught-excluders. The interior was lit by acetylene gas and there was a fully working stove and cooking range. The scientists' workspace was equipped with all the latest kit to enable them do their work as thoroughly as if they were at home. As far as Scott was concerned, their expedition would stand as a landmark, the arrival of civilisation in a primitive world.

But in another letter to Kinsey, Scott revealed that the loss of the tractor had preyed on his mind. It also seemed he had the first inkling that new technology alone might not be enough.

> The loss of one of our motor sledges was a bad blow, as the other two have proved themselves efficient by dragging big loads of stores on shore, but, even so, as I watch them working here I feel rather than know that I was right not to place serious reliance on these machines ...

While Scott and his team scurried around like black ants on that landscape, the Antarctic waited. The home team was ready as well.

Dien Bien Phu

The time had come. It was Saturday 13 March 1954 and the preparations were complete. In position all around the high ground of the slopes surrounding the massive bowl-shaped valley were tens of thousands of soldiers. Hundreds of heavy artillery pieces that had been dragged laboriously up steep mountain tracks the enemy believed impassable were primed and ready for action, overlooking the valley floor. Food supplies, medicines, ammunition and the rest of the paraphernalia required for a siege had been brought into this most remote of locations on foot and on bicycles by uncounted hordes of men, women and children – willing and unwilling alike. It had been a mobilisation of people-power the like of which the world has seldom seen. The last of the civilians had been evacuated from the area and all who remained now were warriors.

In his command post Ho Chi Minh, President of the Democratic Republic of Vietnam, was surrounded by his staff. They watched him closely now as he prepared to speak. Legend has it that he slowly removed his helmet and turned it upside down. Placing it on the table in front of him, he paused briefly and then put one clenched fist inside it.

'The French . . . are here,' he said quietly, without looking up.

Next he ran one index finger slowly around the rim, this time raising his eyes to meet the gaze of his men, each in turn, as he did so.

'And we . . . are here.' He allowed himself to smile at this, and his men smiled back at him.

The coming fight, he told them, would be like the attack of a tiger upon a trapped elephant. Again and again from the darkness of the forest the tiger would reach out to slash and cut at the limbs and belly of its much more powerful, but immobile prey. Slowly, slowly, the elephant would bleed to death.

A defining moment – perhaps the *defining moment – in the history of South-East Asia was rising above the horizon like the sunrise of a new day. The Battle of Dien Bien Phu was about to begin.*

The French had been dominant in Vietnam since 1883. The country had originally emerged as an independent nation in AD 939, when its erstwhile Chinese masters decided to withdraw from the place. Apart from a short period in the 1400s when the Chinese returned to their old haunt, it was self-governing for around 900 years. At first it called itself Dai Co Vet – the Great Viet State – or sometimes the much older name of Annam. In 1802, it took on the name Vietnam for the first time.

During the 1600s French Roman Catholic missionaries had arrived to begin converting thousands of the population. They fell foul of the Vietnamese authorities, however, and for the next two centuries were subjected to periodic persecution and oppression. From 1858 onwards the French sent soldiers into the country. Officially they were there to protect the missionaries, but in reality it was the start of colonisation. France had plans for an Asian empire. By 1883 they had forced their will over the whole country, compelling Vietnam's rulers to sign a treaty splitting it into three parts – which became known collectively as French Indochina.

The German conquest of France at the start of World War II enabled Japan, Germany's ally, to take control of the territory for a while. But their eventual defeat in 1945 opened the door to a new name and a new ideology. Ho Chi Minh had been in China, but returned to his homeland at the head of the Vietminh – the Revolutionary League for the Independence of Vietnam. Emperor Bao Dai, who had been humiliated by the Japanese occupation of his country, stepped aside to make way for the new man.

British and Chinese troops had entered Vietnam following the Japanese surrender, however, and were soon joined by the

French, keen to reassert their control. Ho Chi Minh and his followers refused to accept this reoccupation and the so-called Vietminh War began in 1946. Two years later, France had established a Nationalist Government led by Bao Dai.

Gradually, and with a depressing momentum, the nations of the West lined up to support the Nationalists. The Communist states, predictably enough and following the steps of a now familiar dance, made clear their backing for Ho Chi Minh and his Democratic opposition.

Two opposing governments then began fighting for control of Vietnam – eventually prompting the world's great powers to schedule a peace conference for April 1954, in Geneva in Switzerland, to decide the fate of the country and to try to end their own Cold War in Asia. Due to attend were representatives of the State of Vietnam, the Democratic Republic of Vietnam, Kampuchea, Laos, China, France, Great Britain, the Soviet Union and the United States of America.

In the meantime, both combatants in the war decided a last spectacular victory was required to ensure an upper hand at the peace talks. France believed it had come up with the right place and the right plan.

Time was running out for the colonists. They'd been fighting in Vietnam off and on since 1946, but if anyone had the upper hand it was the Communists under Ho Chi Minh and his gifted military commander – the teacher-turned-soldier General Vo Nguyen Giap. The French Commander in Indochina, General Henri Navarre, had inherited a demoralised army that no longer had any clear objectives beyond its own survival. The Communist forces had waged a successful guerrilla campaign, roamed freely throughout the countryside of the north and enjoyed the support of the Soviet Union and her allies. It was Navarre's job to try to regain some kind of initiative before it was too late.

As 1953 drew to a close, Navarre and his advisers identified the village of Dien Bien Phu, in a remote corner of north-west Vietnam near the borders with Laos and China, as the place for one last roll of the dice. Located towards the rear of their enemy's territory, it promised a double opportunity – to disrupt Ho Chi Minh's supply lines into the neighbouring French protectorate of Laos and to lure his massed forces into an all-or-nothing pitched battle. If France could create an attractive enough target, the thinking went, the Communists would have to attack it. Provided that target was strong enough, it would be the springboard for destroying whatever force was sent against it.

The 10-mile-long valley floor would, Navarre hoped, be turned into a killing field from which the Communists would never escape. If it proved successful, Navarre would be able to use Dien Bien Phu as the blueprint for dealing with the Communist insurgency in the rest of the country.

It sounded simple if you said it quickly enough – but in reality the plan posed enormous logistical problems and challenges for the French. First of all they had to get a large fighting force into the area. Given the location of Dien Bien Phu, and the nature of the surrounding countryside, the only way to move men into the area quickly was by air. The Japanese had effectively started the job for the French by building an airstrip there during World War II. The river valley was flat and wide and therefore presented an ideal location for an air-supplied base – and by March 1954 the French presence had grown to almost 16,000 men, almost all of whom had either been flown or parachuted in. They were French regulars, including members of the elite parachute regiments; French Foreign Legionnaires; veterans of fighting in Algeria and Morocco and Vietnamese soldiers loyal to France and the Nationalist Government of Bao Dai.

Navarre imagined that the battle to come would be a fluid and mobile affair and so placed a cavalryman – Colonel Christian

Marie Ferdinand de la Croix de Castries – in charge of the ground troops. De Castries, from a proud military family and a graduate of the Saumur Cavalry School, set about throwing a ring of seven fortified locations around Dien Bien Phu, and one of the abiding myths of the story is that he named them after his past loves: Anne-Marie, Beatrice, Claudine, Dominique, Gabrielle, Huguette and Isabelle. The fact that those names run in alphabetical order is no doubt neither here nor there, and is certainly less interesting.

The empty buildings of the Vietnamese village that had stood beside the Nam Yum River were dismantled to provide materials for the fortifications. Even the mansion of the French governor was taken apart so that the bricks could be put to use elsewhere. Gone too was every bush and tree in the valley, consumed by the French military engineers as they sought to create an impregnable redoubt.

The preparations had been impressive in terms of the speed of their execution if nothing else – but the ordinary soldiers now hunkered down on that valley floor were filled with foreboding. They were numerous, well trained and well armed – that much was true. The seven fortified positions encircling them housed modern heavy artillery. Numerous tanks and aircraft were at their disposal and they would be supported and supplied by continuous landings by supply planes. Dien Bien Phu had been designed as a hedgehog – and the enemy soldiers were expected to throw themselves on to its spines. But there was no doubting one major and deeply worrying fact: they were occupying the low ground and all around them, overlooking them, were hills and mountains that they did not control.

The army of the Vietminh had occupied that high ground: in fact Giap had managed to mass at least 50,000 men on those slopes and ridges. The French had believed the terrain was too steep and thickly forested – and the trackways leading to it too treacherous – for it to pose a realistic threat. Giap had thought otherwise, and had utilised the strong backs and legs of the local peasant population to manhandle more than 200 heavy guns into positions overlooking the French garrison and strong points.

As the Americans would learn later, the landscape of Vietnam was wholly unsuited to the tactics of conventional European armies and warfare. The French build-up at Dien Bien Phu gave them control of . . . nothing at all. They were entrenched in their position but the army of the Vietminh moved through the surrounding area like grains of sand through loosely linked fingers. Before the battle itself was even under way, the French would suffer more than 1,000 casualties at the hands of Giap's regular divisions.

But much worse was to come. Like the British in South Africa 75 years before, the French in Vietnam had misunderstood their enemy. They believed in their technology and tactics and so underestimated the significance of inferior numbers. They did not understand the terrain and so they were ready to fight the wrong kind of war in the wrong place. Worst of all, they thought Dien Bien Phu would be just another battle – and its outcome of limited significance beyond setting the tone for the imminent peace talks. What they could not know was that part of the future of the world, especially their own future, was being written for them in the hills around and above them. Change was in the air, along with the rains of the coming monsoon.

Colonel Charles Piroth, the good-natured, one-armed commander of the French artillery, had guaranteed he had all the guns he needed to destroy, or at the very least contain, anything the Communists might have managed to cobble together in this unforgiving wilderness. He couldn't have been more wrong, but he wasn't alone.

By teatime on 13 March, the first day of the battle proper, the French guns in fortress Beatrice had been utterly destroyed by Giap's highly trained and superbly camouflaged artillery high in the surrounding hills. Piroth's crews had not even been able to exchange fire with their tormentors – since they couldn't work out where they were – and after less than a single day's fighting the eventual fate of the French at Dien Bien Phu was already ominously clear.

Piroth was devastated – and humiliated. De Castries's deputy, he felt responsible for giving his superior officer a false sense of security and by the following day he was broken – just going through the motions. Under his breath he whispered about being personally responsible, and dishonoured.

Some time during the night that followed, he went alone into an underground bunker and killed himself by lying down and exploding a hand grenade clutched in his one fist.

The Vietminh artillery pounded away at the French positions with devastating accuracy. Giap's crews erected dummy gun positions to trick the French gunners – and moved their own pieces around the valley sides to ensure their locations were never fixed or predictable. The French guns were out in the open, the better to provide 360 degrees of fire, and were sitting ducks. The battle that Navarre had imagined as fast-moving, with French soldiers sallying forth to engage the enemy, swiftly degenerated into the kind of artillery duel familiar to veterans of World War I. From the start the French had to dig in and hide underground in the hope of staying alive long enough for their situation to improve.

For the defenders, Dien Bien Phu was harrowing and dreadful from the moment the Vietminh guns first opened fire. The seven forts were picked off one by one. As quickly as the French replaced the destroyed guns, they were hit again. Within weeks the French guns had fallen silent for good. The ground forces had been expecting to see steady landings of supply planes bringing fresh men and materials on an almost hourly basis. As it turned out, the airstrip was utterly destroyed by 27 March and from then on the men on the ground depended entirely on air-drops. When the fighting started, the defenders of Dien Bien Phu had an estimated eight days' worth of supplies. They needed to have hundreds of tons of material delivered every day just to keep things ticking over – and the fact the siege was endured for as long as it was is testament to the organisational talents of the supply bases outside Vietnam and the bravery of the airmen.

Pilots who had to make the runs down the narrow river valley would later say it was as dangerous as over-flying the Ruhr Valley during World War II. As well as guns for attacking the ground forces, Giap had placed anti-aircraft artillery along the valley sides. Strafed from both sides, military and civilian pilots alike ran a deadly gauntlet as they attempted to drop the thousands of tons of materials needed by the defenders. Civilian pilots Wallace Buford and James McGovern became the first Americans to die in war in Vietnam.

Legionnaires besieged within the defended compound found themselves reliving the fate of their predecessors at Camerone, but on a much greater scale. Who can know now if the legend brought them any comfort, or made it any easier to fight and die.

'Faire Camerone' – do as they would have done. And so they did.

It was Legionnaires who were given the job of recovering the air-drops. As the planes flew higher to avoid the guns, so their accuracy suffered. The territory controlled by the French was also diminishing – disappearing like an oasis exposed to constant sunlight. More and more of the parachutes could be seen falling into enemy territory and it was down to the men of the Legion to go out and bring them back. Under withering fire, men crawled on hands and knees in search of the containers under their telltale white parachutes that now littered the landscape like untimely blooms. True to the reputation of the French, sometimes the life-and-death sorties were made in search of cases of good red wine. On other occasions it was vital military intelligence that went astray – often never to be seen again. De Castries's Brigadier-General's stars, sent out to him by his commander, General René Cogny, were lost along with the bottle of champagne sent to help him celebrate his promotion in the field.

By the start of May, the French situation was becoming hopeless. Giap's strategy had steadily eroded their position until eventually they were in control of a patch of Vietnam not much bigger than a football field. By now the Vietminh had dug something like 300 miles of trenches around and into the French positions. Giap's sappers had undermined the French defences, in the medieval way, so as to blow them sky-high with buried dynamite. He had used modern artillery to knock out virtually every French gun on the ground, and anti-aircraft fire to strangle the compound. His own troops had made countless frontal assaults on every French position. It had been a classic and terrible battle of attrition.

The defenders had been reduced to exhausted, traumatised wraiths. As the siege drew to its close they were existing on a diet of black coffee and cigarettes and getting virtually no sleep while the enemy guns thundered and thundered. Casualties and corpses were piled high and the monsoon rains poured without a halt, creating hellish conditions reminiscent of Passchendaele in 1917. But in among it all there were countless acts of valour. The last medical evacuation by air had been on 26 March. Two days later one more was attempted, but the plane was damaged and could not take off again. Genevieve de Galard, a Women's Air Force nurse, was aboard the stricken flight. She stayed at Dien Bien Phu until the end, and was considered an angel by the sick and the dying.

There was little hope of relief from outside Vietnam – the distances and terrain involved made that practically impossible. The only help came by parachute – many untrained men making their first ever jumps into the blackness of the night skies over Dien Bien Phu. But it would never be enough to turn the tide. Instead the last remaining hope was for a breakout by those soldiers still in a position to make a dash for it.

By May the Vietminh were using World War II Russian Katyusha rockets for final, terrible assaults on the last of the French strongpoints. By mid-morning on 7 May de Castries could see that the last act was being played out in the quagmire conditions all around him, while Stalin's missiles howled and screamed in the air overhead. Time and again human waves of Vietminh soldiers flung themselves against the surviving defenders – time and again they were repulsed. But there were always more.

De Castries radioed General Cogny, safe back in Hanoi, and updated him himself. He was going to order the breakout by those few French forces still holding on to defended positions. He would stay behind with the wounded and surrender to the encircling Vietminh.

'But what you have done until now is magnificent,' Cogny said, horrified by the talk of giving in before the end. 'Don't spoil it by hoisting the white flag. You are going to be submerged, but no surrender – no white flag!'

'All right, mon général,' replied de Castries. 'I only wanted to preserve the wounded.'

Cogny told him: 'Yes, I know. Well … do as best you can … what you have done is too magnificent to do such a thing. You understand, mon vieux?'

Static crackled over the airwaves while de Castries imagined the consequences of what he was being told.

'Bien, mon général,' he said.

'Goodbye, mon vieux,' said Cogny. 'I'll see you soon.'

The radio operator then took the butt of his pistol to the radio set. There would be no more words from de Castries.

Isabelle, manned by 1,000 Legionnaires, as well as Algerians and French regular troops, was the only strongpoint with any hope of breaking out and trying to fight its way through the jungle to friendly Laos. It was not to be, however. Observers would speak later of seeing massive explosions as Isabelle's ammunition dumps were detonated. Vietminh forces were crawling over her defences like ants. If the men inside had even attempted to start their run, they would surely have been spotted before they could leave the cover of their trenches and walls. In the early hours of 8 May a last message came out of the darkness where Isabelle should have been.

'Sortie failed. Stop,' said a voice. 'Can no longer communicate with you. Stop and end.'

Only 70 men out a total of 1,700 ever made it out of Isabelle and through the jungle into Laos.

The final transmission was received from Dien Bien Phu in the early evening of 8 May.

'We're blowing up everything. Adieu!'

It was over.

Into the devastation rushed the massed forces of the Vietminh at last. They would not be turned back this time. A red flag was raised above the bunker that had been de Castries's command post. Dien Bien Phu had fallen, but there had been no surrender.

Out of the carnage and the chaos Giap's men collected nearly 12,000 prisoners. Some 4,500 were too badly wounded to move and were eventually given treatment where they lay, by the Red Cross. Those judged able-bodied began a death march towards prison camps waiting for them 300 miles away towards the north and east. Thousands of them died along the way, their corpses as lost and unmarked as those of more than 2,000 men who had died in the fighting. While imprisoned they were beaten, starved and generally abused. Not many more than 3,000 ever saw their homes again. De Castries was among the survivors. After four months in a prison camp he was returned to his homeland. He retired from the army in 1959 and died in Paris in 1991.

There had been a terrible cost for the Vietminh. Of the 50,000 men who had assembled at the start of the battle 23,000 were casualties now, almost one man in two. An estimated 8,000 of them were dead. But their spilt blood had changed the colour of the map of South-East Asia for ever.

French Indochina was no more and would never be recovered. The French had been on the wrong side of crucial battles before in their history – at Agincourt, Trafalgar, Waterloo – but here in Asia they had felt a shift beneath them like the movement of tectonic plates. Ho Cho Minh had shown his people and the wide world it was no longer necessary to submit to the white man. The time of unquestioned European colonial domination of Asia had been brought to an end in the mud and blood of Dien Bien Phu.

In the Geneva peace talks that followed, Vietnam was split in two, into North and South. By 1959 the Second Indochina War had broken out and before long America was being pulled towards the maelstrom.

Nikita Khrushchev, the Soviet leader, was talking to a Washington official in 1963 when he said:

> If you want to, go ahead and fight in the jungles of Vietnam. The French fought there for seven years and still had to quit in the end. Perhaps the Americans will be able to stick it out for a little longer, but eventually they will have to quit too.

Many more men, the brave and the not-so-brave, were about to add themselves to the body count in the jungles of South-East Asia.

But nothing they would attempt or achieve would ever come close to the dash and the glamour of the valorous doomed of Dien Bien Phu.

The field of human conflict

By late January Scott and his men were hard at work sledding towards the Pole to drop piles of food and fuel that could be used for the attempt proper, later in the year. Scott used ponies to begin with and once again was appalled at how badly they suffered in the snow and ice. By the middle of February they had pushed as far south as the 80th parallel, around 125 miles from Hut Point. It was at this location that they deposited the main dump of stores – the so-called 'One Ton Depot'.

Content that they had gone far enough, Scott decided to turn back and make for the base at Cape Evans. En route they met up with other members of the team – and heard some alarming news. Under the command of Lieutenant Victor Campbell, the *Terra Nova* had been sailing along the Great Ice Barrier with the intention of landing at King Edward VII Land and perhaps identifying an alternative base closer to the Pole. Bad weather had forced them to abandon their plans and take shelter in the so-called Bay of Whales. Another ship was already anchored there – it was the *Fram*, and aboard her were Roald Amundsen and his team of explorers. Campbell, who spoke Norwegian, had paid a visit to the unwelcome arrivals and asked them what their intentions were. Amundsen said they were preparing to make camp for the winter and would set out for the Pole during the Antarctic summer later in the year.

Among other things, the men aboard the *Terra Nova* had noticed and been deeply impressed by the Norwegian's use of dogs. Rather than struggling with the animals, and fighting them every step of the way, Amundsen was in complete control.

His pack pulled efficiently, easily and silently obeyed his every command. It was clear to all who watched that their rivals had a command over the environment that they themselves lacked.

When the news spread to the rest of the British team about the gatecrasher, every man of them was furious. As far as they were concerned it was Scott who had blazed the trail in the Antarctic – it was he who'd made the first journey and endured the first sufferings. It seemed only right, by the standards of English gentlemen, that Scott should be entitled to an uncontested attempt on the Pole.

Cherry-Garrard summed up the general mood when he wrote:

> For an hour or so we were furiously angry, and were possessed with an insane sense that we must go straight to the Bay of Whales and have it out with Amundsen and his men.

But there would be no fighting on the ice – not that day nor any other. Scott and his men quietly swallowed down their rage and indignation and prepared to make the best of things, in the way that manly men do.

Although Campbell had been able to pass on the news of the cuckoos in the nest, he and his team were later caught off guard by the pack-ice. Having taken their leave of the Norwegians, they headed northwards around the coast of King Edward VII Land to continue with their explorations. Landing at Cape Adare, they planned to carry out some geological survey work before rejoining the ship later on. As they made their way back to the prearranged collection point, they found the *Terra Nova* had been driven off by sea ice and the six-man party had to spend the winter in a tiny cave, surviving on a diet of seals and penguins. Had it not been for what was about to happen to Scott and his team, the endurance epic of Campbell's party would have gone down as one of the great survival stories of the whole period.

Unaware of Campbell's predicament, Scott and the rest of the men at Cape Evans settled down for the winter. There was plenty of work for the scientists to be getting on with and Scott would be able to concentrate his mind on the push for the Pole. He confided in his journal that while he would not have behaved as Amundsen had done, he could not allow it to upset him. Above all else, he would not allow the development to panic him or force him to change his plans. The departure date for the run to the South Pole was set for 1 November 1911.

Whether he liked it or not – whether he even admitted it to himself – Scott was about to go to war. Here on territory he considered his own by right he was about to be challenged by an enemy who seemed to have him outgunned. The skies over his kingdom were growing dark, and would remain so for many months to come. But if a fight was coming, then so be it. He would never surrender.

The Battle of Britain

It was towards the end of May 1940 and the Allied armies in north-west France seemed about to be swallowed whole by unstoppable German forces. Hundreds of thousands of British, French and Belgian troops were in fighting retreat, making for the coast at Dunkirk and the only hope of evacuation.

After Britain and France declared war on Germany on 3 September 1939, there was little to report at first. Life on the Home Front carried on as quietly as it always had. Men went to work every day and their womenfolk looked after the houses and cared for the children. It was all so normal. There were Anderson shelters in the back gardens of a million homes – but they were mostly covered in flowers and vegetables. The general inactivity led many to label the first eight months 'The Phoney War'.

But on 9 May 1940 Germany attacked Denmark and Norway – and then Belgium, the Netherlands and Luxembourg the following day. The British Conservative Prime Minister Neville Chamberlain resigned and Winston Churchill was asked to lead a coalition government of Conservative, Labour and Liberal MPs. The Phoney War, if it had ever existed, was over.

In France the German Army rode roughshod over everything ranged against it. The Allied counter-attack, including the Battle of Arras, was a failure and the German advance came on like a rising tide. By 20 May they had reached the French coast. The British and Belgian armies, together with the men of the French First Army, had been neatly separated from their French comrades south of the German spearhead.

At the hamlets of Le Paradis, Le Cornet Malo and Riez-du-Vinage, just over 100 men of the 2nd Battalion of the Royal Norfolk Regiment were holding their own in the face of overwhelming numbers. They were part of the force tasked with covering the general retreat and were as hard-pressed as any. They were well-trained marksmen, though, stubbornly dug in and taking a toll on the Germans trying to force their way further along the road to Dunkirk.

It was tolerable until the 27th, when their ammunition ran out – forcing them to face facts. They were completely cut off and alone, beyond the help of their Battalion headquarters. Reluctantly the 97 survivors of the fight decided to surrender to the force they had so successfully obstructed – Number 4 Company of the First Battalion of the 2nd SS Totenkopf (Death's Head) Regiment. They were 'hors de combat' after all – literally 'out of the fight' and entitled to be treated as prisoners of war.

Many of the British soldiers were injured, but all were summarily disarmed and marched into a field in front of a barn. They were ordered to stand while a pair of machine guns was set up a few yards in front of them. The German commander Obersturmführer Fritz Knöchlein ordered his gunners to open fire, and all 97 men of the Norfolk Regiment fell in a hail of bullets. German soldiers walked among the fallen, finishing them off with handguns and bayonets.

This was the atrocity remembered today as the Le Paradis Massacre. Two men survived it, Privates Bill O'Callaghan and Albert Pooley. Having earlier hidden in a pigsty, they were kept safe for some days by the farmer and her son. They eventually surrendered and were made prisoners of war. After Germany was defeated, in 1945, the pair triggered the investigation that eventually secured Knöchlein's arrest and conviction for the events at Le Paradis. He was hanged in 1949.

Thanks to the sacrifice of men like those 97 of the Norfolk Regiment, nearly 340,000 Allied troops were lifted off the beaches at Dunkirk by the mass evacuation effort known as Operation Dynamo, safe to fight many another day.

The enemy was ruthless. The first part of the Battle of France was over. The Battle of Britain was about to begin.

We were in no condition to fight when we declared war on Germany in 1939. The horrors of the Great War of 1914–18 had persuaded the great and the good that we should all disarm and leave bodies like the League of Nations to find peaceful ways to settle disputes. It was a noble thought. Britain proved spectacularly good at disarming – and energetic in persuading others, like France, to do likewise. Sometimes noble thoughts alone are not enough.

When Hitler came to power in 1933 he ordered the rearming of his country. He was determined the 'Fatherland' would regain a dominant position in the world – while leaving the business of diplomacy to those with the stomach for it. Britain and the rest stood by for years as Hitler amassed the stuff of war and menaced his neighbours.

By the time Hitler's armies began to move in 1939, Britain was still drowsy after years of slumber. There were early jabs by the enemy. On 14 October a German U-boat got into the naval base at Scapa Flow and sank the battleship *Royal Oak*, killing 833 men and boys. Two days later a pair of Junkers 88 bombers attacked warships stationed in Rosyth on the Firth of Forth, the start of the air war.

But the real wake-up call came with the terrifyingly close shave of the Battle of Dunkirk – and the realisation that only the few miles of the English Channel separated us from a terrible foe. France was left to face the German army alone. The enemy entered Paris on 14 June and accepted the surrender on the 22nd. Here at home we were finally wide awake, and caught up in a panicky scramble to get ready for work before it was too late.

Though he would become the embodiment of British will long before the end, Churchill didn't command the adoration of the British people at the start. His colleagues in the House of Commons thought him a heavy drinker and believed his defiance in the face of Hitler was little more than empty bravado.

But if nothing else in those early days and weeks, he was right to fear the Führer – and to call upon every British citizen to stand up and be counted.

'I expect the Battle of Britain is about to begin,' he told Parliament on 18 June 1940. 'The whole fury and might of the enemy must very soon be turned on us. Hitler knows that he will have to break us in this island or lose the war.'

It was also the speech in which he promised that triumph over this enemy would rank above all other possible achieve-ments for 1,000 years to come – 'their finest hour'.

So the Germans were coming. First to face their fury and might would be the men and women of the Royal Air Force (*boys and girls* is just as close to the mark, since so many were teenagers fresh from school). Theirs are the names engraved most deeply into the crumbling monolith of British-ness. The truth of the matter – what it revealed about bravery and the best of men – shines like a golden thread within the confusing tapestry that has been woven around the events of the summer of 1940.

Many historians say the significance of the RAF that summer has been exaggerated and that Churchill invented 'the Battle of Britain' to suit his own ends. They say he used his undisputed powers of rhetoric to persuade us it would be the first of many fights needed to defeat the Nazis; that he was setting the stage for drama and preparing the leading role for himself.

There are certainly good reasons for believing Hitler never planned for the long-drawn-out war the British Prime Minister was predicting in sombre tones. Germany's economy was unpre-pared for such an effort, and in any case it seems he was sure a short-lived, massive assault across Europe would bring victory in weeks or months. By the time his men arrived at Dunkirk, they say, Hitler was on the last page of his own prepared script. Britain was supposed to give up without a fight and settle for a negotiated peace.

Those same people claim Hitler dropped his plans to invade this island not because his Luftwaffe were bested in the air over south-east England, but because he had reluctantly to turn his attentions east towards the USSR. And they say it was the leviathan of the Royal Navy, not planes and pilots, that blocked the invasion. After all, surely no warrior in the world would have dared put men in open boats into the English Channel bound for our coastline while our destroyers still ruled the waves.

To accept this version of events, however, is to miss the point of the kind of tales that make men out of boys. This is not about the global significance of brave men's actions – it's about the way the stories of those actions make us feel as human beings.

You can still visit the sites of some of the airfields that were home to the RAF and Fighter Command during World War II: places with familiar names like Biggin Hill, Hornchurch, Kenley, Debden. Even on those overtaken by modern development there's an atmosphere of times past. But if the sky was ever as blue as the stories claim, the sun as bright or the clouds as still, that time is not now. There was a quality in the air during the perfect summer of 1940 that might as well have been magic, its reality is so hard to believe in any more. But it's the magic that has lasted.

Hitler's plans for the invasion of Britain were codenamed Seelöwe – Operation Sealion. But before he would risk his troops on a Channel crossing, he wanted the RAF swept from the sky. His advisers were nervous about an amphibious invasion under any circumstances. The English Channel had brought calamity to would-be invaders of Britain in the past and was, anyway, controlled by the fearsome Home Fleet. The German Navy – the *Kriegsmarine* – was far too small even to dream of tackling its opposite number head on, and so the only hope of protecting an invasion force lay with aircraft, dive bombers in particular. The Royal Navy's attentions would have to be too distracted, by what was going on above their heads, to have time for dealing with what was happening on the sea. Operation Sealion was scheduled for the middle of September, so the RAF would have to be neutralised by the end of August. Reich-Marshal Hermann Goering promised his master the job would be easily and speedily accomplished.

By 18 June Britain had withdrawn all her forces from France. The RAF had been fighting all the way, covering the retreat and evacuation and harrying the enemy on its own account. The cost had been severe, in terms of both men and aircraft. The only glimmer of hope lay in the fact that the Luftwaffe had been hurt too. The weeks they took to replace their losses and establish control of the airfields in their newly conquered territories gave British factories precious time to build new aircraft – and British families the chance to say goodbye to their young men.

The backbone of the air defence would be provided by the more numerous Hawker Hurricanes, single-seater fighter planes powered by Rolls Royce Merlin engines and armed with eight 0.303-calibre Browning machine guns. They had been in production since 1936 and were simple to build and reliable in action. In the battle to come they would account for by far the majority of RAF kills, as many as seven in every 10. But 'Hurricane' is not the plane or the name that comes most instantly to mind at any mention of the Battle of Britain. That honour goes to the most famous, most eulogised, best loved and most perfect aircraft ever to do a job of work: the Supermarine Spitfire.

Designed by Reginald J. Mitchell, the prototype flew for the first time on 5 March 1936. It had the same engine and armament as the Hurricane but was so much more than the sum of its parts. There was the distinctive outline of its elliptical wing and something more intent and meaningful about its poise in flight. The Merlin engine sang a different song from inside the heart of this younger plane – younger by just a few months. She was as fast and manoeuvrable as anything else in the sky. But none of that is enough to explain why the Spitfire captured and kept the heart of every pilot who saw one or flew one. Talk to any of the surviving Spitfire pilots and he'll tell you the same. They were just a bit special.

Mitchell died suddenly, in 1937, aged just 42. He would never see the triumph of his greatest work. The development of the Spitfire would not stop with him, though. Improvements were made on the basic design throughout the war and beyond. In all, there would be 50 variations on the original. But while the Mark II was already being delivered to bases by June 1940, it was the Mark I – truly the most noble of all the bearers of the name – that fought its way to legend in the Battle of Britain.

Designing a beautiful aeroplane is one thing – seeing its potential is another. Both the Spitfire and the Hurricane were actually acquired for the RAF by the man who would mastermind our side of the fight, Air Chief Marshal Hugh Dowding. A Scottish-born pilot and squadron commander during World War I, he always had a prickly relationship with his superiors and was often close to falling completely out of favour. But all who worked with him were struck by his extraordinary organisational vision and it was this that made him irreplaceable. Before the outbreak of World War II he was placed in charge of Fighter Command, and from there he masterminded the creation of the 'Dowding System', exploiting the brand-new technology of radar to spin a defensive web across the skies over Britain. By June 1939 he was due to retire, but with the storm clouds gathering ominously overhead he was asked to stay in post.

Under Dowding, Fighter Command was split into groups – each of which was responsible for its own patch of sky. Closest to Europe – and preparing to face the brunt of any attack from the Luftwaffe – was Number 11 Group, covering London and the south-east of England. It would be supported by Number 10 group, covering the south-west, and Number 12 Group, covering the midlands and the north.

Throughout the month of June 1940 the Luftwaffe made night-time bombing raids on targets across Britain. As well as weakening our military machine, this was designed to begin the job of wearing down and demoralising the British people. But it also served to demonstrate that the Dowding System worked. By the start of July the RAF had amassed a force of 640 fighters against the Luftwaffe's 2,600 fighters and bombers.

Much is always made of the German numerical superiority – and the doughty underdog role played by our own force. But it should always be remembered that we were fighting over our own land. RAF pilots shot down in dogfights, and surviving the parachute descent, could be back at their airfields within the hour. By contrast their Luftwaffe counterparts were a long way from home, always having to keep back enough fuel for the journey home to base. If they were shot down, they faced the prospect of capture and spending the rest of the war in captivity. And of course there is always an edge for men fighting to defend their own fields, streets and homes. For many RAF pilots this combat in the skies above Britain was as personal as war can ever be.

British historians are generally agreed that the Battle of Britain really began on 10 July, when the Luftwaffe launched their first daylight-bombing raids. This was the tightening of the screws, to see how long the RAF – and the British people – could take the pressure, and on 16 July Hitler decided the preparations for his invasion should begin in earnest.

In harbours and other sheltered places along the coast of the Low Countries, the landing craft and barges for the imminent invasion began steadily to grow in number. The air-fighting up to this point had been sporadic, limited and hesitant, as each side sought to find where the other's weaknesses lay. No one had ever fought a battle entirely in the sky before – there were no rules to follow because the rulebook for this kind of engagement was yet to be written. Pilots tested one another, practising their moves in empty perfect skies.

The pilots: these are the players who've hardly been mentioned so far. The Hurricanes were efficient weapons of war and the Spitfires dazzling, heart-stopping wonders. But they were only machines. They were given life by the men and boys who flew them. It's ironic that the fight remembered as the Battle of *Britain* was fought on our behalf by pilots and crews not just from these shores, but also from Australia, Belgium, Canada, Czechoslovakia, Ireland, France, Jamaica, New Zealand, Palestine, Poland, Rhodesia and South Africa. Some joined the fight from Britain's overseas territories, pulled in by a sense of duty to the mother country. Others were from among the dispossessed of Europe and elsewhere – men whose homelands had been invaded by the common enemy and who were desperate for any chance to strike back, to begin the long struggle towards liberation. The United States of America were still two years away from the war, and yet so many of their young pilots came here to lend a hand that by September 1940 there were enough to form the first American Eagle squadron. In time they would write their own part in the legend.

During the course of the fighting that summer, just over 3,000 RAF men took to the air. This is why Churchill could justifiably talk about 'the few' and why the names of individuals rose to immortality in a way that seldom happened for men fighting upon the land or the sea.

Douglas Bader, who lost both legs in a crash in 1931 but returned to the air, climbing into the cockpit with artificial limbs made of aluminium; Wing Commander James 'Johnnie' Johnson, with 38 confirmed 'kills' the undisputed number one RAF ace of World War II; Pilot Officer Eric Lock, whose 26 kills in the summer of 1940 made him the most lethal RAF flier of the Battle of Britain; New Zealander Flight Lieutenant Al Deere, who won the Distinguished Flying Cross for shooting down three Me 109s and three Me 110s in four days as he fought to cover the evacuation from Dunkirk in May 1940; Paddy Finucane; 'Sailor' Malan. The list of names demanding and deserving of remembrance runs on and on.

And what of the enemy? Their men and boys were just as brave – or else the Battle of Britain would never have gone down in legend the way it has. The name of one of their fliers stands above all others, even alongside the best of the RAF. He was Major-General Adolf Galland, moustachioed, cigar-smoking, a dashing figure straight from the pages of a *Boy's Own* annual. He flew Me 109s during the battle – superb aircraft in their own right – and yet when Goering asked him what would help the Luftwaffe defeat the RAF he replied, 'A squadron of Spitfires.'

Like Deere – against whom he fought in single combat, though both survived the encounter – and like Bader, Galland made it through the whole of the war. Some of that was down to skill and a lot was down to luck, as all three would cheerfully have admitted. But such was the nature of the fight in the skies, one-on-one like the champions of old, there grew between the pilots a certain mutual respect. Galland and Bader became friends in the years after 1945, and when the German died an old, old man in 1996, his funeral was attended by the Englishman's sons.

As July gave way to August, the fight for control of the skies intensified – for the Battle of Britain took months, not hours or days, and was as much about attrition as anything else. Aircraft were no longer the main problem for the RAF – systems of production had been set in place that were capable of turning out ample numbers of Hurricanes and Spitfires indefinitely. Though more numerous than the Spitfires – and the configuration of their guns more effective in action – the Hurricanes were slower than the German fighters and therefore vulnerable to their attack. To cope with this, Hurricanes were used to pick off the lumbering German bombers, while their speedier and more graceful accomplices were held back in readiness to target incoming Messerschmitts.

No – planes were not the problem. Instead we were struggling to find enough men to fly them. The fighting was taking an awful toll, and while every lost aircraft is much like another, easily made again with more metal and plastic, each man is unique and irreplaceable. Exhaustion was a factor too – as pilots had to spend more and more time aloft while the Luftwaffe's superior numbers were thrown against them again and again. Even on the ground there was little real rest to be had. Instead the grounded hours were spent in stressful readiness waiting for the call to 'scramble', when the enervating tension was replaced by fear.

Fighter-pilots, then as now, are a special breed of men. Talk to them and they generally deny it – but they know it too. The best of them have innate abilities that mark them out as natural predators, and also survivors. Their faith in their own abilities enables them to perform actions that can seem plain reckless to the rest of us. I spoke to one veteran of the Battle of Britain who once watched a fellow pilot bring his Spitfire in low over a field, out of sight of his superiors, before flipping it upside down and lowering it steadily towards the ground, inch by inch, until he was able to snag some tufts of grass in the aerial sticking up behind his cockpit canopy. This then, was the stuff of 'the few'.

RAF selection processes also gave priority to men who had been hunters in civilian life. The lightning reactions needed to raise a rifle barrel towards speeding prey – and the ability to judge just how far in front of it to direct the bullet so the animal runs on to it – were skills the flight tutors didn't have time to teach. But these were the skills that were needed to put bullets into enemy fighters passing each other at combined speeds in excess of 700 m.p.h. Here then is part of the power of the story of the Battle of Britain. It was a style of combat from the time of legend: single combat by superheroes.

Across the Channel, Hitler was growing increasingly impatient. Goering had promised him quick success and yet now it was August and still the best efforts of his Luftwaffe were being thrown back across the water. The date of 13 August was given the name *Adlertag* – Eagle Day – when all hopes were pinned on the biggest raid yet launched against the RAF. German pilots flew nearly 1,500 sorties that day and yet the onslaught, designed as a hammer blow, was thwarted. Somehow the Dowding System enabled just enough RAF planes and pilots to be in just the right places enough of the time. Two days later an even greater push was attempted, even more planes and even more sorties. But Fighter Command found its way through the storm.

As August gave way to September, the Luftwaffe tried a change of tactics. First they concentrated their efforts on the airfields themselves – a tactic that might have worked had it been started earlier and sustained for longer. Then from 7 September onwards they made the British people their targets as well. The 'Blitz' came to London that day and would return again and again until the spring of 1941.

Finally, on 15 September, came the day of all days. A total of 162 German bombers pounded London in waves of sorties. The Supermarine factory at Woolston was attacked, so too the town of Portland. Every Me 109 passed fit for action, well over 600 of them, was in the air too, harrying the overstretched British fighters. Time and again our pilots took to the air, returning to base just long enough to refuel and rearm. Spitfires could only stay in the air for around half an hour on a full tank and a single 15-second burst from the machine guns would fire every bullet in the belt. Their presence in the sky was brief and precious. The German attack seemed like it would never end, and defeat for the RAF now might be followed by the long-dreaded seaborne invasion, already weeks overdue.

As dusk began to fall, the German aircraft finally began to withdraw. They had thrown everything they had at the RAF and it had not been enough. Gradually, each pilot in turn looked at his fuel gauge and realised it was time to go home. There would be no final victory this day – nor any day as it turned out.

It's next to impossible to arrive at final figures for losses and kills on 15 September 1940 – the day we remember now as 'Battle of Britain Day'. The British Air Ministry claimed 177 kills – 124 bombers and 53 fighters. They also judged a further 41 'probable kills' and 25 others so damaged they would never have been able to take to the air again, even if they made it home. Lost that day were 30 aircraft and 12 men. During the Battle of Britain, between early July and late October, something of the order of 1,700 German planes were shot down, with the loss of over 500 RAF airmen from 14 countries. Another 400 had been wounded, many seriously and permanently.

There had been other costs to pay and other lives lost. Between July and December 1940 more than 23,000 civilians were killed and more than 32,000 wounded by German bombing raids on British cities. As a result of a single raid in December, nearly 3,000 innocent people lost their lives. There would be many more civilian deaths to come. Centres of British industry had been badly damaged too – though not our industrial *capability*. But Dowding and the RAF had won the Battle of Britain and the Luftwaffe had been so severely damaged it would never fully recover. By the end of 1940, Hitler had postponed Operation Sealion indefinitely.

Was it the battle in the sky that persuaded him to change his plans? Did 3,000 RAF pilots turn back the tide? Those questions don't require answers. What is true is that the Battle of Britain was part of the long story that ended with Allied victory in Europe, and then in the Far East. It's also impossible to deny the immortal bravery of the pilots and ground crews who ensured the survival of the RAF at a time when its destruction seemed inevitable. Perhaps most importantly of all, the Third Reich had been made to experience its first defeat.

Another fragment of the legend of that summer has Churchill, together with his Chief of Staff 'Pug' Ismay, monitoring events, one late August day, inside Number 11 Group's operations room at Uxbridge.

The tension in the room crackles like electricity in the moments before a thunderstorm. Churchill turns to Air Vice-Marshal Keith Park and asks for an update on whatever force he's holding in reserve. Park tells him there's nothing in reserve – that every pilot and plane is in the sky above them.

The minutes and hours drag by and still Churchill waits, desperate to know the outcome. Finally word begins to filter through that the German planes, once thick as flies, are now thinning in number. As the light goes out of the sky, so too do the last of the bombers and Me 109s and 110s. It's not even the beginning of the end, but at least this day is over.

Churchill and Ismay leave the operations room to return to Chequers. As they're getting into their staff car, Pug starts to say something to his boss. Churchill, sitting down and staring straight ahead, slowly holds up one hand.

'Don't speak to me just yet,' he says quietly to his friend. 'I have never been so moved.'

A few seemingly endless minutes pass in silence, the only sound the purr of the car's engine and the hum of its tyres over the tarmac. Finally Churchill leans forward.

'Never in the field of human conflict,' he murmurs, as much for his own ears as for Pug's, 'has so much been owed by so many to so few.'

Ismay would later note in his diary that those words burned

themselves into his brain and that he had to repeat them to his wife as soon as he got home that night. Some days later, on 20 August, Churchill would address Parliament and reveal they had stayed with him too.

Their finest hour

It's fashionable now to play down the achievements of 'the few'. They were stubborn and they were brave – not to mention stylish – but their efforts didn't really make any difference to the course of the war. That's what they say.

But that's not the point. What matters is that 'the few' did what they set out to do. Getting the job done is the important thing. The victory of the Royal Air Force over the Luftwaffe in 1940 was part of a noble tradition of knuckling down, seeing it through to the end. Scott carried that torch through the darkness of his own journey and passed it on.

Manly men don't concern themselves overmuch with the big picture – they don't weigh up whether their sacrifice will win the war or guarantee the applause of a grateful nation.

When all's said and done it's about having '*"Done things" just for the doing, letting babblers tell the story.*'

Manly men do what they set out to do because anything less is to let the side down.

Scott was the underdog when he set out with his team on the evening of 1 November 1911. He was accompanied by Edward Wilson, Edward Atkinson (expedition surgeon), Henry 'Birdie' Bowers, Titus Oates, Apsley Cherry-Garrard, Charles Wright, and Petty Officers Tom Crean, Edgar 'Taff' Evans and Patrick Keohane. A two-man team using 23 dogs would bring up the rear.

Despite the pall cast over the proceedings by the knowledge that Amundsen and his more experienced party were out there ahead of them on the ice, Scott remained determined that they should and would do their duty. The Pole was the target and that was all he would allow himself to think about.

In his journal he wrote:

The future is in the lap of the gods; I can think of nothing left undone to deserve success.

What he couldn't know was that Amundsen and his team of four companions had set out two weeks before – and by the time Scott and his men were bidding farewell to their comrades at Cape Evans, the Norwegians were the best part of 200 miles further down the route towards the Pole.

Scott's main party was using ponies – the tractors having left the week before, heading for the Great Ice Barrier with heavy loads of food and fuel. Right from the off the animals found the going heavy and covered only a handful of miles a day. On 21 November they caught up with the tractor team – Teddy Evans, Chief Stoker Lashly, Day and Hooper, the tractors having been abandoned miles back in the snow. The new technology had failed and the men had been reduced to the old nightmare of man-hauling.

The Norwegians, many miles ahead, were having no such problems. They'd set out with 52 dogs, and Amundsen had calculated, with ruthless precision, the day on which each animal would become more useful as a future food supply than as a beast of burden. When that day came the animal was dispatched with a bullet to the head and set aside as food for the journey home.

Trailing 200 miles or more behind him, Scott was being reminded that he was not – had never been – a lucky man. By the time they were on the Beardmore Glacier they were suffering badly in atrocious weather conditions. The first week in December brought the worst blizzard Scott had yet experienced in the Antarctic. For four days the men were trapped in their tents eating food that should have been propelling them towards the Pole. When the snowfall finally stopped, the temperature was unseasonably warm, creating a scum of slush that ensured everything from clothes to sleeping bags remained soaking wet, day and night. By now, and just to compound the misery, they were man-hauling too. The ponies had found the going impossibly hard and had been shot, skinned and turned into a food supply.

On 14 December, Scott ordered the dog team to turn back. They had delivered their food stores to the lower part of the Beardmore Glacier – ready for the main party's return – and there was no point in their going any further or consuming more of the dwindling supplies. On the same day, Amundsen and his men reached the Pole. They had experienced next to nothing of the hardship that was a daily reality to the British team. Their experienced handling of their dogs – their suitability for the job in hand – meant the two parties might as well have existed on different planets.

Towards the top of the glacier Scott made his first decision about which of the 12 men should keep going, and which foursome should be sent back to Cape Evans. Only four would make the final push and so this was just the first of two heart-breaking judgement calls for the leader. Atkinson, Cherry-Garrard, Keohane and Wright were the first to turn around and head for home – and were bitterly disappointed. So much struggle and sacrifice could surely only be made worthwhile by a share of the final glory? The remaining eight split into two teams of four – one consisting of Scott, Oates, Wilson and Taff Evans; the other of Bowers, Crean, Lashly and Teddy Evans.

Beyond the Beardmore Glacier, out on the polar plateau itself, spirits were briefly raised as for the first time they felt they could almost see the end of the journey. On 3 January Teddy Evans, Lashly and Crean were told they would be going home. Scott had changed his plans at the last possible moment and would lead four, rather than three, over the last stage. There's no general agreement among historians about why he suddenly added an extra man to the party bound for the Pole. Perhaps he just wanted to allow as many of them as possible to share the glory. The homeward-bound trio accompanied Scott, Wilson, Taff Evans, Bowers and Oates for a few more miles the following day. Eventually, and amid much sadness, Scott insisted they had come far enough and the final farewells were said.

On 16 January, Bowers spotted a dark speck off in the distance. It seemed out of place in the landscape. A few more miles of painful hauling in the traces revealed the truth. It was a flag on top of a cairn and stretching away from it in two directions were the tracks of sleds. By then, the Norwegian flag had been flying at the South Pole for the best part of a month, but for Scott and his men the disappointment was fresh, and cut as deeply as a newly sharpened blade.

They erected their own Union Jack, given to them by Queen Alexandra, and posed for photographs. A thread was used to let them operate the shutter remotely and take the famous snap of all five of them together.

Scott wrote in his journal about how sorry he was for his 'loyal companions' and how he expected the journey back to Cape Evans would be 'dreadfully tiring and monotonous'.

With hope and expectation gone from their souls, the men began to falter. Wilson suffered bouts of snow blindness and for the rest there was frostbite to hands, feet and faces, as well as strain injuries to muscles in legs and backs. The swelling of one of Oates's feet began to give cause for real concern.

At no point did they get any breaks from the weather and every step of every mile was a dreadful slog through bitterly cold temperatures and thick snowfalls. On 3 February, Petty Officer Evans took a heavy fall from which he never fully recovered. As the days wore on his mood changed and his personality seemed to disintegrate. Wilson thought concussion might have been to blame, but more recent thought suggests the man may have been suffering the early symptoms of scurvy.

Whatever the cause, on 16 February Scott wrote: 'Evans has nearly broken down in brain, we think. He is absolutely changed from his normal, self-reliant self.'

The following day, as they hauled and dragged as usual, Evans stepped out of the traces. He lagged further and further behind and, when his companions lost sight of him, they struggled back to find him collapsed in the snow. They carried him on a sled until they could make camp and then got him inside one of the tents. He never regained consciousness and died at around 10 p.m. that evening.

'A very terrible day,' wrote Scott.

Down off the glacier and on towards the Barrier. Still there was no respite and no help from nature. To add to their woes, the men were finding a shortage of fuel at each successive supply dump. Now even the prospect of a hot meal at the beginning and end of the day became too much to ask.

Oates was the next to be lost. His condition had deteriorated steadily and as March progressed his badly frostbitten feet became too inflamed and painful to walk on. At this point, Scott became understandably confused about dates, but around 16 or 17 March the men awoke to yet another blizzard and Oates asked to be left in his sleeping bag. His companions refused and the Soldier struggled on for one more day. He hoped not to wake next morning, but did – to hear the blizzard still howling.

He roused himself one last time and told the rest of them: 'I am just going outside and may be some time.'

He was never seen again.

Scott wrote:

He went out into the blizzard and we have not seen him since. Though we tried to dissuade him, we knew it was the act of a brave man and an English gentleman.

The date of 17 March would have been especially significant to Oates: it was his 32nd birthday.

Scott, Bowers and Wilson were, by then, within 10 or 11 miles of One Ton Depot. Cherry-Garrard had waited there with the dog team for several days, until shortage of fuel and worsening weather forced the return to Cape Evans.

The same unrelenting blizzard forced the trio into their tent once more. They had mere scraps of food and no more fuel for heating or cooking.

They knew how close they were to the depot and the hope of salvation, but every time they thought about attempting the final push, the weather defied them.

'I do not think we can hope for any better things now,' wrote Scott. 'We shall stick it out to the end, but we are getting weaker, of course, and the end cannot be far. It seems a pity, but I do not think I can write more.'

It was 29 March 1911.

Thermopylae

The battlefield of Isandlwana in kwaZulu Natal, South Africa, is marked here and there by memorials to the dead. It's a vast and wild place dominated from every angle by a mountain shaped like the back and loins of a resting lion. Scattered among stunted trees, aloe bushes and endless swaths of parched grass, the monuments of stone and bronze seem incongruous – not least the iziqu that remembers Zulu valour. Another is dedicated to 22 men of the Royal Natal Carbineers and has written on it:

> Not theirs to save the day
> But where they stood, falling to dye the earth
> With brave men's blood for England's sake and duty
> Be their names sacred among us
> Neither praise nor blame add to their epitaph
> But let it be simple like that which marks Thermopylae
> Tell it in England, those who pass us by
> Here, faithful to their charge, her soldiers lie.

The comrades of 22 South African soldiers killed in 1879 found the need to recall a battle fought by Greeks and Persians 5,000 miles away and 2,359 years before. It was the greatest honour they could bestow, this comparison, this self-conscious echoing of words in Greek on another stone in another place. They wanted to believe their fallen had been part of something as deserving of eternal memory as that other battle, fought in the shadow of another lion.

Looming over all of it was a man more legend now than real. The place where he fell was marked for a time with a stone lion – a deliberate choice, since 'leon', the Greek word for lion, recalled the first four letters of the hero's name. He was Leonidas, King of Sparta and

commander of 'the 300' who, in the summer of 480 BC, fell alongside
him on a low hill overlooking the Malian Gulf of the Aegean Sea at
the place they called Thermopylae.

The seeds of the trouble that would lead to war and the immortal
battle had been sown in that ancient world around the year
491 BC. Heralds of the expanding Persian Empire of King Darius
the Great had arrived in the independent Greek city-state of
Sparta requesting proof that the inhabitants would submit to
imperial rule.

'Greece' in the 5th century BC was not the unified country
of modern times but rather a collection of perhaps 1,000 tiny
independent states, many openly hostile to one another and
scattered around the rims of the Mediterranean and Black Seas.
Plato described them as frogs around the edge of a pond.

The Persian Empire, founded around 550 BC, stretched from
India to the eastern coast of the Aegean Sea and had spread
from its source in modern Iran faster than anything the world
had seen before. The proof required by those heralds was an
offering of earth and water, symbolic of submission, and samples
had already been peacefully handed over by many other Greek
states. The citizens of Sparta, however, were made of sterner
stuff than many of their neighbours. For them, freedom was all
and death preferable to life lived beneath a tyrant's yoke. When
the heralds requested Spartan earth and water they were put
to death – in fact they were told to get it themselves and thrown
down a well. The heralds who arrived in Athens were also killed
and now both states were united – willingly or unwillingly – by
the blood of a vengeful foe.

The Persian Empire had placed the shadow of its hand over
scores of different peoples and civilisations – but it's the way
of the Spartan that is most alien, most incomprehensible, when
viewed with our modern eyes. Yet it is their way of thinking
and of *being* that has set the standard by which countless acts

of valour and self-sacrifice have been measured ever since. Great indeed was the shadow cast by the Persian multitude, but the blinding light of Leonidas and his 300 would not be dimmed by all the years from then until now.

Sparta was the principal city within a territory more accurately described as Lacedaemon. It was regarded, by its neighbours of the 5th century BC, as the strongest military power on mainland Greece – and the reason for this supremacy lay in the way it governed its subject population. Full Spartan citizens – those living as free men and women – were a privileged minority greatly outnumbered by an underclass of Greek people they called 'helots', literally slaves. These people the Spartans forced, under perpetual pain of death, to work as labourers and domestic staff. It was helots who toiled in the fields, cooked and cleaned in Spartan homes and provided every other menial function necessary to the smooth running of the society.

All of the Greek city-states depended to some extent upon the labour of slaves but everywhere else these were 'barbarians' – people of other races or civilisations captured in war or by invasion. Only in Sparta did Greek enslave Greek.

Freed from normal labours, Spartan men were ordered to devote all their time and energy to preparing and training for war. War was the ultimate occupation and the Spartans its ultimate practitioners. They were forbidden by law to practise any other trade or craft but soldiery, and from the age of seven boys were taken from the family home and lodged in barracks where they embarked upon a harsh and relentless military training that set the pattern for the rest of their lives. Every Spartan man was a soldier in what was effectively a standing army – but an army with no clear objective beyond the borders of its own territory. Rather than a force primed for invading or oppressing its neighbours, the primary concern of the Spartan Army was to hold itself in readiness to suppress any revolt by the helots within Lacedaemon itself. In fact every year the state declared 'war' upon the helots. At the first sign of revolt any ringleaders could be slaughtered with impunity – thus absolving their Spartan executioners of any 'contamination' of the soul as a result of such an otherwise unclean act.

The Spartans – men and women, children and adults – led lives so foreign to our own that they might have been lived on another planet, let alone in another time. Soon after birth infants were dunked into bowls of wine and, depending on how they reacted in front of the elders tasked with administering the test, were either allowed to live or were taken and thrown to their deaths in a ravine outside the city. Babies born with any kind of defect or disability were similarly dispatched. This was merely the start of a life of endless tests – of constant scrutiny by self and by others to ensure each citizen was worthy of the name ... Spartan.

Death and the expectation of death lived within and among this civilisation like members of the family. Rather than being buried in separate cemeteries or burial grounds outside the city, the dead were cremated or inhumed close at hand. Mortal remains were not to be shunned or feared but accepted, inevitable as the passage of time.

While living in the barracks, boys in their early teens were routinely paired with older boys who became their mentors, minders and usually their lovers. The influence of the older man over the life of the younger might continue into adulthood – long after the marriage of both to Spartan women. A powerful senior partner might secure a path to promotion and social advancement for his younger protégé.

The greatest aspiration for any Spartan man – his duty, in fact – was to die a beautiful death in combat. Spartan burial rites forbade the inclusion of much in the way of grave goods or even a headstone for the vast majority of the deceased. Only the greatest warriors, who had given up their lives in a way admired by their fellows, were accorded the honour of a stone bearing their names and the two-word acknowledgement, 'in war'. Spartans called themselves Lacedaemonians – or Lakones – and it is from this root that we get our English word 'laconic', descriptive of a man of few words. This brevity extended even to the veneration of their war dead.

(In 346 BC Philip II of Macedon was busy conquering everyone within reach. To the Spartans he sent this message: 'You are advised to submit without further delay, for if I bring my army into your land I will destroy your farms, slay your people and raze your city.' The Spartans' one-word reply stopped Philip in his tracks: 'If.')

For Spartan women the principal obligation was the production of healthy children, preferably sons who would become soldiers. Those who died in childbirth – like men who died the most beautiful deaths in battle – were granted headstones over their graves. Women too had their wars to fight in the name of Sparta, and valiant deaths suffered in that single combat commanded as much respect as any won upon the edge of a sword or at the point of a spear.

With the domestic duties around the home being performed by helots, Spartan girls and women were free to concentrate on higher matters – like encouraging their boys and men to seek glory in war. They were expected to shun any man or male behaviour that was not brave or valorous. Their instruction to husbands, brothers and sons departing for battle was 'with it, or on it', a reference to the warrior's shield. Spartan infantry-men were called 'hoplites' – literally shield bearers – and to throw away or otherwise lose a shield guaranteed ridicule and, worse, dishonour. The women were telling their men they expected to see them return carrying their shields in victory or carried home dead upon them by their comrades.

Spartan women enjoyed freedoms unknown by those in other Greek states, including the right to own property. It's worth pointing out that while homosexual relationships were accepted between unmarried boys in the barracks, such behaviour was expected to stop once the men married and took on their part of the job of making children. Sparta was about being a soldier and making soldiers.

Parallel to the belief in the rightness and the glory of war was a profound belief in the overarching power of their gods. If Spartans believed themselves subject to anything, it was to the will of a pantheon of gods – all of whom they visualised armoured and armed for battle. Central to their religion was a dependency on divination. It was normal, even expected, for commanders to delay decisions in the thick of battle while they repeatedly examined the entrails of sacrificed animals or consulted other oracles, signs or portents in hope of being told what to do for the best.

Here was a society that had evolved with the intention of inuring its citizens to hardship, pain and any fear of death. Armed with their commitment to the beauty of combat, the rightness of death and an unquestioning belief in the power of their gods, Spartans were known to smile in the face of near-annihilation of their warriors – just so long as the news of the bloodbath included references to brave lives lived and beautiful deaths won.

And this then was the tree of life and death that produced Leonidas, its finest flower. As the younger half-brother of King Cleomenes I, he could hardly have expected ever to come into one of the twin kingships of Sparta. But he was married to Gorgo, Cleomenes's only daughter, and when the king died without male issue Leonidas found himself elevated to the throne as its most rightful heir. (It has been suggested that Leonidas had a hand in the death of his predecessor, but historians are undecided.)

Having grown up without the expectation of kingship, he had experienced the rites of passage of the fighting men he now commanded. As a rule crown princes are sheltered or otherwise removed from the lives of other men, and had Leonidas been born to kingship, this story might have been altogether different. As it was, he had spent his boyhood and early manhood in the barracks and had acquired the same mindset as the men he would take with him to Thermopylae.

The threat from the Persian Empire had certainly not been removed by throwing its heralds down a Spartan well in 491 BC. Instead it loomed and rumbled beyond the horizon like a coming storm. Darius the Great was dead now and had been succeeded by his son and heir Xerxes, self-styled King of Kings. When it came to extending the reach of the empire it was very much a case of like father, like son. The disparate Greek states had reacted to the imperial threat in different ways over the years – some by throwing in their lot with the would-be conqueror – but by 480 BC a coalition of resistance had formed around the hard core of Athens and Sparta.

Intent on conquest and domination as he was, Xerxes had, by 480 BC, already ordered his Egyptian engineers to construct a huge, double-pontoon bridge two kilometres long across the Hellespont – more familiar to us as the Dardanelles. This was impressive – but as nothing compared to the might of the naval and land forces he now mobilised against the Greeks. Herodotus – regarded by many as the father of history, and certainly blessed with a gift for hyperbole – reckoned Xerxes might have sent as many as 5 million infantry and cavalry, along with more than 1,200 ships. Huge exaggeration though this undoubtedly was, most historians are agreed that the Persian land force could have numbered at least 80,000 men and perhaps as many as 200,000. As well as the fighting men came the camp-followers – the wives, womenfolk and servants as well as the hangers-on and bounty-hunters that follow in the wake of war like flies. In any event, it seems fair to imagine a veritable host on the move towards the Greek heartlands.

If there was any uncertainty about the size of the invading

army, there was no doubt among either the Persians or the Greeks regarding the route the invasion would have to take. Xerxes's path towards south and central mainland Greece – and towards the cities of Sparta and Athens that had so gallingly defied him – would force him along a narrow pass bounded by steep mountainsides to the south and by the sea to the north. At its three narrowest points the roadway was barely wide enough to let two wagons pass one another. These pinch points were the 'gates', and since there were naturally occurring hot springs nearby, they were known locally as the 'hot gates' – in Greek, *Thermopylae*.

It was to the middle of the three gates that King Leonidas, tasked with holding back the might of Persia, had brought his much smaller army. Here the cliffs were steepest and closest by the road; here the bottleneck created by geology was his strongest ally.

By the time Xerxes's force arrived at the gates his navy was also in position in Cape Sepias, to the north. The Greek ships were lying in wait for them at Artemisium, a harbour at the north-western end of the island of Euboea, in the Malian Gulf. The subsequent naval engagement would be crucial too. Without being challenged, the Persian Navy might have been able to land an outflanking force on land towards the Spartan rear. The stage was set.

During the month of August, the pass of Thermopylae can be a hard place to be at the best of times. The temperatures rise well into the 30s Centigrade and flies and other biting insects add to the discomfort. For several days of that August of 480 BC Xerxes held his horde at the ready, but made no move.

When tens of thousands of people stay in the same place for even a handful of days, they add to their own discomforts with every passing hour. The sun beat down by day, heating the rock and the earth so that the nights brought little relief. Worse than any heat of sun or land though, or the reek of massed humanity, was the pressure of waiting. For the Persian force as well as for the defenders that time of waiting must have drawn out with the grating rasp of sword blade against sheath. Thermopylae can be a hard place to be at the best of times, and these were not the best of times.

The force commanded by Leonidas was perhaps 4,000 strong. It comprised soldiers from several parts of mainland Greece, including Thespes and Thebes, as well as around 1,000 helots. Elite among all of these fighting men, however, were 300 Spartan hoplites, hand-picked for the job by Leonidas himself. These were the best of the best – the few – but that this was a suicide squad ready and expecting to die is revealed by the king's order that only the fathers of sons could make up this contingent. Such a condition ensured that the men's family lines would be able to continue after their death – and it was guaranteed that boys left fatherless by such a battle would be hungriest of all among their peers for their own chance to live up to such deaths.

How can we imagine what was said between husbands and wives, parents and children, as the soldiers made ready to leave their homes and families for ever? Had their upbringing really been enough to make it easy for those goodbyes to be said? Was the faith of every man and woman, son and daughter, strong enough to make those partings happy? Herodotus wrote that when Gorgo asked Leonidas what she should do when he was gone, he told her to marry a good man and have strong children.

Everyone in Greece knew the quality of the Spartan hoplite. He was the best trained, best equipped and best motivated of any fighting men in the known world. He wore his hair very long, clearly visible down his back beneath a helmet fashioned from a single sheet of bronze and topped with a horsehair crest. It afforded fine protection from blows aimed with sword or spear but made it hard to see and hear. Hoplites fought shoulder to shoulder with their comrades in the phalanx for the simple reason that to lose physical contact with the man either side was to cease to be a functioning part of this otherwise unstoppable fighting machine. On his chest and back he wore a moulded sheet of bronze armour over a tunic of red wool. His lower legs were shielded by lightweight greaves, like shin pads, and he was barefoot – the soles of his feet toughened to leather by a lifetime spent running and marching over rock and thorn. On his left arm he carried a large, circular wooden shield faced with a thin sheet of bronze. Held in front and overlapping the shields of the hoplites on either side, it meant that a disciplined advance by such a phalanx presented its opponents with an impenetrable wall moving inexorably forwards. He was armed with a short stabbing sword or, better yet, a spear.

While the stand-off continued, Xerxes ordered one of his men to approach the Greeks and see what they were doing. The spy returned to say they were practising gymnastics completely naked or combing their long hair! Xerxes laughed out loud at the news – this would surely be a walkover!

But Demaratus, once a Spartan king, now dispossessed and in the pay of the Persians as an adviser, put his master straight. In the first place, he said, 'Spartans are the equal of any man when they fight as individuals; fighting together . . . they surpass all other men.'

But this detail about the hair, he said, was the blackest news the spy could have brought back. Hoplites prepared this way only when they had decided they would never be going home, would never stop and never surrender. This was the final preparation for a deliberate fight to the death. Only death would end the day for the Spartans.

Undeterred, Xerxes sent emissaries to say this was the last chance to submit to Persia without a fight. Leonidas curtly dismissed them, and an enraged Xerxes delivered his final word

– that the Spartans should hand over their weapons now while there was still time.

Leonidas's reply has gone down in history – to be repeated many times since by commanders given similar threats:

'Come and get them,' he said.

Xerxes unleashed a frontal attack by thousands of infantrymen – those taken into the Persian Army from conquered or otherwise submissive states. These 'medes' were far from his best men, but surely force of numbers would carry the day? More lightly armed than their opponents, they charged, howling, into the narrow space left by crowding mountain and sea – and in such a place, where perhaps only a dozen could pass at a time, their numbers counted against them. As they crowded into the narrows and emerged in handfuls on to the far side of the 'gate', the waiting Spartans cut them down like grass.

There is a spur worn by men fighting to defend their homes, fighting in the defence of family and of a way of life that is missing from the armour of invaders. Those Spartans, outnumbered though they were, had nowhere to run to even if they wished to flee – and they did not. The rock and dust beneath their bare feet was where they belonged. Added to this was the technical superiority that comes from lifelong training and experience as a fighting unit. Fighting as one, as Demaratus had warned Xerxes they would, the hoplite infantry were capable of deploying tactics with a finesse that was beyond the wit of conscripts. In later centuries, Roman legions would make their advance irresistible by deploying their front-line fighting men in relays. A legionnaire would spend no more than 15 minutes at the front before being replaced by a fresh man. Pulled to the back and given time to get his breath back, he could fight all day if need be. This ploy was known to the Spartans first, and meant that though their total force at Thermopylae was small, its muscles and lungs were constantly being renewed as though by extra forces. More impressive still, the instinctive command of drill meant whole companies of hoplite infantry were able to feign withdrawals, pulling pockets of the enemy into reckless pursuit, before wheeling about on command and cutting down their would-be tormentors.

Hour after hour it went on, until it was said the ground beneath the soldiers' feet became slick with spilt blood, the air heavy with its metallic stink. Frustrated by the inability of the medes to make any headway, Xerxes reinforced them with waves of his crack troops – a 10,000-strong royal bodyguard known as the 'Immortals'. It was believed by enemies of the Persian Empire that as one fell he was instantly replaced by another waiting in the wings – and so the Immortals' number could never be worn down. History would show there were only 300 Immortals at Thermopylae and none of them was Persian.

Dusk was making inroads on the full light of day and still the Greeks held the pass. Finally the heaps of Persian slain blocking the gates – so-called Immortals plentiful among them – became an impossible hindrance to any hope of victory that first day. The invaders were forced to withdraw.

Now there was the blood and gore of dead Persians to be combed from the hair of the hoplites, waiting in the sudden silence of this space between life and death.

Wounded but still mighty, the Persian host rose like the dawn on the morning of the second day. Immortals and medes alike were flung at the gates by the king of kings, impatient for a final victory he knew must soon be his. But still the invaders had to endure killing and dying by the hundreds and by the thousands while the disciplined, better-armoured hoplites shrugged off the torrent, falling only in ones and twos.

It is now that one of those tantalising 'what ifs' of history arises. If the narrow gates of Thermopylae had remained the only entrance for the Persians, might they eventually have lost their appetite for the fight in this place now reeking with the corruption of their bloated and fly-blown dead? Perhaps, given another roll of the dice, victory might have come not to Xerxes, but to Leonidas.

As it was, fate was to place a traitor on the stage in the form of a local Greek farmer called Ephialtes. He it was who told the Persians about another way towards the cities of Athens and Sparta – a way that bypassed the lowland narrows of Thermopylae. Brought before Xerxes, he promptly divulged the details of a route up into the mountains that would offer easy passage even for armed men.

As the second day of the battle came to an end – still without any breach in the Spartan defence – a force of Immortals was dispatched into the mountains to find the high road. Some say word of the betrayal reached Leonidas and that his response was to send an assassin charged with killing Xerxes himself. True or false, Xerxes was not killed that night and by morning his Immortals had overcome the Greek force stationed on the high road. They were now behind the Spartans and travelling quickly towards them. Perhaps this was the single failure of Leonidas – proof that he was human after all: that he knew that high road was his Achilles heel and yet he placed only a small guard there that was too easily overcome.

When word reached the Spartan king that he was outflanked, he ordered the bulk of his army to withdraw while there was still time – the better to fight another day. Maybe this is wishful thinking – maybe many Greek soldiers simply saw the game was up and took themselves away to safety rather than face the inevitable. But even that possibility takes nothing away from Leonidas, his 300 and the few hundred other Thespians and native Greeks who remained to fight in the jaws of death.

Over breakfast that morning of the third day, Leonidas coolly informed his comrades that they would take their next meal in Hell. In hope of goading the defenders, Persian emissaries approached the gates to say that bowmen would be joining the fray – so many, their arrow shafts would blot out the sun and turn day to night.

'Good news,' said the Spartan Dieneces, in true laconic style. 'At least we'll be fighting in the shade!'

And the arrows flew and swords swung and spears were thrust and men fell. The defenders fought with impossible will and the invaders were dying faster even than before. Perhaps for those Spartans there was a freedom in those last hours and minutes, the freedom of death foretold. Before coming to Thermopylae they had consulted the oracle at Delphi and it had told that either Sparta would fall or one of her kings would die. Death then – even the death of Leonidas himself – was the price that had to be paid if Sparta was to remain free. In any case the king and his men fought with a savage recklessness and the enemy dead were piled high around them. Finally, surrounded by uncountable numbers of the enemy, Leonidas and his comrades fought their way towards a small hill over-looking the gates and the sea.

It was here in this moment that the king was cut down, and now the remaining few fought desperately to keep his body from the enemy. Their efforts were in vain, and Leonidas's corpse was dragged away by the invaders. Later, in a fit of rage at the price he had been made to pay for passage through the hot gates, Xerxes ordered its crucifixion. In a final act of desecration, the head was cut off and impaled on a stake for all to see.

And there on the slopes and summit of that hill the Spartan few found their finest hour. All shields and weapons broken, they threw themselves at the enemy armed only with hands and teeth. Grappling, gouging and biting for the throats of the foe, they died to the last man. Even at the end the Persians could find neither the courage nor the strength to break these last men face-to-face. Instead it was their archers, keeping a safe distance and unleashing storm after storm of arrows on to Persian and Spartan alike, that finally brought the matter to a close.

So Xerxes and his Persians passed through Thermopylae. Their stay in Greece, however, was brief and unhappy. The Spartan stand at those gates and the death there of Leonidas poured steel into the backbones of those Greeks now facing the invader. There were no Athenians at Thermopylae – but there were many on the ships at Artimisium. Their bravery in the face of the Persian Navy – aided and abetted by winds unfavourable to the foe – brought a victory of sorts. Dispersed, their morale broken, the Persians withdrew, leaving the Greeks in control of the sea. There would be no landward invasion now.

A year later, inspired by the immortal sacrifice of the few, a united Greek force stiffened by yet more Spartan hoplites finally defeated the Persian Army at the Battle of Plataea and tossed Xerxes out of mainland Greece for ever.

Visitors to Thermopylae today – coming in hope of feeling the claustrophobic confines of the gates that did so much to defy Xerxes – will likely find only disappointment. Centuries of sediment in the estuary of the River Sperchius that runs through the site have pushed the sea back more than three miles to the north. Rather than thundering past the gates, it merely glints in the distance, a shadow of its former presence.

The Greeks have built a main road right through the former battlefield and the din of trucks and cars all but drowns out any sounds of a distant battle. There are modern memorials to visit – fine and impressive statues of hoplites standing guard in front of smooth walls.

Off to one side of the modern road, however, the more determined visitor might pick out the low hill recently identified as the most likely site of that last stand. Excavation by archaeologists has uncovered heaps of bronze arrowheads – evidence of that final execution of the last of the Few.

Even here the only memorial is a modern one, a block of local stone quarried nearby and already all but lost among the long grass. But engraved upon it are two lines of a poem composed 2,500 years ago by the poet Simonides. These are the sentiments that were to find an echo 23 centuries later on a bronze plaque on a stone in far away South Africa after the war of 1879.

Much more than that, they are *the* sentiments in praise of valour and they ring out from uncounted stones in countless places around the globe. Wherever men have stood and fought, straight-backed and clear-eyed when all hope is gone, comrades will seek to make sure those places are not forgotten. To do that, they look again for the words shaped to remember Leonidas and his 300:

> Go tell the Spartans, passer-by
> That here, obedient to their laws, we lie.

For the boy

A search party left Cape Evans in late October 1912 tasked with the sad job of finding out what had happened to the missing men. They found the bodies of Scott, 43, Wilson, 39, and Bowers, 28, on 12 November, still nearly 150 miles from the home base. Their tent was all but buried in the snow and just six inches or so of the top of it was still visible above the surface.

When the searchers dug away the drift and opened the tent, they found the dead men wrapped in their sleeping-bags. Scott was in the middle with his companions either side. It looked as though Wilson and Bowers had died peacefully in their sleep. Scott was half out of his sleeping-bag, reaching one arm towards Wilson. In the opinion of the searchers, it hadn't been an easy death for the captain. The men's diaries, letters and other personal items were carefully gathered up for return to their families, before a simple funeral service was conducted beneath the endless sky. The tent was then collapsed on top of the bodies and a cairn of snow raised above it.

The search party looked for Captain Oates as well, but found only his sleeping-bag and one of his boots. They erected a cairn of snow and placed a wooden cross on top of it with a note that read:

Hereabouts died a very gallant gentleman.

News of the deaths was made public back in Britain on 13 February 1913. There was a memorial service in St Paul's Cathedral the following day – but Kathleen was not there. Unaware of the tragedy that had overtaken her husband and the other men nearly a year before, she was by then en route to New Zealand, in hope and expectation of a happy reunion, and temporarily out of touch when the story broke. It was on the 19th of the month, aboard a mail steamer crossing the Pacific Ocean, that she received the news.

By the time she returned to Britain in April, Scott's adventure was already in the process of being made legend. Prime Minister Herbert Asquith announced that had he lived Scott would have been made a Knight Commander of the Order of the Bath. Kathleen was therefore ennobled as Lady Scott, in his absence.

It is Scott's journal and letters that reveal what kind of man he was by the end of his long march, what he had learned about himself and about mankind. The words scratched upon page after page, in careful handwriting, ensured his immortality. Trapped at the end by merciless weather, out of food and fuel, the trio had had no choice but to bed down and wait for death. Though they had taken suicide pills with them for just such an eventuality, the seals on the bottles were intact when they were recovered.

'Had we lived,' wrote Scott in his 'Message to the Public', 'I should have had a tale to tell of the hardihood, endurance, and courage of my companions which would have stirred the heart of every Englishman. These rough notes and our dead bodies must tell the tale.'

There is a long straight line connecting Captain Scott and his fellows to all the other manly men of history – those who came before and those who have followed since. Scott's own story seems to me the most moving of all because his reach exceeded his grasp. He made it to the Pole, but the getting home again was beyond him. And yet he understood what he must do even at the last.

Success is counted sweetest, by those who ne'er succeed
To comprehend a nectar requires sorest need
Not one of all the purple host that took the flag today
Can tell the definition so clear of victory
As him defeated dying, on whose forbidden ear,
The distant sounds of triumph burst agonised and clear.

Scott's writings reveal that he was the last to die, alone in that pitiless place. And yet he devoted many of his last hours to updating his journal and writing letters to friends, acquaintances and loved ones. Practical and unflappable to the end; there's not a note of self-pity in any of it.

His letter to Kathleen was addressed 'To my Widow', and among other things makes clear he wished for her what King Leonidas of the Spartans had wished for his wife Gorgo. Leonidas was laconic in his choice of words, as demanded by his culture and upbringing: 'Marry a good man,' he had told her, 'and have strong children.'

Scott was an English gentleman and addressed his widow accordingly.

I want you to take the whole thing very sensibly, as I am sure you will. The boy will be your comfort. I had looked forward to helping you to bring him up, but it is a satisfaction to know that he will be safe with you. You know I cherish no sentimental rubbish about remarriage. When the right man comes to help you in life you ought to be your happy self again – I wasn't a very good husband, but I hope I shall be a good memory. Certainly the end is nothing for you to be ashamed of, and I like to think the boy will have a good start in his parentage of which he may be proud.

Was Scott a student of Spartan history? Had he learned from those long-lost heroes how manly men conduct themselves when all is lost? Did he learn from Leonidas that it was right to hope his wife and son would be happy again, after he was gone?

Kathleen continued her work as a sculptor and her first effort after Scott's death was to create the bronze of him, wearing his Antarctic kit, that stands now in Waterloo Place, in London. As Scott had wished, she married for a second time, becoming the wife of Edward Hilton Young MP. The couple had one son, Wayland, also an MP. Kathleen died in 1947.

Scott had found the strength of character to reveal in simple words how he planned to face the end. His journal and his memory came back to a world close to a war that would change everything and everyone. Scott had shown how men might meet their deaths with dignity and without complaint. A generation would shortly try to measure themselves against the standard set by Captain Scott of the Antarctic. In many ways the men and boys of Flanders would fight in the shadow he had cast. Their name liveth for evermore.

Spare of visible emotion though the letter to Kathleen is, somehow it aches with the longing of a breaking heart.

> You must know that quite the worst aspect of this situation is the thought that I shall not see you again. The inevitable must be faced ... I think the last chance has gone. We have decided not to kill ourselves but to fight to the last ... but in fighting there is a painless end, so don't worry.

He knew it was the memory that mattered, and the story – an amazing story for his son, and every son:

> Make the boy interested in Natural History if you can. It is better than games. They encourage it in some schools. I know you will keep him in the open air. Try and make him believe in a God, it is comforting.

What lots and lots I could tell you of this journey. How much better it has been than lounging about in too great comfort at home. What tales you would have had for the boy ...

Further reading

Captain Scott

Robert F. Scott, *Journals: Captain Scott's Last Expedition*, ed. Max Jones, Oxford University Press, 2006.

Reginald Pound, *Scott of the Antarctic*, World Books, 1968.

Robert F. Scott, *The Voyage of the Discovery*, Smith Elder and Co., 1905.

Michael Smith, *I Am Just Going Outside: Captain Oates, Antarctic Tragedy*, Spellmount Publishers, 2006.

Susan Solomon, *The Coldest March: Scott's Fatal Antarctic Expedition*, Yale University Press, 2003.

The Penlee lifeboatmen

rnli.org.uk

The SAS and the Battle of Mirbat

Michael Asher, *The Regiment. The Real Story of the SAS*, Viking, 2007.

Barry Davies, *Heroes of the SAS. True Stories of the British Army's Elite Special Forces Regiment*, Virgin, 2000.

Tony Jeapes, *SAS. Secret War. Operation Storm in the Middle East*, Greenhill Books, 2005.

Nigel McCrery, *The Complete History of the SAS. The Story of the World's Most Feared Special Forces*, Carlton Books, 2003.

Stewart McLean, *SAS. The History of the Special Raiding Squadron. 'Paddy's Men'*, Great Northern Publishing, 2006.

Ian McPhedran, *The Amazing SAS*, HarperCollins, 2005.

The Demons of Camerone

Douglas Boyd, *The French Foreign Legion*, Sutton Publishing, 2006.

Douglas Porch, *The French Foreign Legion: Complete History of the Legendary Fighting Force*, HarperCollins, 1991.

James W. Ryan, *Camerone. The French Foreign Legion's Greatest Battle*, Praeger Publishers, 1996.

The Battle of Isandlwana

Saul David, *Zulu. The Heroism and Tragedy of the Zulu War of 1879*, Viking, 2004.

Ian Knight, *Isandlwana 1879. The Great Zulu Victory*, Osprey, 2002.

Ian Knight, *The Zulus*, Osprey, 1989.

Ian Knight, *Zulu War 1879. Twilight of a Warrior Nation*, Osprey, 1992.

John Laband, *Lord Chelmsford's Zululand Campaign, 1878-1879*, Stroud, 1994.

The Cockleshell Heroes

Bill Hawkins and Sarah Jane Walker, *The Other Cockleshell Heroes*, Trafford Publishing, 2006.

C. E. Lucas Phillips, *Cockleshell Heroes*, Pan Books, 1974.

Bill Sparks DSM, *Cockleshell Commando: The Memoirs of Bill Sparks*, Casemate Publishers and Book Distributors, 2002.

The Yangtze Incident

Lawrence Earl, George C. *Yangtse incident: the story of H. M. S. Amethyst, April 20, 1949, to July 31, 1949*, Harrap and Company, 1950.

L. Frank, *Yangtse River Incident 1949: The Diary of Coxswain Leslie Frank*, Naval and Military Press, 2004.

Sir John Moore, the Iron Duke and the retreat to Corunna

J. H. Anderson, *The Spanish Campaign of Sir John Moore*, Hugh Rees Ltd, 1905.

Roger William Day, *The Life of Sir John Moore: Not a Drum Was Heard*, Leo Cooper, 2001.

Robert Harvey, *The War of Wars. The Epic Struggle Between Britain and France: 1789-1815*, Constable, 2006.

Philip J. Haythornthwaite, *Corunna 1809. Sir John Moore's Fighting Retreat*, Osprey, 2001.

Lawrence James, *The Iron Duke. A Military Biography of Wellington*, Vintage, 2002.

Christopher Summerville, *March of Death: Sir John Moore's Retreat to Corunna, 1808-1809*, Greenhill Books, 2003.

Sir Ernest Shackleton and the Imperial Trans-Antarctic Expedition

Harding McGregor Dunnet, *Shackleton's Boat: The Story of the James Caird*, Neville and Harding Publishers Ltd, 1996.

Leonard Duncan Albert Hussey, *South with Shackleton*, Low, 1949.

Sir Ernest Shackleton, *South. A Memoir of the Endurance Voyage*, Heinemann, 1919.

Michael Smith, *An Unsung Hero. Tom Crean – Antarctic Survivor*, Collins Press, 2001.

Frank Worsley, *Endurance. An Epic of Polar Adventure*, W. W. Norton and Company, 2000.

The Flight of the Nez Perces

Dee Brown, *Bury My Heart At Wounded Knee. An Indian History of the American West*, Vintage, 1991.

Mark H. Brown, *The Flight of the Nez Perce*, University of Nebraska Press, 1982.

E. Jane Gay, *With the Nez Perce: Alice Fletcher in the Field, 1889-92*, University of Nebraska Press, 1981.

Kent Nerburn, *Chief Joseph and the Flight of the Nez Perce: The Untold Story of an American Tragedy*, HarperOne, 2005.

The Birkenhead Drill

A. C. Addison and W. H. Matthews, *Deathless Story. The Birkenhead and its Heroes*, Naval and Military Press, 2001.

Norman Clothier, *Black Valour - The South African Native Labour Contingent, 1916-1918 and the Sinking of the Mendi*, University of Natal Press, 1987.

Douglas W. Phillips, *The Birkenhead Drill*, The Vision Forum, 2004

The Thin Red Line and the Charge of the Light Brigade

Saul David, *Victoria's Wars*, Penguin, 2006.

Richard Holmes, *Redcoat: The British Soldier in the Age of Horse and Musket*, HarperCollins, 2002.

Hugh Small, *The Crimean War. Queen Victoria's Wars with the Russian Tsars*, Tempus, 2007.

John Sweetman, *Balaclava 1854. The charge of the Light Brigade*, Osprey, 1990.

The Battle of Trafalgar

Max Adams, *Trafalgar's Lost Hero: Admiral Lord Collingwood and the Defeat of Napoleon*, Wiley, 2005.

Tim Clayton and Phil Craig, *Trafalgar. The Men, the Battle, the Storm*, Hodder, 2005.

Gregory Fremont-Barnes, *Trafalgar 1805. Nelson's Crowning Victory*, Osprey, 2005.

Peter Padfield, *Maritime Power and the Struggle for Freedom*, John Murray, 2003.

John Sugden, *Nelson. A Dream of Glory*, Jonathan Cape, 2004.

John Terraine, *Trafalgar*, Wordsworth Editions Ltd, 1998.

Moonwalkers and Apollo 13
Mark Beyer, *Crisis in Space: Apollo 13*, Children's Press, 2002.
Jim Lovell and Jeffrey Kluger, *Apollo 13*, Mariner Books, 2006.
Andrew Smith, *Moondust. In Search of the Men Who Fell to Earth*, Bloomsbury, 2006.

Constantinople
Roger Crowley, *Constantinople. The Last Great Siege 1453*, Faber and Faber, 2005.
Donald M. Nicol, *The Immortal Emperor: The Life and Legend of Constantine Palaiologos, Last Emperor of the Romans*, Cambridge University Press, 1992.
Donald M. Nicol, *The Last Centuries of Byzantium*, Cambridge University Press, 1993.
David Nicolle, *Constantinople 1453. The End of Byzantium*, Osprey, 2000.

Dien Bien Phu
Howard R. Simpson, *Dien Bien Phu. The Epic Battle that America Forgot*, Potomac Books, 2004.
David Stone, *Dien Bien Phu 1954*, Anova Books, 2004.
Martin Windrow, *The French Indo-China War 1946-54*, Osprey, 1998.

The Battle of Britain
Patrick Bishop, *Fighter Boys: The Battle of Britain, 1940*, HarperCollins, 2003.
Peter Brown, *Honour Restored. The Battle of Britain, Dowding and the Fight for Freedom*, Spellmount Publishers Ltd, 2005.
Tim Clayton and Phil Craig, *Finest Hour*, Coronet Books, 2001.
R. J. Overy, *The Battle of Britain*, Penguin, 2004.

David E. Fisher, *A Summer Bright and Terrible. Winston Churchill, Lord Dowding, Radar and the Impossible Triumph of the Battle of Britain*, Shoemaker and Hoard, 2006.

Tony Pollard and Neil Oliver, *Two Men in A Trench II. Uncovering the Secrets of British Battlefields*, Michael Joseph, 2003.

Thermopylae

Ernle Bradford, *Thermopylae. The Battle for the West*, Da Capo Press, 2004.

Paul Cartledge, *The Spartans. An Epic History*, Channel 4 Books, 2002.

Paul Cartledge, *Thermopylae. The Battle that Changed the World*, Macmillan, 2006.

Nic Fields, *Thermopylae 480 BC. Leonidas' Last Stand*, Osprey, 2007.

Steven Pressfield, *Gates of Fire* (novel), Bantam Books, 2000.

Illustration acknowledgements

1. *Captain Robert Falcon Scott* © Bettmann/CORBIS

2. *The Penlee lifeboatmen* © Mick West

3. *The SAS and the Battle of Mirbat* © David Pentland/ Cranston Fine Arts

4. *The Demons of Camerone* Reproduced by kind permission of Ladybird Books Ltd © Look and Learn

5. *The Battle of Isandlwana* © National Army Museum, London/Bridgeman Art Library

6. *The Cockleshell Heroes* Every effort has been made to contact the copyright holders. The author and publisher will be happy to correct any omission at the earliest opportunity.

7. *The Yangtze Incident* © PA Photos

8. *Sir John Moore at Corunna, January 16th 1809* by B. Granville Baker. Every effort has been made to contact the copyright holders. The author and publisher will be happy to correct any omission at the earliest opportunity.

9. *Sir Ernest Shackleton* © Photolibrary

10. *The Nez Perces* © CORBIS

11. *The Birkenhead Drill* © Imagestate/Photolibrary

12. *The Charge of the Light Brigade* © The Print Collector/ Alamy

13. *The Battle of Trafalgar* © Bettmann/CORBIS

14. *Apollo 13* © Bettmann/CORBIS

15. *The Siege of Constantinople* © Classic Image/Alamy

16. *Dien Bien Phu* © Keystone/Stringer/Getty Images

17. *The Battle of Britain* © Hulton-Deutsch Collection/CORBIS

18. *Leonidas at Thermopylae* by Jacques-Louis David © Hulton Archive/Stringer/Getty Images

Acknowledgements

The easy part of a book like this one is the writing. Long before I started typing, I had a pin-sharp idea in my head of how the stories would *sound*. There's a very specific tone that always works for me in an adventure story when I hear it – and all I had to do with *Amazing Tales* was listen to the voices in my head. For most of the time, I just took dictation.

Like I said, that was the easy part, and it was my part. The hard jobs were everyone else's problem, and to all of those individuals I owe a huge debt of thanks. My editor at Michael Joseph is Rowland White and if it hadn't been for him, this wouldn't have seen the light of day. From our first words at our first meeting, I knew that Rowland could hear the same voices in his head. In fact, with the benefit of hindsight it's clear to me now that before I started speaking to him that day, he already knew these stories, and how they should sound. Throughout the process, we have talked together like overgrown schoolboys, and it has been his boundless enthusiasm for, and commitment to, the project that made the whole enterprise huge fun from start to finish.

My literary agent at William Morris, lovely Eugenie Furniss, had the wisdom to put Rowland and I together in the first place – and so to her too goes another huge helping of my thanks. She listened to, understood and reassured me all the way, and the sheer force of her no-nonsense commonsense bowled me along helplessly. Massive gratitude, as usual, goes to my agent, dearest Sophie Laurimore, also at William Morris, who has looked after me for longer than anyone else and who has followed the progress of this project with the kind of enthusiasm I might have expected from a fellow chap.

Both Sophie and Eugenie are, most importantly as far as I'm concerned, the mothers of sons. Two more potential readers – so obviously, well done there.

With the hardback edition of this book, almost above all other considerations it had to look right. It had to have the appearance of a treasured annual returning to the sunlight after long incarceration in a trunk in the attic. And so it does. This is down to Andrew Smith, who took care of the overall design, and to Tom Sanderson, who created the jacket. Further thanks are owed to Nick Lowndes, for copy editorial; James Blackman, for production; Chantal Gibbs, for researching all the pictures; Annie Lee, for scrupulous attention to detail when editing my stream of consciousness; Jennifer Doyle, for marketing and Catherine Duncan, for publicity. I am also in debt to Naomi Fidler and Ana-Maria Rivera and the whole of the Penguin Sales Team.

To Trudi, Evie and Archie, all my love.

All I can offer to all of the people above are my grateful thanks. Responsibility for any and all mistakes and omissions is down to me, and me alone.

He just wanted a decent book to read ...

Not too much to ask, is it? It was in 1935 when Allen Lane, Managing Director of Bodley Head Publishers, stood on a platform at Exeter railway station looking for something good to read on his journey back to London. His choice was limited to popular magazines and poor-quality paperbacks – the same choice faced every day by the vast majority of readers, few of whom could afford hardbacks. Lane's disappointment and subsequent anger at the range of books generally available led him to found a company – and change the world.

'We believed in the existence in this country of a vast reading public for intelligent books at a low price, and staked everything on it'
Sir Allen Lane, 1902–1970, founder of Penguin Books

The quality paperback had arrived – and not just in bookshops. Lane was adamant that his Penguins should appear in chain stores and tobacconists, and should cost no more than a packet of cigarettes.

Reading habits (and cigarette prices) have changed since 1935, but Penguin still believes in publishing the best books for everybody to enjoy. We still believe that good design costs no more than bad design, and we still believe that quality books published passionately and responsibly make the world a better place.

So wherever you see the little bird – whether it's on a piece of prize-winning literary fiction or a celebrity autobiography, political tour de force or historical masterpiece, a serial-killer thriller, reference book, world classic or a piece of pure escapism – you can bet that it represents the very best that the genre has to offer.

Whatever you like to read – trust Penguin.